...e Newspaper Readers of Southern New England from Robert F. Tasca

And...NOW!...Is The Time...In Fact,

There Never Was A Better Time To Get The Buy... You've Been Looking For On A Brand New 1963

Falcon...Fairlane...Galaxie or Thunderbird

Believe Us... If You Have Any Intention Of Buying A New Car... You Should Investigate The Offer We Are In A Position To Give You.

Remember!... We don't care where you've been or what you've been offered... You'll Sure Go For Our Offer and You'll Be Glad You Did Business with Tasca.

THE WORLD'S SECOND LARGEST FORD DEALER

Tasca FORD SALES Inc.
WHERE YOU SAVE ALL-WAYS...ALWAYS

777 TAUNTON AVE. EAST PROVIDENCE   GE 4-7474

1963 COBRA
The World's Fastest Production Sports Car
Exclusive at Tasca's in the Northeastern States

January 27, 1963

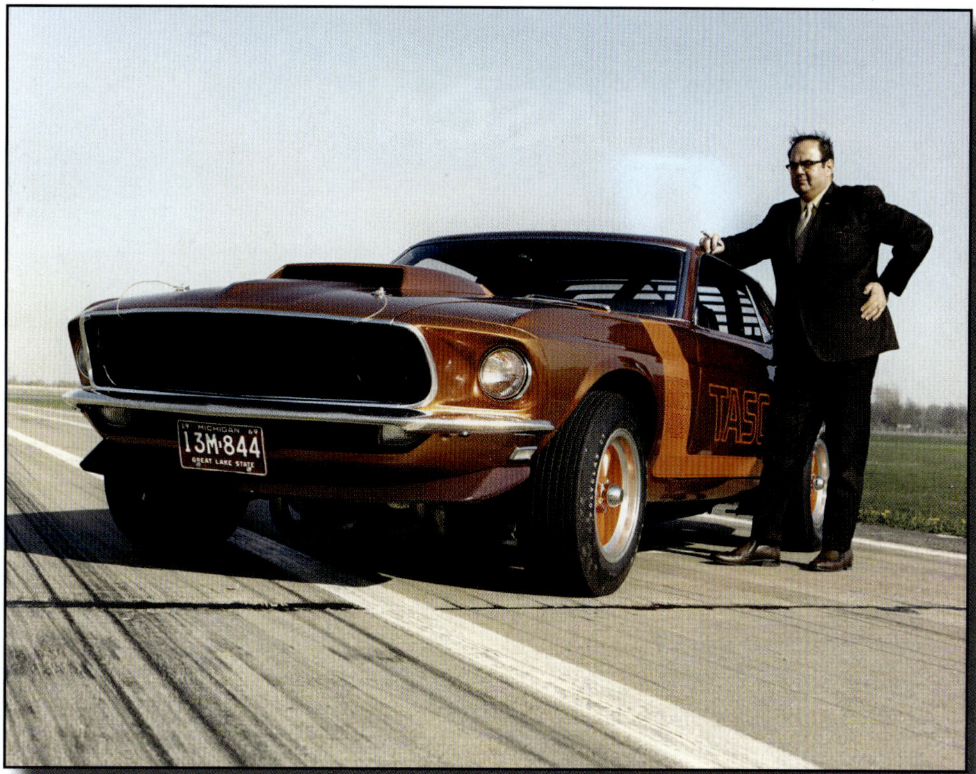
MICHIGAN
13M·844
GREAT LAKE STATE
TASC

The TASCA
FORD LEGACY

Win on Sunday, Sell on Monday!

Bob McClure

CarTech®

CarTech®, Inc.
39966 Grand Avenue
North Branch, MN 55056
Phone: 651-277-1200 or 800-551-4754
Fax: 651-277-1203
www.cartechbooks.com

© 2014 by Bob McClurg

All rights reserved. No part of this publication may be reproduced or utilized in any form or by any means, electronic or mechanical, including photocopying, recording, or by any information storage and retrieval system, without prior permission from the Publisher. All text, photographs, and artwork are the property of the Author unless otherwise noted or credited.

The information in this work is true and complete to the best of our knowledge. However, all information is presented without any guarantee on the part of the Author or Publisher, who also disclaim any liability incurred in connection with the use of the information and any implied warranties of merchantability or fitness for a particular purpose. Readers are responsible for taking suitable and appropriate safety measures when performing any of the operations or activities described in this work.

All trademarks, trade names, model names and numbers, and other product designations referred to herein are the property of their respective owners and are used solely for identification purposes. This work is a publication of CarTech, Inc., and has not been licensed, approved, sponsored, or endorsed by any other person or entity. The Publisher is not associated with any product, service, or vendor mentioned in this book, and does not endorse the products or services of any vendor mentioned in this book.

Edit by Bob Wilson
Layout by Monica Seiberlich
Design concept by Connie DeFlorin

All photos courtesy the Tasca Family/Tasca Automotive Group Archives unless otherwise indicated.

ISBN 978-1-61325-128-7
Item No. CT526

Library of Congress Cataloging-in-Publication Data
McClurg, Bob.
 The Tasca Ford legacy / by Bob McClurg.
   pages cm
 ISBN 978-1-61325-128-7
 1. Automobile dealers–United States–History. 2. Tasca family.
 3. Tasca, Bob, 1926-2010. 4. Ford Motor Company. I. Title.

HD9710.U52M435 2014
381'.4562922200922745–dc23
[B]
                    2013043954

Written, edited, and designed in the U.S.A.
Printed in China
10 9 8 7 6 5 4 3 2 1

Front Flap: Tasca Ford received the first H-M–built 1965 427 SOHC engine A/FX Mustang, drove straight to Pomona from Charlotte, North Carolina, and proceeded to win the Top Stock Eliminator at the NHTRA Winternationals. Left to right is Dean Gregson, John Healey, Bill Lawton, and Bob Tasca Sr.

Frontispiece: Bob Tasca Sr. may have been down on fuel floppers, but he was totally upbeat when it came to the Tasca Street Boss a 494-ci, Can Am aluminum-engine Boss 429 (KK-1214), which ran 11.00 at 136.00 on a G60XD 15-inch Goodyear Polyglas street tire! In the October 1969 issue of Super Stock & Drag Illustrated magazine ("Top This, If You Think You Can!"), Editor Jim McCraw wrote, "If you can beat the Boss with a street car (street tires, closed exhaust system with tail pipes to the rear bumper, and driveline components by the manufacturer) you can get $1,000 in cash!"

Title Page: This beautiful night shot of the Tasca Automotive Group's 165,000-square-foot facility certainly does the place justice. Styled by former Ford Land Architectural Design and Development chief Sadd Chehab, the design is modular so that it can continuously be added upon.

Table of Contents: Tasca Ford's famous "A-1 Useful Cars" sign, the word "useful" being a Bob Tasca inspiration.

Back Cover Captions:

Top Left: To the winner goes the spoils as Bob Tasca Sr. (left) and Billy Lawton (right) congratulate each other while John Healey looks on. Bob's widow, Josephine, still has all of these early trophies.

Top Right: Here is the Tasca Ford Thunderbolt restored back to its original Super Stock specification. It is currently owned by New Hampshire muscle car collector Steve Ames.

Bottom: Hubert "Hube Baby" Platt drove a Tasca Ford CJ at both the AHRA and NHRA Winternationals competing in C/SA. Of course, Platt did double duty at Pomona, also driving the Paul Harvey Ford SS/E Cobra Jet Mustang and was runner up to eventual Super Stock Eliminator winner Al Joniec in class. (Photo Courtesy Steve Reyes)

End Papers: This January 7, 1963, advertisement from Tasca says a lot because there is a lot to say. Note the lower right-hand photo reference to the 1963 Cobra, billed as the "World's Fastest Production Sports Car." They were right!

OVERSEAS DISTRIBUTION BY:

PGUK
63 Hatton Garden
London EC1N 8LE, England
Phone: 020 7061 1980 • Fax: 020 7242 3725
www.pguk.co.uk

Renniks Publications Ltd.
3/37-39 Green Street
Banksmeadow, NSW 2109, Australia
Phone: 2 9695 7055 • Fax: 2 9695 7355
www.renniks.com

TABLE OF CONTENTS

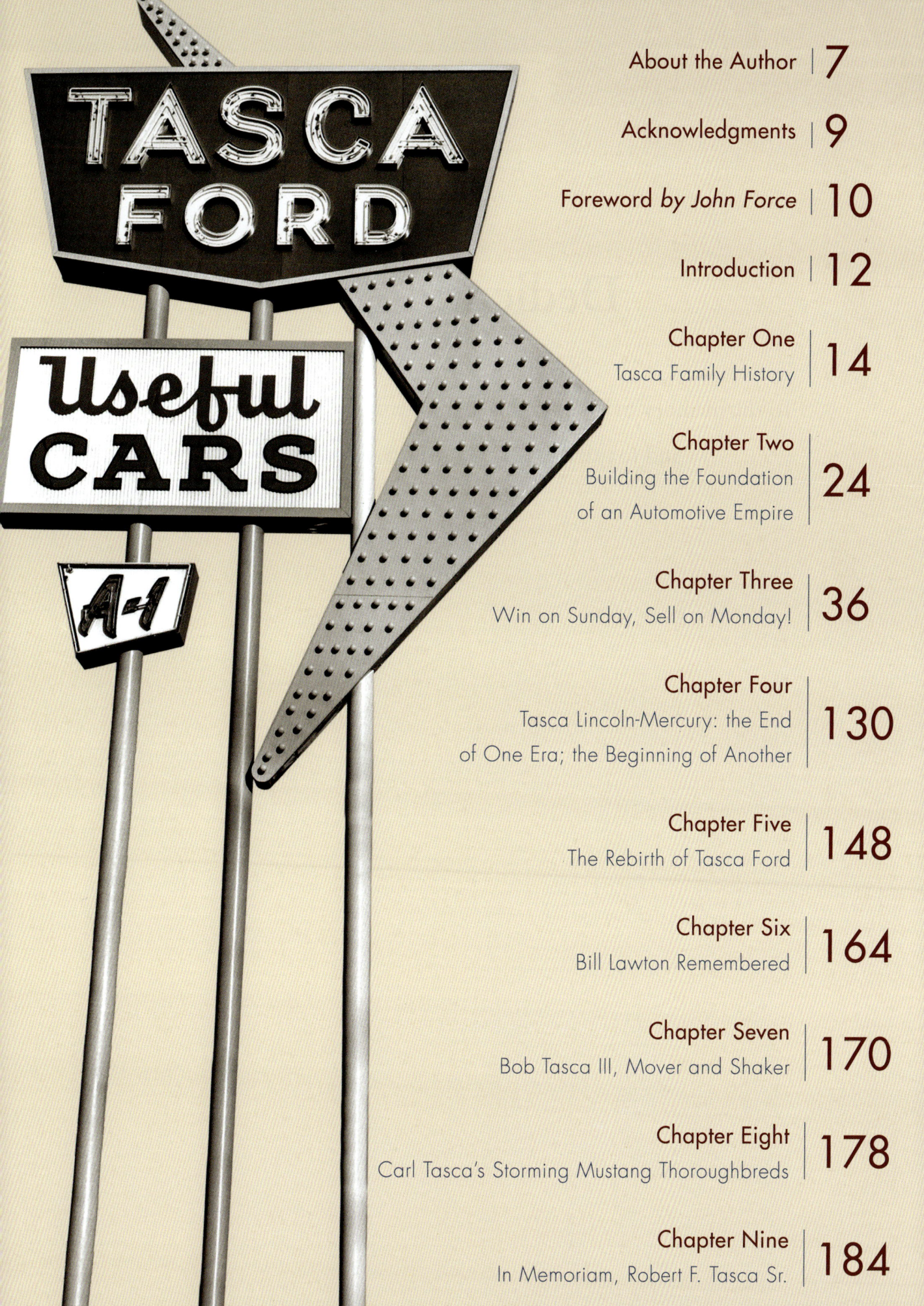

About the Author | 7

Acknowledgments | 9

Foreword *by John Force* | 10

Introduction | 12

Chapter One
Tasca Family History | 14

Chapter Two
Building the Foundation
of an Automotive Empire | 24

Chapter Three
Win on Sunday, Sell on Monday! | 36

Chapter Four
Tasca Lincoln-Mercury: the End
of One Era; the Beginning of Another | 130

Chapter Five
The Rebirth of Tasca Ford | 148

Chapter Six
Bill Lawton Remembered | 164

Chapter Seven
Bob Tasca III, Mover and Shaker | 170

Chapter Eight
Carl Tasca's Storming Mustang Thoroughbreds | 178

Chapter Nine
In Memoriam, Robert F. Tasca Sr. | 184

Dedication

To the memory of Tasca racing team member Michael F. Conte
and to my father, Robert H. S. McClurg

About the Author

Bob McClurg has been writing about cars and car people for the past 47 years. He is a widely acclaimed automotive photojournalist whose specialty was photographing erratic fuel altereds, wheel-standing gassers, vintage funny cars, fire-breathing front-engine dragsters, and early Pro Stock cars in drag racing's halcyon days. He has stood on the starting lines of some of the most famous drag strips in the history of the sport, and has pretty much seen and done it all.

This book, *The Tasca Ford Legacy: Win on Sunday, Sell on Monday* is Bob McClurg's sixth book for CarTech and as you will soon see, it kind of comes full circle. McClurg's previous works have included *Diggers, Funnies, Gassers & Altereds; Drag Racing's Golden Era; Nitro, Fire, Rubber & Smoke; Bob McClurg's Drag Racing Memories; How to Build Supercharged and Turbocharged Small-Block Fords; Yenko! The Man, The Machines, The Legend;* and *How to Install and Tune Nitrous Oxide Systems.*

As a youngster, Bob McClurg grew up in Southern California's pre-urban-sprawl era when many smaller communities were still separated by orange groves and rows of eucalyptus trees. The McClurg family ultimately settled in the City of Orange after moving from upstate New York in July 1954, seeking milder climates and seemingly unlimited opportunities offered by the Golden State. Bob's father, Robert H. S. McClurg, had grown up as part of a large Irish immigrant family in New York's post-Depression recovery era, which haplessly evolved into the World War II era. Like countless other young Americans, Bob's father went off to war, and was among the fortunate ones to return. However, with a growing family to feed, there was never enough money or leisure time in the McClurg household to indulge oneself in something as expensive and irrelevant as hot rods. As far as Bob's father was concerned, cars were strictly a mode of transportation to get from point A to point B.

"Unfortunately, my father used to call hot rods 'jalopies,' or even worse, 'junkers.' I was absolutely befuddled by that. He just had no use for cars other than as basic transportation. He just didn't see the beauty in them or marvel at the incredible amount of engineering put into them. I remember the time he tried to change the main bearings on the flathead V-8 engine in his 1941 Ford work car. I learned a whole new (and quite colorful) vocabulary that weekend. But then, he *was* a former sailor in the United States Navy!"

Fortunately for Bob there were outside (automotive) influences he could draw from. The late Jack Hart, who went on to become the first Competition Director for the fledgling National Hot Rod Association (NHRA), owned Hart's Texaco Service located at the corner of Chapman Avenue and Parker Street and kind of took him under his wing. One block down was Towne Barber Shop where Bob worked as a shoeshine boy. It was during that time that he discovered *Hot Rod* and numerous other car magazines stuffed in the barbershop reading rack. Directly across the street from Towne Barber Shop was Selman Chevrolet's "A-1 Used Car" lot, which usually had a handful of Tri-Five Chevrolets and a Corvette or two.

Walking crosstown to St. John's Lutheran School every day was another adventure with plenty of places for a car-crazy kid to get sidetracked. Along the route, directly across the railroad tracks, was Selman's new-car showroom, and right across the street from Selman's was Bill Corwin Ford. If that wasn't enough temptation, there was also a Goodyear tire retreading shop, the Blake & Nation Body Shop, Hoffman's Radiator Shop, and the local Mobil gas station. You get the picture.

In the early 1960s, the McClurg family moved across town to Villa Park, which seemed light years away from Bob's old hangouts. Fortunately for him, there were three different hobby shops located on nearby Tustin Avenue, two of them with slot car tracks, and all of them easily within walking distance!

"I was a sophomore on half-day sessions at Orange High School, and walked down to either Gish's Toys or Frank's Hobbies every morning to race slot cars until about 11:30 a.m., then went to school. On the way home again, it was even more slot car racing!"

To help pay for his "slot car addiction," Bob took a weekend job at Gish's Toys. One afternoon, owner Roger Clausen asked Bob if he would like to accompany him to Lions Associated Drag Strip.

"Big Daddy" Don Garlits was match racing Chris "Greek" Karamesines, Don "Snake" Prudhomme, and Kenny Safford. Talk about sensory overload! The sights, the sounds, the smells of nitro and burnt rubber: Wow! You just don't get that from simply reading a car magazine. From that point on, he was hooked!

"Hooked," yes, but not able to do very much about it. "I didn't get my first car until I was 18 years old so I had to 'mooch' rides to the drags from whomever I could. I usually was the one who paid, and sometimes I got left there. Even worse, I had almost zero mechanical skills, so for me, becoming a big-time drag racer was pretty much out of the question. There had to be another way!"

Fortunately, McClurg excelled in journalism. He wrote his first real newspaper article on traffic safety for the *Orange Daily News*; it was published when he was in the fifth grade. That led to a brief stint as editor of the ninth-grade junior high school newspaper. Then it was on to high school yearbook class, but all the writing jobs had already been taken. His journalism teacher, John Osborn, handed him the school camera, a couple of rolls of film, and gave him a little piece of advice, "You can either take pictures, or transfer to another elective!"

"I knew very little about photography. My uncle had given me his old 35-mm Argus C3 a few years before, but it involved quite a bit of math, and I was lousy at math!"

Then one night McClurg sneaked onto the starting line at Lions Associated Drag Strip with camera in hand. It was a short visit, just enough time to click off about a half-dozen pictures before being escorted back to the stands by track security, but it proved to be a real game changer.

"From then on, all I wanted to do was photograph drag racing. Fortunately, I was able to obtain a starting-line photo credential through the sports editor at the *Orange Daily News*. By then I was attending Fullerton Junior College and met a classmate who photographed football for the *Anaheim Bulletin* newspaper. I wasn't particularly interested in photographing football, but sports editor Doug Miles made me a deal that if I would do that on Thursday and Friday nights, he would arrange for a permanent starting-line photo credential for me at Lions, Irwindale, and OCIR on Saturdays and Sundays. Doug also made good on the deal by publishing a weekly feature story I did on one of many local Orange County racers!"

In April 1969, Bob got his first big break with *Super Stock & Drag Illustrated* and headed east. His first assignment was none other than photographing Tasca Ford's last in a series of Mustang funny cars, the Tasca Super Boss.

The prolific McClurg has gone on to become published in practically every car magazine in America as well as a number in Europe and Asia. Along the way he's worked for the *Los Angeles Times* Orange County Bureau, he's served as photo editor for Petersen Specialty Publications, photo editor for *Hot Rod*, and editor for *Hot Rod Corvette* and *Petersen's Kit Car*. He's taught school at Chatsworth, California's Learning Tree University and served as editor at McMullen and Yee's *Mustang Illustrated* and editor at McMullen/Argus *Ford High Performance* magazines. Today, Bob and his dog "Itchy" reside just outside Hilo, Hawaii, and Bob is still writing and taking in select car events on the mainland.

"After all those years, I finally have my own shop on the property. I also have an IHRA-sanctioned drag strip [Hilo Raceway Park] 3 miles in one direction of town, and a dyno shop less than 3 miles in the other direction of town. This truly is paradise!"

Acknowledgments

The author and publisher wish to thank the following people and organizations for their invaluable assistance in the research, development, and preparation of *The Tasca Ford Legacy: Win on Sunday, Sell on Monday!*

Ralph "Father Al" Almonte; Jere Alhadaff; Steve Ames of Ames High Performance, Marlborough, New Hampshire; Robert "Yeager" Andriossi; Sam Auxier Jr.; Garrett, Laura, and Chantal Balberde; Daria Baraga; R. F. "Bob" Bissell; Phil Bonner; Richard H. "Dick" Brannan; Brandon, Ashley, and Frankie Bregel; G. K. Callaway; Peter Caldwell; Jesus Christ Our Savior; Patty Cicerone; Austin Coil; Eric Dahlquist-Vista Group, Van Nuys, California; "Uncle Gene" De Graide; Randy Delisio, Delisio's Performance and Restoration, Lyons, New York; Darwin Doll; John Force; and John Force Racing, Yorba Linda, California.

Ford Motor Company: John Clinard, Jessica Enoch, Mark Fields, Edsel Ford II, Elena Ford, William "Bill" Ford Jr., Susan Krusel, and Alan Mulally.

Donald Farr; Bob Frey; Anna Gattone; Charles E. "Charlie" Gray Jr.; Billy Gilbert; Dean Gregson; Al and Ellen Hanna; John Healey; Roy Hill, CEO, Roy Hill Drag Racing School; William "Bill" Holbrook; Jim Inglese; Tommy Iverolino; Al Joniec; John Justo; Jim Kelly; Lee Kelley; Rick Kirk; Bill Kolb Jr.; Maddeline, William, Christopher, Todd, Christopher II, Conner, Nicholas, and William II Lawton, Lawton Moving & Storage; Butch Leal; Tom Madigan; Louis Marciano; Tim Marshall; Buddy Martin; Tom and Kathy McClurg; Jim McCraw; Dick Towers, Match Race Madness; Julio Marra; Bob McCardle; Kenn Mitsunaga; J. B. Myer Hilo Office Max/Impress employees Kristy, Lydia, Chelsea, Caysha, Kayla, Tarcel, and Brooke; Hubert Platt; Ralph Poirier; T. P. "Jack" Redd; Photo Restorations by Donald Sarian, donaldsarian.com; Lachelle Seymour Motorcraft/Quick Lane; *Ford: The Performance Years*, Martyn L. Schorr; Source Interlink Media Archives; Steve Reyes; Gas Ronda; Talladega & Spoiler Registry; Louis Tullie; Mike Perlini; *Providence Journal* Archives, Providence, Rhode Island; Shelby American Automobile Club (SAAC); Rick Kopec; Vincent Liska; Howard Pardee; Dan Reiter; Ned Scudder; Ed and June Veader; "Thai" VFW Hall, Bristol, Rhode Island; Ms. Linda Vaughn; Curt Vogt, Cobra Automotive, Wallingford, Connecticut.

And the entire Tasca Family: Josephine Tasca; Robert F. Tasca Jr.; Carl A. Tasca Sr.; David J. Tasca Sr.; Patricia A. Tasca-De Cristofaro; Nicholas J. De Cristofaro Jr.; Robert F. Tasca III; Mike Tasca; Carl A. Tasca Jr.; David J. Tasca Jr.; Carrie Tasca; Nicole, Rebecca, and Nicholas De Cristofaro.

Foreword

by John Force

The first time I heard the name "Tasca," I was a young man from Bell Gardens, California, attending the NHRA Winternationals in Pomona, California. At the time, I think I was so young that I had to sneak into the pits! That was the year (1965) that Tasca Ford won Top Stock Eliminator with their 1965 427 A/FX Mustang and a legend was born! As I said, that was the first time I had heard the name "Tasca," but it certainly wasn't the last!

I formally met Bob Tasca Sr. and his family in December 1996. I was in East Providence, Rhode Island, on business, it was snowing, and as I drove along Fall River Avenue I saw this big sign that said "Tasca!" I remembered the name from racing. I was cold enough and just curious enough to stop in.

I was met on the lot by Tasca Lincoln-Mercury Sales Manager Mike Perlini, who looked at me and said, "You're John Force, aren't you?" We shook hands and Mike escorted me into the showroom. The first thing I noticed was all the pictures on the walls of the late Bill Lawton and the entire Tasca family.

Then I heard Perlini tell someone in the nearby office, "You're never going to guess who I found walking around on the lot."

The voice said, "Who?"

Mike said, "John Force."

Then the voice says excitedly, "John Force. The only 'John Force' I know of is the world-famous funny car driver."

Well, I just so happened to be standing right around the corner, so once again I said, "Yup! That's me!"

The "voice" belonged to some kid no more that 19 or 20 years old. We shake hands and he's got me test driving this car, and that car, and finally I said, "Kid, listen; you're doing a great job here but I need to talk to one of the Tascas."

Then he said, "John, I'm Bob Tasca III."

Long story short, I wanted to know if Bobby III's grandfather, Bob Tasca Sr., was still around. Well, I got to tell you; it was like meeting Wyatt Earp and his brothers. They (Bobby Jr., Carl, and David) all walked out of their offices and shook my hand. Then everyone from the shop came in once the word got around that I was there. I mean, it was really huge! Mr. Tasca said, "We're just getting ready to go to dinner. Want to go along with us?"

I said "Hell, yeah," so we all went out and had Italian food, and I mean *the best* Italian food! What an evening that was. When Grandpa Tasca spoke, nobody else spoke; know what I mean? I don't mean to sound quirky, but if you ever saw the movie *The Godfather*, that's what it reminded me of; the respect was so immense."

At dinner, we got to talking about racing, and I mentioned that my number-two driver, Tony Pedregon, didn't have a sponsor, and that my deal with Pontiac Motor Division was also a bit shaky. He looked at me and said, "How would you like to have a Ford body on that hot rod of yours? I'll get Tony a [Ford] sponsorship in 24 hours!"

I said, "Bob, with all due respect, I've been trying to get Ford to return my telephone calls for the last 15 years. You're telling me you're really going to get me a sponsor in 24 hours?"

"Yup, but I don't just want Tony; I want you!"

Of course, Grandpa Tasca had the power to make that call to Ford Motor Company; they took his call and you would have thought *he* was the president of Ford Motor Company. I mean the guy bled Ford Blue, and that ain't no b*#l s%*t! At that time Ford was walking away from drag racing. They weren't actively sponsoring Bob Glidden anymore. Glidden wasn't dominating Pro Stock as he had for so many years previously and the eliminator seemed to be heading off in another direction. Of course, Bob Tasca wasn't at all happy about the situation, and perhaps this chance meeting could change all that.

Tasca used to tell Ford's Bob Rewey, "You know, you spend all this money on Indy car racing and go look out in the parking lot. None of your customers are there. It's all foreign cars. Then go look at the parking lot at the drag races. That's where your customers are. You guys are crazy for walking away from drag racing."

Anyhow, he called Jacques Nassar on the Ford Corporate jet and said, "Hey! I'm here in the restaurant with John Force, and you really need to take a good look at this kid. He's going to be a big star and he'll take you where you want to go!"

I don't remember whether it was 24 hours or not. It couldn't have been much longer than that. Anyhow, he just made it happen. Both Tony and I got a Ford sponsorship.

When I showed up in Dearborn they said, "Okay, you've got a deal. We talked to Mr. Tasca, and if he says you're good for the image of Ford Motor Company, then you're good." And that's kind of how the Tasca and Force family friendship was cemented. Ford supplied John Force Racing [JFR] with the Mustang bodies, they supplied us with the trucks, and Bob got us the sponsorship money and the publicity machine that goes along with it.

Of course, Bobby III really loved his grandfather, and the two of them just loved drag racing; in fact, the whole family does. That family is very well connected and very close, and that's their strength. They've raised all these children and now they've got a ton of grandchildren. Speaking for myself, I keep my family close together and there are a lot of similarities. I've been to their home many times. Their house is like a compound, and I'll tell you one thing. If Grandpa Tasca was the boss, grandma Josephine was surely number two! Their Christmases, the way they get together, just the respect, it's unbelievable.

Grandpa Tasca sat with me and he talked about his children and I talked about my family and what we were both trying to accomplish in the future: to protect our children and pass along to the next generation and the next generation what we've created. I pray that my family never stops. But I'm telling you, his won't. I guarantee you that much!

I lost my dad, Bill, so many years ago. He was my hero and then he was gone. That's why I really latched onto Grandpa Tasca. I've had mentors in my life, some family, some people that successfully ran big companies; it was just amazing how I related to him. It didn't matter whether it was on a personal level, or professional problems with my racing operation; he was there to give me advice. In my lifetime, there have been a few key people along the road.

The first was my father. I was also very close to my Uncle Gene Beaver. He was the one who gave me my start in drag racing. Another one of them was Grandpa Tasca. He was key to my career. Our association was a major turning point. Whenever I had a problem, and didn't know how to solve it, he listened to what I had to say. Then he would say, "Here's what I think." If you wanted Grandpa Tasca to tell you that you were right, but that you were actually wrong, he'd say that you were wrong. He'd say, "John, I can't help you until you accept that you were wrong."

You know, Ford Motor Company didn't love Bob Tasca only because he was a successful car dealer. They loved him because he related to the common man. He spoke the common man's language. He dealt with so many people in the unions. If Ford had a problem, Grandpa Tasca went to the unions, he went to the factories, and he talked to the workers and the workers talked to him. He really strengthened the bond between the workers and management at Ford.

When I attended his funeral, I couldn't believe how much traffic there was. It was the biggest church I've ever been to in my life, and the place was packed. It was as if everybody in the state of Rhode Island came to pay their respects to this great man. You know, I'm an emotional guy. I may cuss, I may fight, I may drink a little, but I'm God fearing. When I'm really down in the dumps and in need of some emotional comfort I think about my father, I think about my Uncle Gene, I think about Eric Medlin, and I think about Grandpa Tasca. Those people were key figures in my life, and they are with me every day in my prayers.

Foreword 11

Introduction

This is a classic American success story about the life and times of the late Robert F. Tasca Sr., a man who by all accounts could have very well become the governor, senator, or congressman of Rhode Island (or any other state in the union for that matter) had he chosen to enter the world of politics rather than the world of the automobile. Lucky for us Bob Tasca regarded cars, and, more specifically, Ford cars, a higher calling.

For me, it has been an honor to author *The Tasca Ford Legacy: Win on Sunday, Sell on Monday!* However, no one person wrote this book; many people did. At this juncture, I feel it vitally important to thank Bob Tasca Sr.'s wife, Josephine; sons Robert F. Tasca Jr., Carl A. Tasca Sr., David J. Tasca Sr.; and daughter Patricia Ann Tasca-De Cristofaro, along with the entire Tasca family and extended Tasca family members, who are acknowledged elsewhere in this book. Had it not been for their untiring efforts and intense dedication to this project, this book might have never happened. I thank each of them for their vote of confidence. I also want to thank and credit Tasca University's Mike Perlini, who has acted as the corporate liaison or "point man" between the Tasca Automotive Group and me on this project. Mike contributed crib notes, vignettes, organizational skills, and expended shoe leather. Perini's initial comment was, "I don't know how in the hell you're going to be able to cram every fact and figure about the Tascas into just 192 pages! You could do volumes on these people." And he was right!

Of course, as a 29-year veteran of the Tasca Automotive Group, Perlini would know. Like the Tasca clan, Mike was born with "gasoline in his veins." Mike's father, Gino Perlini, was initially a body man who later became a body shop owner. When Gino returned from World War II, he became involved in fixing up wrecked cars for Pawtucket, Rhode Island, junk man Charlie Steingold (Broadway Auto Sales). There was a genuine need for safe and reliable transportation in early post–World War II America. Once the automotive factories got up and running again, Steingold obtained a De Soto franchise, and Gino signed on as foreman, and then graduated to salesman, then sales manager, and ultimately general manager.

Eventually the De Soto franchise gave way to Pontiac, and Gino became the public face in the new Steingold Pontiac franchise. Gino's son, Mike, had the good fortune to be able to work in every single department at the dealership including serving time as lot boy, new-car prep, painter, body man, and service technician. He worked on the parts counter, did warranty work, and ultimately became an accomplished salesman.

However, Perlini wanted to assert his independence and strike out on his own. After working at a number of different dealerships where he got the education of a lifetime seeing what the underbelly of the automobile business really looked like, he became somewhat disillusioned. At the urging of a good friend who worked at Tasca Lincoln-Mercury, Mike applied for a job in 1985, and was interviewed by none other than Bob Tasca Sr.; so, some 29 years later, Mike's initial good fortune has now become our good fortune.

I first met Bob Tasca Sr. in April 1969 after having just assumed the job as Photo Editor at Eastern Publishing Company's Alexandria, Virginia–based *Super Stock & Drag Illustrated (SS&DI)* magazine. At the time, I was a wet-behind-the-ears California kid of 21½ years of age who up to that time "lived" on the starting lines of Lions Associated Drag Strip, Irwindale, Carlsbad, and Orange County International Raceways. That was my world. As a lad, I just couldn't get enough of cars and car people, and I was the only kid in the fifth grade, I might add, to have my own subscription to *HRM*! Having also been a loyal subscriber to *SS&DI* in my teenage years, I was well aware of just who Robert F. Tasca Sr. was, and the major role that he and his East Providence, Rhode Island, Ford dealership had played in the shaping of Ford Motor Company's "Total Performance Era."

By comparison, Tasca Ford Sales, Inc., was to the Ford Motor Company what other 1960s muscle car retailers such as Nickey Chevrolet (GM), Royal Pontiac (GM), Century Oldsmobile (GM), Mr. Norm's Grand Spaulding Dodge (Chrysler-Dodge), and Yeakel Plymouth (Chrysler-Plymouth) were to their corresponding automotive franchisers.

That fateful day in April, I found myself standing in the middle of "Ford High Performance Heaven"; Falcon Sprints, Hi Po Fairlanes, Mustangs of all "flavors," Torinos, Shelbys, and Cobras; I was surrounded by them. It was kind of like being a kid in a candy store. Do you smell? Do you look? Do you touch? Do you eat? Then up walked the man behind the legend that was all things Tasca. He extended an open hand to my boss, *SS&DI* Editor Jim McCraw and gave him a hearty handshake.

I had always pictured Bob Tasca as sort of a cross between P. T. Barnum and Vince Lombardi. I wasn't far off. He was dynamic, friendly, entertaining, well-spoken, product savvy, and above all, strictly business. At 6 feet 1 inch and weighing approximately 275 pounds, the native Rhode Islander cast an ominous shadow. Nonetheless, I felt as though I knew Mr. Tasca almost as well as I knew my own father because there were numerous similarities. Both men came from immigrant families. Both men had lost their mothers at an early age. Both men were creative, hard working, fun loving, strict yet fair, good family men, and men of great spiritual devotion.

Anyhow, that was the Bob Tasca that everyone knew on a national level. But you don't get to be the second-largest Ford dealership in the world (and especially one from as small a state as Rhode Island) without first establishing a rock-solid customer base at the local level. Tasca's time-honored credo, "You Will Be Satisfied," was based on attending to the wants and needs of one customer at a time. Bob Tasca Sr. knew full well that to be successful in auto sales or leasing of bread-and-butter cars to "Mr. and Mrs. John Q. Public," it was an absolute necessity that they were provided with the best service and technical support available. Therefore, in the earliest days of Bob's business he instituted after-hours and weekend service, two important stepping stones in Bob's "Principle of (giving) 100 percent."

"When it comes to Rhode Island residents, Tasca Ford is to automobiles what Dell's Frozen Lemonade is to Rhode Islanders," commented TasCafe General Manager Patty Cicerone. Being an "out of stater" I was initially perplexed by that comment. That is, until I learned from a number of the local residents that, just like Tasca, Dell's Lemonade is a local institution; an astute analogy, Patty.

Probably one of the things that impressed me the most about the entire Tasca family organization is that were you to ask any one of them what their particular job description is, they would tell you (and I mean every one of them) that nobody in the Tasca family has titles. Theirs is a family-run business!

"When you're one of the owners you have to do everything corner-to-corner," says David Tasca Sr. "If you see something wrong, you fix it!"

"We all work together as a group," says Bob Tasca Jr. "It's not always a walk in the park but we agree that we stay together and stay strong. To quote our late uncle Wallace, '"Wally"' Tasca, God rest his soul, 'The family should always speak as one.'"

That kind of thinking is what made this country great; it's what this country used to be all about. In today's high-speed society where everything is newer, shinier, faster, and of course much less personal, the Tasca Automotive Group is a family-run American "business machine" fueled by people.

As for me, I am happiest when I am writing about cars and car people. One of the last things I remember Bob Tasca Sr. saying to me as we concluded our final interview together for the October 1992 issue of *Mustang Illustrated* magazine, "Well, do you think that you've got enough material here to write a good story about us?" to which I replied, "Enough? There's enough material here to write a complete book about you and your family, Mr. Tasca." He looked at me and said, "Well then, maybe after I see what you've written, if I happen to like it, you just might be the right person to help me write my book about my life in the car business."

As many of you know, Bob and author Peter Caldwell collaborated on the 1996 release, *U WILL B SATISFIED*, a book that by all accounts is regarded as the Holy Grail of automobile sales and personal motivational primers.

Anyhow, so here I am a little more than 30 years later writing books about the automobile and the men who loved them with an unbridled passion. In the course of doing so, I am most happy when afforded the opportunity to "wax nostalgically" about two different subjects, vintage drag racing and Ford Motor Company products and the "Genuine Ford People" who made that company what it is. For me, this book is what you might call a "two for," and the folks at CarTech didn't have to ask twice if I would be interested in doing it. Let's see now, the working title should be something like *The Tasca Ford Legacy: Win on Sunday, Sell on Monday!* Yeah, that works!

You may notice that Chapter Three, titled "Win on Sunday, Sell on Monday," is particularly lengthy. The reason is obvious. It covers the time when the bulk of Tasca Ford history was made. And when I say "history," I'm talking about dealership history *and* racing history, as they go hand-in-hand. This book has been two years in the making, but it represents a lifetime's worth of acquired knowledge. When meeting with the people who were actually there back in the day, you get a sense of being there along with them, almost as if you were the proverbial "fly on the wall." The remembrances are distinct. The story accounts are not only historical fact but also lasting experiences and indelible impressions frozen in time. Bob Tasca Sr. was such a dynamic man, and the Tasca family is such a dynamic family.

Enjoy!

Tasca Family History

With a family tree that extends back to the late 1700s, the name Tasca (which means "pockets" in Italian) is deeply steeped in old-world tradition and time-honored values. As a young man, Carlo A. Tasca's (or "Grandpa Charlie's") family migrated to America in the late 1800s from his hometown of Cupello, Italy (which is located 26 miles northeast of Naples in the Campania Region), and settled in the Providence, Rhode Island, area. A diamond setter in the jewelry industry by trade (the east side of Providence was known as the jewelry district), Grandpa Charlie was a relatively small man who smoked a big cigar.

In 1925, he married Maria Carmena ("Carrie") Colavecchio, whose family had likewise migrated to the United States from the province of Frosinone, which is located approximately 46 miles southeast of Rome in the Lazio Region.

Robert Francis Tasca was born October 4, 1926, on the Feast of St. Francis of Assisi (hence the middle name "Francis" in honor of the patron saint of animals). Sadly, Maria Tasca died of pneumonia (March 1927) when Bob was only six months old. Carlo and Maria had lived upstairs from her parents, Benedeto and Antonia ("Mamela") Colavecchio, in a little tenement house in Providence located on Sisson Street. Because Carlo was a young widower and could not raise a six-month-old baby boy on his own, Maria's parents co-raised young Bob. It was crowded in the Colavecchio household with young Robert's two Colavecchio uncles, Octavio Leonard ("Uncle Jake") and Thomas, plus five Colavecchio aunts, Angela ("Aunty Angie"), Anna, Philomena, Theresa ("Aunty Tess"), and Jean ("Aunty Jean"). Living conditions were cramped, but it was a house full of love, as Bob Sr.'s

This extremely rare photograph shows six-month-old Robert being bottle-fed by his birth mother, Maria Colavecchio-Tasca, who tragically succumbed to pneumonia in March 1927. From that point on, young Robert was jointly raised by his father, Carlo, and Maria's parents, Benedeto and Antonia Colavecchio.

CHAPTER One

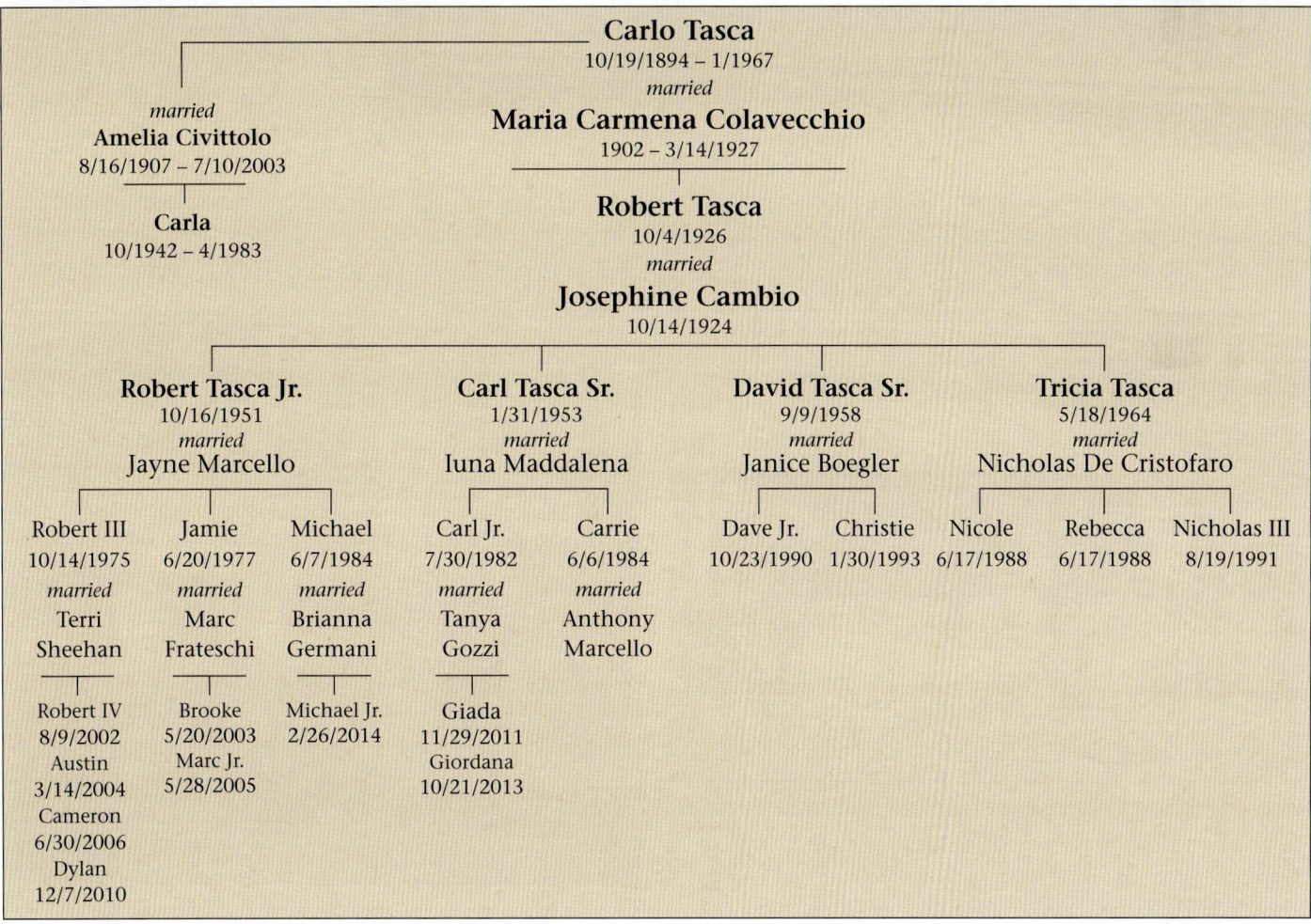

The Tasca Family Tree.

Carlo Tasca
10/19/1894 – 1/1967
married

married
Amelia Civittolo
8/16/1907 – 7/10/2003

Maria Carmena Colavecchio
1902 – 3/14/1927

Carla
10/1942 – 4/1983

Robert Tasca
10/4/1926
married
Josephine Cambio
10/14/1924

Robert Tasca Jr.	**Carl Tasca Sr.**	**David Tasca Sr.**	**Tricia Tasca**
10/16/1951	1/31/1953	9/9/1958	5/18/1964
married	*married*	*married*	*married*
Jayne Marcello	Iuna Maddalena	Janice Boegler	Nicholas De Cristofaro

Robert III	Jamie	Michael	Carl Jr.	Carrie	Dave Jr.	Christie	Nicole	Rebecca	Nicholas III
10/14/1975	6/20/1977	6/7/1984	7/30/1982	6/6/1984	10/23/1990	1/30/1993	6/17/1988	6/17/1988	8/19/1991
married	*married*	*married*	*married*	*married*					
Terri Sheehan	Marc Frateschi	Brianna Germani	Tanya Gozzi	Anthony Marcello					

Robert IV 8/9/2002
Austin 3/14/2004
Cameron 6/30/2006
Dylan 12/7/2010

Brooke 5/20/2003
Marc Jr. 5/28/2005

Michael Jr. 2/26/2014

Giada 11/29/2011
Giordana 10/21/2013

Chapter One: Tasca Family History

As this birth certificate clearly shows, Robert Francis Tasca Sr. was born in Providence, Rhode Island, on October 4, 1926, to parents Carlo Albert Tasca and Maria Carmena Colavecchio-Tasca.

This picture shows young Bob on his second birthday. He grew up among five aunts (Angela, Anna, Philomena, Theresa, and Jean) and two uncles (Octavio and Thomas Colavecchio). It was a crowded but loving household.

That's little Bob in the left foreground along with other family members on Highland Beach at the family summer cottage at Warwick, Rhode Island. Left to right are: Richard and Angie Tasca, Charlie Tasca, Bob, cousin Robert E. Tasca, Anna and Wallace "Wally" Tasca.

Well, it looks as though cars are in young Bob's future, although this particular set of wheels happens to be "Brand X."

16 The Tasca Ford Legacy

daughter, Patricia A. Tasca-De Cristofaro, fondly remembers.

"Grandpa Benedeto Colavecchio had this small workshop, or to be more precise, a 'shed' out in the back yard. It was place of refuge where he would escape when he had enough of all the kids and could no longer stand the noise. I guess today you would call it a Man Cave. He would go out there and lay on the bench, and my great-grandmother (who was a relatively small woman) would bring him out a huge pitcher of lemonade, and he would just chill out. When my great-aunts moved from that house, my brother Bobby moved that shed, and now has it in his back yard."

Aunty Anna Tasca-Gattone, with whom Bob spent his summer months at Warwick, Rhode Island's Highland Beach, remembers her nephew as being slightly overweight and doted on by his father, Carlo. Bob was extremely smart and, in a cute sort of way, somewhat mischievous.

"He was always doing something to gain attention. One time when he was quite young, he pulled all the heads off all my dolls. I remember he also got into trouble with one of the neighbors for re-arranging all the decorative stones in the man's front yard. He used to kink the hose on my father while he was trying to water the garden. That stopped once father turned the hose loose on him. He always used to warn Bobby, 'If you don't behave, you're going off to military school!'"

A positive trait Bob Tasca Sr. learned from his grandfather is expressed in the Tasca Automotive Group's basic principles of (giving) 100 percent. No matter what grade Bob earned on the front of his report card, the only grade that mattered to his grandfather Benedeto was found on the back, and that was the grade given for "effort." Nothing less than an "E" for "excellence" was acceptable, thus a lifelong trait of pursuing excellence became a Tasca family tradition.

Grandpa Charlie Begins Anew

Carlo Tasca spent the first 13 years of young Robert's life attending to his son's every want and need. He was a terrific father. However, the life of a widower can be a lonely one. Once Grandpa Charlie was confident that young Bob (who was knocking on the door of teenage adolescence) would be fine, Carlo began courting Amelia Civittolo and married her in June 1939. In October 1942, Amelia presented Carlo with a daughter and 16-year-old Bob with a half-sister named Carla, whom Bob dearly loved. For Tasca, it was the opportunity to happily assume both roles of big brother and stepson.

Family Helping Family

Of course, a number of Bob's aunts and uncles played an important role in the shaping of his adult life. Probably the exact moment in time that set young Tasca on the road to automotive

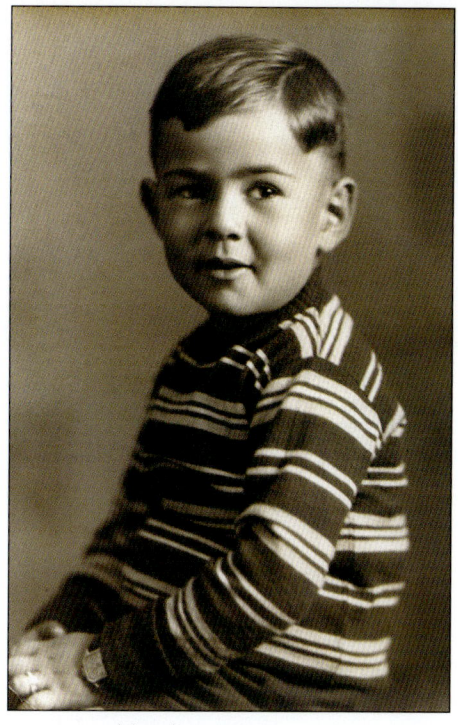

A 5-year-old Robert F. Tasca Sr. puts on his best (angelic) face at the local photo studio. Tasca's Aunty Anna-Tasca Gattone described Bobby as "extremely smart but somewhat mischievous. He was always doing something to gain attention."

Bob and his Aunt Theresa Colavecchio posed for this photo on July 19, 1934, on the boardwalk at Spring Lake, Rhode Island. "Aunty Tess" went on to run the front office at both Tasca Ford and Tasca L-M. In fact, she and her sister, Jean (a Certified Public Accountant), were two of Bob's first employees.

Chapter One: Tasca Family History

"stardom" was most certainly the day when (at just four years old) Bob's Uncle Jake Colavecchio put a wrench in his hand (most likely to discourage young Tasca from causing any further mischief) and in the process taught him how to fix a Model A Ford. That defining moment led to eight-year-old Robert Tasca writing an essay for his teacher at George J. West Elementary School (145 Beaufort Street, Providence, Rhode Island) titled, "When I grow up, I want to be a Ford dealer," and the rest, as they say is, "history."

As longtime Tasca family friend and former Mt. Pleasant District High School chum Louis Marciano related, "Bob was a big kid and kind of aggressive (or could that be "dynamic"?) but in a friendly sort of way. He was a good student. He and I went to Mount Pleasant High School [established 1939] together, which was located in Providence. I was a defensive end on the Mt. Pleasant Highlanders football team, and Bob was a saxophone player [Tasca occasionally played the clarinet as well] in the Mt. Pleasant High School Marching Band, so our paths frequently crossed, especially at football games. Bob also loved automobiles. He loved them so much that he could take an old Ford apart, and put it back together with his eyes closed!"

"Whatever he did, he did it well," commented his cousin Anna.

However, Bob's schooling and his love for the automobile were ultimately on a collision course, and in more ways than one. His family did not approve of his desire to get into the car business. They preferred that he follow his father, Charlie, into the family jewelry business, viewed by them as more noble, much cleaner, and a considerably more profitable pursuit. In his pre-adolescent days, Bob was frequently sent to bed without supper because of his constant chatter about fixing cars. While he sat in his room he vowed that not only would he follow his dream, he would be far more successful with cars than if he went into the jewelry industry, according to Louis Marciano.

"After Bob took his final exams [May 1943] he stopped going to classes and went to work at Harry Sandager Ford. That is until the Mt. Pleasant High School Vice Principal caught up with him and asked, 'Where have you been? You haven't been coming to classes.' Bob said, 'Well, I've finished with my exams, and I'm now working.' The principal said, 'You get back to school. You come to class every day. You have ten days left until you get your diploma [June 1943]. Then you can go out and get a job!'"

That same summer Bob's Uncle Jake Colavecchio graduated from M.I.T. and nephew Bob permanently replaced him at Harry Sandager's. Young Tasca started out as a forty-cent-an-hour grease monkey. However, by the middle of 1948, he had worked his way through the company and was named to the position of General Manager. The future looked bright for 23-year-old Robert F. Tasca, and there would be no turning back.

For Love and Family

Josephine Cambio-Tasca, who was named after her grandmother Josephine Cambio, was born in the North Providence town of Lymansville, Rhode Island, on October 14, 1924. She was the oldest of five girls (Josephine, Edith, Vera, Ann, Ester) and two boys (Pat and John). Josephine's mother, Dora, was a homemaker, and her father, Pasqual, worked at the Esmond (Rhode Island) Mills Textile Plant. Dora and Pasqual Cambio had migrated separately to America from the towns of Pratella and Cionlana located near Naples, Italy, and were married stateside.

"My mother lived with her sister, my Aunt Margaret ("Maggie"), when she came to Providence, and once she and Pasqual met, they went through a traditional Italian courtship, and married."

During her formative years, Josephine attended Lymansville Grammar School and later North Providence High School.

"Being the oldest of seven children, I wanted to become a schoolteacher. Unfortunately, my parents couldn't afford it. One of my aunts offered to pay my tuition to college but my mother wouldn't accept it because she knew that she could not pay the money back. So, at 16 years old, I went to work in the jewelry business at Uncas Manufacturing. That's when I first met Bob. You won't believe it, but I was making a novena at St. Thomas Catholic Church on Fruit Hill. He had a 1939 Ford that he used to drive by in.

"One day, he followed me home. Now, my mother was very a strict Italian. At first, she wasn't very happy about it because I was the oldest of the five girls, and I was expected to set an example for the other girls to follow. She came out onto the porch and said, 'If you want to talk, come in the house.' From then on everything was fine. Bob was a big guy and he loved to eat and that really endeared him to my mother, not to mention the fact that he spoke fluent Italian. She always had something cooking on the stove and he kind of charmed her. My parents really liked him. On Sundays he and my kid brother, Pat, would always wash the car. Then after dinner, we would all go out for ice cream."

Another trait that endeared young Tasca to Josephine's parents was the fact that he was hard working. On December 30, 1950, at age 25, two momentous events occurred that forever shaped Bob Tasca Sr.'s destiny.

First, Bob and Josephine were married at St. Thomas Catholic Church, after which the couple honeymooned for three days in New York City before moving into their new home in North Providence. Did the newly married Mr. and Mrs. Robert F. Tasca go sightseeing in the Big Apple like regular tourists? Well, maybe a little, but according to Josephine, they mostly went shopping. "Bob just loved to shop!"

And second, while on their honeymoon the new Mrs. Robert F. Tasca received a bit of a shock when her husband sat down and wrote his resignation letter to Harry Sandager announcing that he would be leaving his post as General Manager at Sandager Ford. He would be starting a Ford dealership of his own.

The Next Generation of Tascas

Bob Sr. and Josephine had four children, who were the lights of their life: Robert Francis Jr., Carl Albert Sr., David Joseph Sr., and Patricia Ann.

Robert Francis Tasca Jr.

Robert F. Tasca Jr. ("Bobby II") was born October 16, 1951, at Providence, Rhode Island's Roger Williams Hospital. The oldest of four, Bob Jr.'s destiny from the cradle was to become president of the Tasca Automotive Group. As Tasca Jr.'s father once commented, "Bob is in charge of the company. He's in charge of marketing, merchandising, advertising. He goes to all the weddings, funerals; he's the fun guy. He promotes good will and he's a super salesman!"

In his formative years, Bob Jr. was your typical all-American kid. He was handsome, smart, and popular. Bobby first attended St. Mary's Academy (Bayview) in 1969, then graduated from Scituate High School. He then matriculated to Providence College (PC), where he graduated with a degree in business in spring 1973.

Bob Jr. loved cars just like his father did, and began tinkering with them at age seven. That love for the automobile led to a series of jobs at the dealership, starting at the bottom as a lot boy. Among numerous assignments, Bobby II worked as a mechanic before becoming involved in management. During the Tasca L-M days, he ascended to the presidency of that enterprise.

On February 4, 1968, Bobby II was introduced to his future bride, Jayne Marcello, by his cousin (get ready for it) Robert Tasca. The couple was married on June 14, 1974, and has three children and six grandchildren.

Their oldest son, Robert F. Tasca III is vice president of the Tasca Automotive Group. He married Therase Sheehan and they have four children, Robert F. Tasca IV, Austin T. Tasca, Cameron J. Tasca, and Dylan Anthony Tasca.

Daughter Jaime M. Tasca is the Tasca Automotive Group's Customer Relations Manager. She married Mark A. Frateschi and they have two children, Brooke Alexandra Frateschi and Marc A. Frateschi Jr.

Bobby II's youngest son, Michael Joseph Tasca, is the principal dealer at Tasca Jeep, Ram, Chrysler-Dodge. He married Brianna Germani.

"I've been truly blessed," says Bobby II. "I've got three great kids, and six terrific grandkids. I work with two dedicated brothers, as well as most of my nieces and nephews. I guess you could say that my mother and father did a lot of things right."

Carl Albert Tasca Sr.

Carl A. Tasca Sr. ("Carly") was born January 31, 1953, at Providence, Rhode Island's Roger Williams Hospital. Carl and

On December 30, 1950, 25-year-old Robert F. Tasca Sr. took the plunge, and married sweetheart Josephine Cambio during a ceremony at Saint Thomas Catholic Church in Providence, Rhode Island. During a brief honeymoon in the Big Apple, Bob surprised and shocked his bride by writing his resignation letter to Harry Sandager announcing that (upon his return) he would be starting his own Ford dealership.

This Christmas photo shows Bobby II (seated, top left) and his brother Carl along with a handful of Tasca and Colavecchio cousins. I think that's David to the upper right in the cowboy hat.

Chapter One: Tasca Family History

older brother Bobby II had one of those typical older brother/younger brother sibling-rivalry type of relationships.

"Bobby and I were always together. One time I was playing basketball against a guy who was quite a bit bigger than I was and he kept hogging the ball. That got old very quickly. I said, 'Wait a minute, I'm going to get my older brother Bobby, and he's going to kick your ass!' I went to Bobby and he took one look at the guy, who was bigger and older than both of us. And Bobby said to me, 'Fight your own battles, will you?'"

Today, Carl is the Corporate Treasurer of the Tasca Automotive Group.

"I've always been good with numbers," he says. "My father sat me down when I was a young kid (1966) and taught me how to read a financial statement. He said to me, 'Profit is what's on paper. Cash in the bank is reality. Make sure that the cash in the bank is right.'"

Then Carl quickly added, "But

The Glenn Miller Band Story

As previously mentioned Bob Tasca played saxophone in the Mount Pleasant District High School Marching Band. However, playing the traditional marching band songs that every red-blooded American kid learned to play back in the day bored him and he often improvised, according to Louis Marciano.

"Bob was an excellent player. However, every once in a while, he would make a mistake on purpose, or he would put in a few extra notes just to make the band master upset. The marching band wore kilts [aka: The Providence High School Kilties]. Some of the boys in the matching band didn't particularly like that idea (Bob included), so after some protest they let the girls wear the kilts and the guys wore light blue trousers."

What Bob Sr. really wanted to do was follow in the footsteps of his musical idol, the immortal Glenn Miller. Tasca learned the famous songs and stylings of the Glenn Miller Big Band sound. To earn extra pocket money and see some of the traveling big bands of the era, Bob worked as a stagehand at popular venues around the Greater Providence area. He carried his saxophone with him everywhere he went and played it whenever he had the occasion.

One night while the Glenn Miller Band was performing at the Metropolitan Theater, the stage manager was asked if there was a musician's hall in Providence. Apparently, one of the band's saxophone players had split his lip and could not play. The stage manager suggested that he listen to young Tasca. After reeling off

Not only was young Robert F. Tasca mechanically inclined, he was also musically gifted. Tasca played the saxophone in the Mount Pleasant High School Kilties Marching Band. This picture was taken during his junior year in front of the school while hanging out with a couple of his band buddies.

20   The Tasca Ford Legacy

I wasn't big on school. I went to St. Mary's Academy in East Providence for eight years. Then we moved to Scituate, Rhode Island, where I graduated from Situate High School. I went off to Providence College for two years. I was more interested in going to work than going to school. The priest (who was also the principal) at PC noticed this and called my father and said, 'Carl's not coming to school.' My father said, 'Well, I guess that means that he wasn't meant to go to college!' Then he says to me, 'You don't go, I don't pay,'" so I transferred to 'Tasca University,' and that's where I stayed."

When it came to the applied art of the automobile, Carl was tutored by some of the best minds in the business. His father, Bob Sr., taught him the financial end of it. Dean Gregson was instrumental in teaching Carl the sales end of things. At the time he had John Healey in the High Performance Department and Ralph Poirier

several of Miller's most popular tunes young Bob was asked to sit in with the band that night.

"Glenn Miller said, 'When I come back from the war, I want you to play in my band.'"

Although the overall experience of being asked to play in the Glenn Miller Band was personally rewarding, it was nonetheless a bittersweet experience as Glenn Miller died in a World War II airplane crash on December 12, 1944. Along with his passing went Bob's aspirations of becoming a professional big-band musician. Tasca said, "When he [Miller] died, I took my saxophone and put it away. That was the end of my career in music."

"As children, we all grew up on Glenn Miller," says daughter, Tricia. "My father played his music every Saturday night. We would sit in the beautiful living room that he designed; he had a wall-to-wall, reel-to-reel sound system. When I was a little girl, I would dance around the living room, and even now, when I hear Glenn Miller's music, I get very choked up because those are memories that you never lose. I almost wish that I had lived in that era; it was such a simple time."

It should be noted that toward the end of Bob Sr.'s lifetime, when he was in poor health and in need of something to keep himself occupied, the Tasca Automotive Group's Mike Perlini suggested that "the Bopper" (what his really close friends called him) take up the saxophone again. Bob Jr. still has his father's prized saxophone. He keeps it in tip-top condition just in case the Bopper's spirit should ever feel like playing a tune.

Bob Tasca Sr.'s idol was the big-band musician Glenn Miller. Tasca wanted to follow in Miller's footsteps and become a professional musician. He even filled in one night at Providence Metropolitan Theater when Miller's saxophone player split his lip and couldn't play. Sadly, Captain Glenn Miller died in a World War II airplane crash over the English Channel. Bob put his saxophone away, and never played it again.

Chapter One: Tasca Family History   21

and Billy Gilbert in the Service Department; how could you lose?

"I was a lot boy. I prepped cars. I did oil changes. I learned how to set valves on Ralph Poirier's 1965 Shelby GT350 when I was very young. He put me up on a box so that I could reach over the fenders into the engine compartment. We used a set of cut-off valve covers on the engine, lowered the idle, and I set my first set of valves.

"I was always around the mechanical side of the business and still love hanging out with the mechanics today. I have a second office out in the shop and I spend about 80 percent of my time out there. I have a lot of respect for our technicians because they know how to properly fix a car. There's nothing worse than when something goes wrong on a customer's car and you don't know how to fix it."

Carl Sr. married Iuna Maddalena on November 24, 1979. They have two children, Carl A. Jr. and Carrie Ann. Carl Jr. married Tania Gozzi and they have a daughter, Giada. Carl Jr. works with his cousins on overall corporate strategy and operations and is currently involved in the re-organization of Tasca's newly acquired Nissan dealership. Carrie Ann works in the Fixed Operations (Fixed Ops) Accounting Department.

David Joseph Tasca Sr.

Like his two older brothers, David J. Tasca Sr. was born at Providence, Rhode Island's Roger Williams Hospital, on September 9, 1958.

"Because I was the third and youngest son, I was home with my mother and father a lot more than my brothers Bobby and Carl were. They were 16 and had their driver's licenses. So, when my dad wanted to do something in the yard with the sprinkler system [which was practically a fixation with Bob] I would always be the one home, so . . . Not that I felt stuck with the job, mind you. That was how I learned, by working with him. When I got married and had my own home, I knew how to fix something when it broke! I would say the most memorable time I spent with Dad was every time that I was with him."

David Sr. was extremely athletic and just *loved* sports. He played baseball from age eight all the way through high school. He played in little league, senior league, the farm team, and Sr.'s team. You name it, he played it.

"The farm team was called the Elks. My father's L-M dealership sponsored our little league team, called the Cougars, and that name carried over to my senior league team, which my father also sponsored. Whenever he was home, he came to watch me play. He even coached third base and occasionally umpired for the team. I was a pretty fast runner as a kid and used to steal bases. That was one thing I was really good at. That was great fun. I always liked to play rather than watch because baseball's a long game."

David also played basketball and

Go Elks! A slightly distracted David J. Tasca, Jr. is seen here in the bottom row, second from right. Young Tasca played baseball from age eight all the way through high school and was pretty darned dedicated to the sport.

22 The Tasca Ford Legacy

W il concittadino Roberto F. Tasca

In the mid-1960s, Bob, Josephine, Tricia, and David visited father Carlo's hometown of Avellino, Italy, where they were given a hearty Italian welcome.

street hockey with his two older brothers. "Even in the snow, we would shovel off the basketball court and shoot hoops."

David attended St. Mary's Academy in East Providence and graduated from Scituate High School in 1976. Instead of going off to college, however, David elected to go right to work at Tasca L-M in Seekonk, where in 1982 he helped start the "Tasca Two-Year Pre-Trade Program," among numerous other projects. He worked in conjunction with his father and financial wizard Eustace Wolfington. Today, David is the Corporate Secretary of the Tasca Automotive Group, which involves taking care of inventory re-stocking, etc.

David married Janice Boegler on July 16, 1983, and they have two children. David J. Tasca Jr. handles many of the managerial facets of the dealership, such as trucks and acquisitions. Christie L. Tasca is currently attending Quinnipiac University in Hamden, Connecticut.

"When it comes to the automobile business, I learned from the bottom up. A lifetime's worth of education came from my father. He was the best teacher anyone could ever ask for."

Patricia Ann Tasca-De Cristofaro

"Tricia," as she is known, is the youngest of the Tasca siblings, and the only daughter born to Bob and Josephine Tasca. Tricia was born May 18, 1964, also at Providence, Rhode Island's Roger Williams Hospital.

"I was given the name 'Tricia' because when my father was a Ford dealer, he saw a cute little toddler in a hotel lobby. He walked over to her and asked her what her name was. She said, 'My name is Tricia,' and that's how my father named me!" As the only daughter she was known as "daddy's girl."

"When it came to the Tasca women and their role in society, my father was definitely a traditionalist. Or I guess today he would be called a male chauvinist. It wasn't easy being the only girl in the family, and I don't think that it's that easy for my nieces either!"

"Education was very important to my father. First I went to St. Mary's Academy. I went on to graduate from Scituate High School and then studied nursing for two years at PC as I really wanted to become an RN!"

Like her brothers, Tricia Tasca worked part time and during the summers at Tasca L-M and then Tasca Ford. She worked in the office. She shuttled around customers and did whatever was required of her.

"I said to myself, 'As much as I love nursing, I'm expected to be in the family business.' So I switched my major and ended up graduating with a business degree in Liberal Arts."

Patricia met husband-to-be Nicholas J. De Cristofaro Jr. (who ironically comes from a jewelry manufacturing background) while picking up his car for service.

"I said to my girlfriend, 'Who's that guy?' And he said to her, 'Who's that girl?' And that was it. It's kind funny; everything in the Tasca family businesses is either car or jewelry related!"

Nick and Tricia were married August 1, 1987. They have three children. Twin daughters Nicole J. De Cristofaro and Rebecca J. De Cristofaro are currently attending Stone Hill College in Easton, Massachusetts. Son Nicholas III is a Lance Corporal in the United States Marine Corps, and is stationed in Norfolk, Virginia, where he serves as Crew Chief on a CH46 helicopter.

"My father gave me a lot of advice over the years, but I think one of his better quotes was, 'If you love what you do, you'll never work a day in your life.'"

A beaming Bob Tasca stands alongside his daughter, Tricia, on her wedding day, August 1, 1987. The newly married Mrs. Nicholas De Cristofaro met her future husband while shuttling cars at Tasca. It was love at first sight.

Chapter One: Tasca Family History

Building the Foundation of an Automotive Empire

Chapter One concluded with Bob Tasca Sr. announcing to his somewhat astonished bride Josephine and the entire Tasca family that he was quitting his job as General Manager at Cranston, Rhode Island's Harry Sandager Ford with the intention of becoming a Ford dealer himself.

After growing tired of selling Hudsons, Bob became a Ford franchisee on November 17, 1953. This empty building, located at 1282 Hope Street, is the former home to not only DuPont's Garage, but to the newly established business enterprise, Tasca Ford Sales, Incorporated. Would you believe that Tasca sold 26 new Fords within his first month in business?

CHAPTER TWO

In just seven years, Bob Tasca worked his way up from a forty-cent-an-hour grease monkey to general manager at Harry Sandager Ford in Cranston, Rhode Island. In this photo, Tasca is shown handing the keys to a new 1950 Ford to nationally famous midget racer Bill Schindler.

In a little more than five years (1943–1949) Bob Tasca had ascended from a forty-cents-an-hour job as one of Harry Sandager's grease monkeys to mechanic, to salesman, to sales manager, and eventually to general manager of the dealership. Although Bob was well paid and enjoyed what he later termed "a father-and-son relationship" with his employer, the job posed something of a philosophical dilemma. He later wrote, "I can't sleep at nights when my customers are unhappy; I really mean that. When it got to the point at which I wasn't able to satisfy the customers as I wanted due to company policy, I left."

Bob Sr. wanted to be his own boss; he wanted to be the master of his own destiny. In reality, he was just making good on his grade-school declaration, "When I grow up, I want to be a Ford dealer." Those who were closest to Bob would be the first to tell you that when he made up his mind to do something there was no stopping him.

An indignant Harry Sandager wrote a letter to Ford Division Sales Manager Walker A. Williams expressing his dissatisfaction with the 25-year-old Tasca, making a series of false accusations in hopes that it would block Bob from realizing his goal and force him to return to the dealership. Although the content of the letter was more fiction than fact, Sandager was able to temporarily thwart Bob in his quest. Ford cited Tasca's relatively young age and lack of experience as two of the numerous reasons to deny him a franchise. Both Harry Sandager and the Ford Motor Company clearly underestimated the resolve of this native son of Rhode Island.

While Harry Sandager got his "revenge" in a manner of speaking, it was a hollow victory. Sandager lived long enough to see Tasca Ford Sales flourish and become a major competitor. His agency, however, went out of business shortly after his passing.

Bob's next move was to partner with Ralph Pari, acquiring the Ferncrest Motors Hudson franchise (a temporary experiment, some would say) located at 6 Smith Street in Providence. But a Ford was a Ford, and a Hudson was anything but one.

"My father used to deliver the Hudsons at night because the cars were so damned homely looking," says Bob Sr.'s second-oldest son, Carl. "Customers used to come in the next morning, and say, 'Bob, what kind of car did you sell me? This thing is *ugly!*' My father would say, 'Ah, but it rides nice. You'll get used to the looks.'"

By mid-1953, Bob saw the handwriting on the wall, and wanted to back a winning horse. He began buying new Fords from other dealers in the Greater Boston area using the old Hudsons taken in on trade from the dealership. He turned around and sold the new Fords (at least four that we know of) out the back door of his Hudson franchise! Of course, today's franchise rules would never allow such a thing but in those post–World War II days, you could bend the rules a little without any major repercussions. Also, at that time Hudson was in serious financial trouble and needed all the dealers they could get, as longtime friend Louis Marciano tells it.

"I was one of the first people to buy a new Ford through Bob via Ferncrest Motors. I said, 'Bob, I would like to buy

> "The long and the short of it was that Bob Tasca was outselling all the local Ford dealers and he didn't even have a Ford dealer franchise."

a nice, new [1951] Ford convertible so I can go out and have a good time. He said, 'Give me a few weeks, and I'll check around for you.' About a month later, I met Miss Gloria Petrucci, my future wife. Within three months I decided that I was in love and wanted to buy her a diamond ring. I went back to Bob and said, 'Bob, I'm going to get married, and I need to buy my girlfriend a diamond ring. You've got to sell this car for me

Chapter Two: Building the Foundation of an Automotive Empire

After two months, Bob had outgrown his one-horse operation at Du Pont's Garage, and rented this huge Quonset hut–like building (from a former Packard dealer), which was located at 811 Hope Street. All was well with the business until August 31, 1954, when Hurricane Carol roared up Rhode Island Sound's Narragansett Bay with its record-setting waves of nearly 14½ feet. (Photo Courtesy *Providence Journal*)

Hurricane Carol wiped out Tasca Ford within a matter of minutes. Bob, his cousin William "Bill" Tasca, and employees Matt Gervasio and Tommy Iverolino waded up Hope Street in waist-high water to seek refuge in the steeple of the Trinity Presbyterian Church. To add insult to injury, Bob's office had been looted of $3,200. (Photos Courtesy *Providence Journal*)

This is the former Trinity Presbyterian Church building at 850 Hope Street; it has been a VFW Hall since 1963. The rooftop bell tower where Tasca and company stood and viewed the destruction was a post–Hurricane Carol addition.

This sales contract jacket is a rare memento from Tasca's ill-fated 811 Hope Street dealership, which is now a municipal parking lot. Note the slogan, "You'll Save All Ways Always at 'America's Highest Trader,'" no doubt some of Bob's late-night-inspired prose.

The Humblest of Beginnings

The long and the short of it was that Bob Tasca was outselling all the local Ford dealers and he didn't even have a Ford dealer franchise. There were rumors of Hudson's imminent merger with Nash. In January 14, 1954, Hudson became part of the Nash-Kelvinator Corporation (which ultimately morphed into the American Motors Corporation). By then, Bob was even more convinced that it was time to end the experiment, and seriously considered purchasing a Chevrolet-Cadillac franchise that was for sale in eastern Connecticut.

However, when the local Ford factory representatives, R. F. Leonard and Ray Sweeney, heard of Bob's plans, they convinced their superiors to ignore the derogatory Sandager communiqué. At just 27 years of age, Bob Tasca became an officially licensed Ford dealer on November 17, 1953. He was one of the youngest entrepreneurs in Ford Motor Company history to be, ahem, "af-FORD-ed" this golden opportunity.

Bob Tasca now had his Ford franchise, although his father was dead set against it. When approached for financial assistance, Tasca's father replied, "What the hell do you want to do that for? Why would you want to come home covered in grease every night when the jewelry business [Providence, Rhode Island's Tasca Jewelry] is so clean and you can make a good living at it?"

Tasca replied, "Pop, I'll make more money on a Saturday than you'll make in a week because I'll be doing what I really want to do!"

Charlie Tasca loaned his son the two grand he needed to buy his Ford franchise, and that was the end of the discussion. That's what Bob Tasca Sr. wanted, and that's exactly what he got. "I began

and find me a cheaper one. I can't afford both the car and the ring.' We became engaged Valentine's Day 1952. Bob got me a second car (a 1951 Ford coupe) that was cheaper and I was able to buy a diamond ring for my bride to be!"

In 2006, Louis Marciano came in to see Bob at the Tasca Automotive Group's new Cranston, Rhode Island, facility and presented him the two original Ferncrest Motors Sales Contracts on those cars.

Chapter Two: Building the Foundation of an Automotive Empire

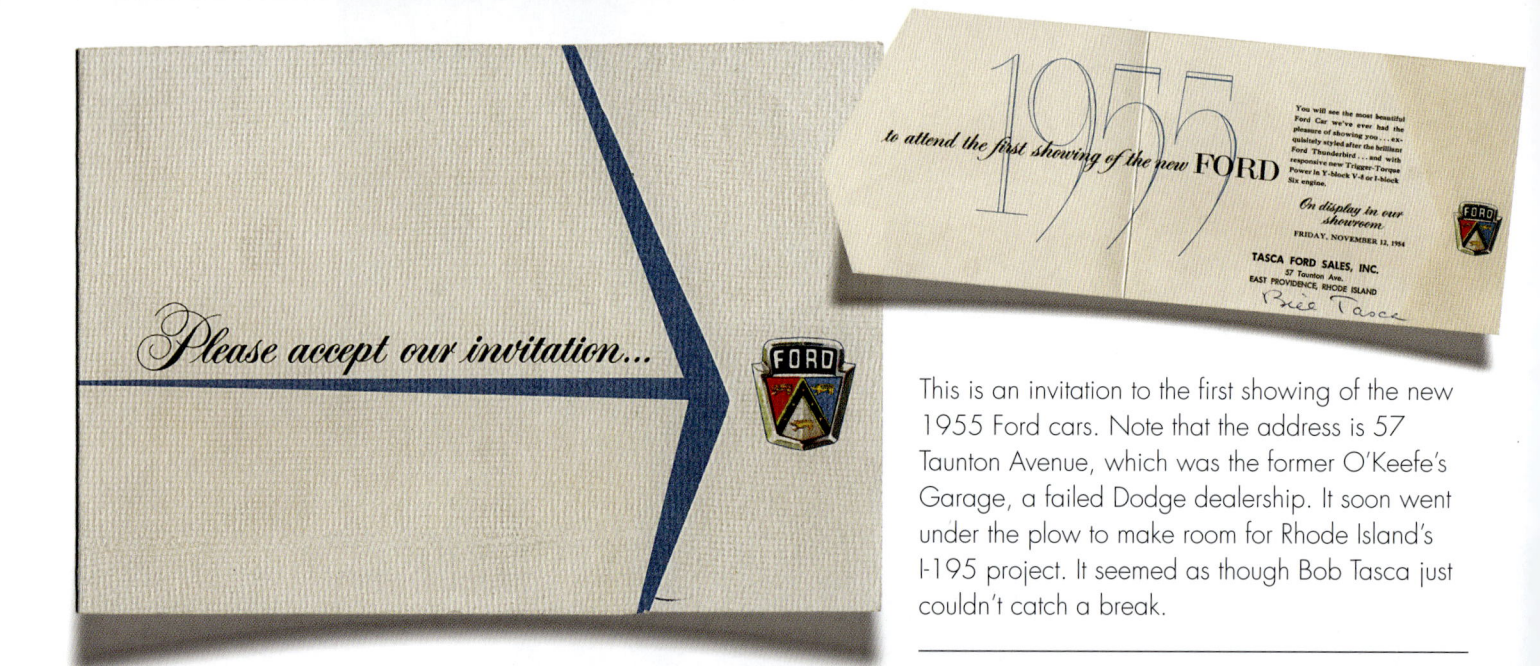

This is an invitation to the first showing of the new 1955 Ford cars. Note that the address is 57 Taunton Avenue, which was the former O'Keefe's Garage, a failed Dodge dealership. It soon went under the plow to make room for Rhode Island's I-195 project. It seemed as though Bob Tasca just couldn't catch a break.

with $2,000 cash, which was more than $30,000 less than the normal minimum Ford required."

In those days, most Ford dealers were small, community-based operations. As chief mechanic, salesman, and general manager of Tasca Ford Sales all rolled into one, Tasca's early days were anything but easy. He had to be creative, and often had to improvise. Tasca and his Aunt Tess (as office manager and bookkeeper) rented a single stall in a gas station known as DuPont's Garage, located at 1282 Hope Street, Bristol, Rhode Island, and hung out his shingle. Tasca paid DuPont $10 per car to prep his new Fords as he sold them. Aunty Jean controlled the purse strings, Bob later wrote.

"From the very beginning, I'd known what kind of business I wanted to run; one focused on selling and servicing [Ford] automobiles; one that would give customers satisfaction that they had never dreamed before. I figured that if I could do that, the bottom line would take care of itself!" That became Bob Tasca Sr.'s mantra for the rest of his life.

Tasca was supposed to sell 35 new Fords a year, which was about three cars a month. However, in his first month of business, Bob sold 26 units, well within target range of Ford's yearly sales quota. This level of sales necessitated the hiring of three additional employees, Bob's cousin William "Bill" Tasca, "Tommy Tasca" Iverolino, and Matt Gervasio. Within two months, Tasca Ford Sales had become fully capitalized with $35,000 in the bank and was ready to move from its humble beginnings to an address more fitting of its status.

Tasca rented a huge World War II Quonset Hut located at 811 Hope Street in Bristol, right on the shore of Rhode Island Sound's Narragansett Bay. All was well with the new enterprise until Hurricane Carol roared through Narragansett Bay on August 31, 1954; its record-setting waves of nearly 14½ feet

This photo was taken at the National Guard Armory Car Show, Providence, Rhode Island, in 1956 while Tasca's franchise was still operating out of the 57 Taunton Avenue address. Shown is a 1956 Thunderbird accompanied by a 1956 Ford Sunliner with the ultrarare plexiglass top.

28   The Tasca Ford Legacy

virtually destroying everything in its path, Tasca Ford included.

"At ten o'clock that morning the waves were starting to wash over the railroad tracks that ran alongside the shore behind the dealership," commented Tommy Iverolino. "Bob called the Chief of Police and asked him what he should do. 'Don't worry,'" the chief said, 'We'll let you know if there is any real danger.' Right about then a big wave came crashing over the railroad tracks and smashed in the showroom windows!"

Bob Sr., his cousin Bill Tasca, Iverolino, and Gervasio waded through waist-high water and literally swam up the street seeking refuge in the steeple of the Trinity Presbyterian Church [at 850 Hope Street], where they safely viewed the carnage. To add insult to injury, Tasca Ford's sales office had been looted. All Bob found was an empty money bag, and a handful of uncashed checks.

Youngest son David commented, "After Hurricane Carol, my father could have thrown in the towel and said, 'I just lost my business. I don't have any money. Maybe I shouldn't be doing this.'

But he kept going. He never took an exit. He stayed on the highway."

We Didn't Borrow Any Money, and Came Back Stronger Than Ever!

With only $875 in his pocket Tasca regrouped and assumed the reins of a failed Dodge dealership in East Providence, known as O'Keefe's Garage,

> " With only $875 in his pocket Tasca regrouped and assumed the reins of a failed Dodge dealership in East Providence, known as O'Keefe's Garage. "

located at 57 Taunton Avenue. He renamed it Tasca Ford Sales, but according to Bob's widow, Josephine Tasca, that too was a "washout." First, the local Ford dealer vehemently objected to Tasca's setting up shop in such close proximity to his dealership. In light of this, Bob was temporarily granted the license to only service Fords, not sell them.

Second, the state of Rhode Island ultimately exercised its right of eminent domain as its newly planned Interstate 195 project was routed right through the middle of Bob Tasca's showroom. An exasperated Bob Tasca found a piece of undeveloped farmland farther up the road at 777 Taunton Avenue and began making plans to build the ultimate (for its time) Ford dealership.

"This was really the beginning of Tasca Ford as we know it," commented Carl Sr. "My father had already been through hell and high water but he had a vision and he was determined to see it through. He wanted to become the nation's largest Ford dealer and he wasn't going to take no for an answer!"

At first, not everyone shared equally in Bob Tasca's vision.

"When my father went to the bank to secure financing they threw him out, saying, 'That's out in the middle of farm country. Why do you want to build [a dealership] there? Nobody's going to come there!' My father said, 'Don't you worry, they'll come!'"

Breaking Ground

In 1956 Bob Tasca broke ground on his new dealership at 777 Taunton Avenue. One of the photos taken during that landmark occasion is of a group of men standing out in the middle of what appears to be nothing more than a pasture at the time but that soon changed. On December 20, 1956, Tasca Ford

This display featuring a 1956 Thunderbird as the centerpiece was a joint promotion between Tasca and Shepard's Department Store located in downtown Providence.

Chapter Two: Building the Foundation of an Automotive Empire 29

"If you build it, they will come," is a famous line. It is also a fitting one when it came to the new-from-the-ground-up Tasca Ford Sales, Inc., erected on a piece of farmland off Taunton Avenue in East Providence.

In this widely circulated publicity photo taken at the ground-breaking ceremony are (left to right): Tasca consigliere William "Bill" Corvese, Ford Motor Company representative Ray Sweeney, Bob's father Charlie "Carlo" Tasca, Bob Tasca Sr., and Ford District Manager R. F. "Bob" Leonard.

Young Bobby Jr. (left) and Carl pose with the official, specially engraved shovel used in the ground-breaking ceremony.

Sales opened to the public. Its new home was an ultra-modern, 25,000-square-foot, split-level, two-story building. It had been designed by Leonard "Uncle Jake" Colavecchio, the very same Uncle Jake who launched a six-year-old Robert F. Tasca on the path to automotive immortality.

"777" (as it became known to Ford enthusiasts worldwide) featured a wall-to-wall glass showroom and sales offices fronting Taunton Avenue with the administrative offices and parts and service departments located directly behind it. On the lower level (or basement) were the used car department, vehicle prep, and new-car storage. Out front on the billboard-style marquee right below the east-side front door, a neon sign proclaimed, "Ford By Tasca." The sign located at the service entrance underscored Tasca's customer satisfaction credo, "May We Service You?" Off to the right at the end of the lot was where the Tasca Ford "A-1 Useful Cars" sign stood. Tasca also erected a huge billboard at the bottom of College Hill to advertise all the latest Ford models.

According to current Tasca University Dean of Instruction and 28-year Tasca Automotive Group veteran Mike Perlini, "Before the I-95 onramp was built, the College Hill intersection proved to be the ideal location to erect a billboard. Mr. Tasca knew this because all the executives and people who worked in downtown Providence had to commute through College Hill on their way to work every morning. When they stopped at the red light at the bottom of College Hill, they would be staring straight at that huge billboard."

"When I was a young kid, my father took me out on the lot and gave

These photos were taken of the new Tasca Ford Sales dealership at 777 Taunton Avenue during the Grand Opening. The split level, three-story facility boasted 25,000 square feet with a wall-to-wall glass showroom and sales offices fronting Taunton Avenue. Administrative offices and parts and service departments were located directly behind the showroom as well as downstairs.

Chapter Two: Building the Foundation of an Automotive Empire

TASCA

"Win on Sunday, Sell on Monday!"

Bob Tasca Sr. may have been a Ford man by profession but above and beyond everything else in life he was first and foremost a family man. As you can imagine, having a daughter and three car-crazy young boys running loose around the Tasca household could at times become a little hectic.

"About 85 percent of the time the boys were well-grounded kids and a real pleasure to have around," commented Josephine Tasca. "It was the other 15 percent of the time when you needed to worry as they could become little hellions."

When Bobby II and Carl were no more than four or five years old, their father decided that he would lift some of the burden off Josephine by bringing the boys to work with him. After all, that is how he got started in the car business, and it hadn't hurt him any. Imagine what a great reality-TV series that might have made had there been such things back in the day.

Carl says, "Bobby and I used to get picked up from parochial school, I'm talking about second or third grade, by the parts driver and go right to the

Tasca Ford Sales' initial entry into drag racing was with the sponsorship of customer Gordon Carlson's 1962 406-ci 405-hp Galaxie 500 4-speed car. Depending on the way the car was set up (Stock or Super Stock) it ran 13.4s to 13.5s at more than 105 mph.

36   The Tasca Ford Legacy

Young Bobby Jr. (left) and Carl pose with the official, specially engraved shovel used in the ground-breaking ceremony.

Sales opened to the public. Its new home was an ultra-modern, 25,000-square-foot, split-level, two-story building. It had been designed by Leonard "Uncle Jake" Colavecchio, the very same Uncle Jake who launched a six-year-old Robert F. Tasca on the path to automotive immortality.

"777" (as it became known to Ford enthusiasts worldwide) featured a wall-to-wall glass showroom and sales offices fronting Taunton Avenue with the administrative offices and parts and service departments located directly behind it. On the lower level (or basement) were the used car department, vehicle prep, and new-car storage. Out front on the billboard-style marquee right below the east-side front door, a neon sign proclaimed, "Ford By Tasca." The sign located at the service entrance underscored Tasca's customer satisfaction credo, "May We Service You?" Off to the right at the end of the lot was where the Tasca Ford "A-1 Useful Cars" sign stood. Tasca also erected a huge billboard at the bottom of College Hill to advertise all the latest Ford models.

According to current Tasca University Dean of Instruction and 28-year Tasca Automotive Group veteran Mike Perlini, "Before the I-95 onramp was built, the College Hill intersection proved to be the ideal location to erect a billboard. Mr. Tasca knew this because all the executives and people who worked in downtown Providence had to commute through College Hill on their way to work every morning. When they stopped at the red light at the bottom of College Hill, they would be staring straight at that huge billboard."

"When I was a young kid, my father took me out on the lot and gave

These photos were taken of the new Tasca Ford Sales dealership at 777 Taunton Avenue during the Grand Opening. The split level, three-story facility boasted 25,000 square feet with a wall-to-wall glass showroom and sales offices fronting Taunton Avenue. Administrative offices and parts and service departments were located directly behind the showroom as well as downstairs.

Chapter Two: Building the Foundation of an Automotive Empire

me some sound words of advice," commented Carl Sr. "Pointing to the cars in the showroom he said, 'Those cars you sell for Henry!' Then pointing to the Tasca Useful Cars lot he said, 'And those cars you sell for Bob!' It was right then and there that I realized just how really important used cars were."

Service, Service, Service!

Many people contend that Tasca Ford Sales practically invented customer satisfaction. Early on, Bob Sr. arrived at the conclusion that the average working man couldn't necessarily afford the luxury of taking the time off work to bring his car or truck in for weekday service. This became a major concern from a personal service/business growth viewpoint as well as from a vehicle warranty perspective.

"It wasn't long after I started the business that I'd committed to evening and weekend service. Nobody else, anywhere, offered that back then [1958]. It was unheard of but I knew I had to do it to make my customers happy. At first my people balked at working evenings and Saturdays; they changed their minds though when I told them we'd have extended hours within a month or I'd padlock the doors and go out of business. This is called a 'creditable threat' and I felt that strongly about it. They believed me, and after awhile, they discovered that night service and weekend service wasn't so bad after all."

"Bob was a work-a-holic, said Tasca Sr.'s widow, Josephine. He wanted a family business and he knew that it would take a great deal of commitment ("24/7") to make it a financial success. I used to bring his dinner down to the dealership on Sunday afternoons and I would put out a tablecloth but he would quite often end up using the hood of a car as his table."

Tasca later wrote, "I can remember getting out of bed in the middle of the night and driving down to Fall River, Massachusetts [more than 17 miles], to pick up a customer's car that had broken down. The customer phoned, saying, 'I broke down on the highway and I left the car right there. I was able to get a ride into Providence, and I got home in a cab, but my car is right in the middle of the road. I wish you'd have it picked up!'

"What was I supposed to tell him? 'Call us in the morning, and we'll take care of it.' He was concerned about the car being left the way it was, afraid that it might be towed, and that he'd get cited for leaving the car improperly parked. So, I went down and handled it. You know what? Than man bought cars from me for the rest of his life; I probably sold him eight or ten cars because of that incident."

The Fat Mechanic Out Back!

What started as part of Bob Tasca's business agenda with customer satisfaction being the dealership's top priority was parlayed into a long-term business relationship with the upper echelon of management at Ford Motor Company. A chance meeting one hot sunny Saturday afternoon in the fall of 1957 ultimately set Bob Sr. on the road to success.

"People often ask how my relationship with the top brass at Ford Motor Company began. Well, it all started by helping someone who had a problem with his car, someone I did not sell a car to nor would I ever sell a car to, but I didn't care about that, I satisfied him anyway.

"It was one of those clear, hot summerlike September days that everyone who lives in New England knows very well; a day that, had it occurred earlier in the year, would have sent everyone to the beaches. It was so hot that the tarmac outside the service area had turned soft, and you could see the heat waves rising from it. As I wiped the sweat from my forehead, I watched as a car drove into my dealership with tires squealing and billows of smoke pouring out from underneath the hood. It looked like a pre-production car, perhaps a new Edsel, Ford's big upcoming entry into the new mid-priced field.

"Only a factory executive would be driving such a car. The car pulled up to where I was working and the man [hurriedly] got out and said, 'Boy, am I lucky

> " Arranging swaps with my customers was just something I would do to make them happy. "

to find you here working on a Saturday. My car is overheating and I've got to get to a wedding being held on Cape Cod and I'm already late. Can you fix it?' This man was in a hurry, a man who was used to giving orders. Well, I knew I could fix it but when I confirmed that it was in fact an Edsel I knew I wouldn't even have parts for it.

"'I can fix it for you but I can't do it right now. Let me tell you what I can do. Leave your car with me and you take my car. Tell me where on the Cape you will be staying. I'll fix your car tonight and tomorrow I'll bring it to you and we can swap back.'

"'You'll do that?' he asked.

"'Sure!' I didn't even ask the guy's name. I wasn't worried, though, because I knew his car was worth [way] more than mine. It was no big deal because arranging swaps with my customers was just something I would do to make them happy.

32   The Tasca Ford Legacy

This aerial photo from 1959 shows the immensity of 777 Taunton Avenue, which was considered by many to be state-of-the-art for Ford dealerships at the time. The 25,000-square-foot structure designed by "Uncle Jake" Colavecchio sat on 80,000 square feet of land.

"The next day my wife and I drove out to Cape Cod estates. The gatekeeper told me where on the property I could find my car. I'd brought an extra set of keys so I just left his car and took mine. We went on our way to morning Mass and then enjoyed the Cape for the rest of the day.

"Several weeks later as I was opening the day's mail I noticed an official-looking letter from Ford Motor Company addressed to Robert F. Tasca, President of Tasca Ford Sales. The letter read as follows:

> Dear Mr. Tasca,
> I had occasion last Saturday to stop at your dealership in East Providence, Rhode Island. My car had overheated and needed repairing. Never in my 40 years in the automobile business have I ever encountered such an extraordinary example of customer service as I did at your dealership that day!" [The letter went on to recount the details of the customer satisfaction incident.]
> I wish to congratulate you on the very fine dealership organization you run.
> Incidentally, please give my thanks to the fat mechanic out back.
>
> Sincerely,
> Ernest R. Breech,
> Chairman

"Well I just leaned back in my chair and laughed. The fat mechanic was me!"

Oldest son Bob Jr. relates, "About a month later, my father went to a Ford Dealer Meeting in New York. He was told that a Ford Motor Company executive who was there wanted to meet him. Who do you think it was? Ernie Breech, of course, and he wanted to introduce him to his boss, Henry Ford II, or the 'Deuce' as he was known."

Bob Tasca and Henry Ford II got along famously. In fact, in a high-profile industry where the Deuce was surrounded by yes men, "HF II" admired Bob for his forthrightness, honesty, and keen insight into New Car Product Development.

Chapter Two: Building the Foundation of an Automotive Empire

According to the Tasca Automotive Group's Mike Perlini, "Bob was quite vocal when it came to product quality, and this endeared him all the more to Mr. Ford. What made Bob Tasca different, however, was that he also had ideas on how Ford could *fix* the problems. Henry Ford II affectionately came to nickname him Tasca 'the Critic.'

"Assembly plant visits became an outgrowth of Bob Sr.'s passion for quality and from what Henry Ford II perceived as Tasca's ability to correct them. It was difficult for a young Bob to convince Ford Assembly Plant managers and Ford engineers to accept his ideas as he was initially viewed as an interloper and with great mistrust and skepticism. For Bob, it was a slow and frustrating process but he never gave up."

The Customer Satisfaction Ten Commandments

In 1953, Bob Sr. sat down and wrote up a business plan as an integral part of his business based on customer satisfaction. This business model was of course revised and expounded upon as Tasca Ford Sales grew and developed. "The Customer Satisfaction Ten Commandments," as he liked to call them, are fundamentally basic rules of fair play, which could be, and in many cases have been, applied to any customer-driven enterprise. Tasca's explanation is fairly simple and straightforward: "There are five negative rules, which one mustn't do, and there are five positive rules, which one should do!"

1. Never gouge a customer: Once you gouge a customer, you can't buy him back; you have to earn him back. And that's a lot tougher than if you had never gouged him in the first place.

2. Never pay a co-worker on a percentage of gross profit: To be sure you never gouge a customer, never give any co-worker an incentive to do so; pay on volume and on customer satisfaction, but never pay on a percentage of the gross.

3. Never tell a customer that something can't be fixed: When the customer bought the product from you, he didn't do it with the understanding there'd be problems you couldn't fix. When he's not satisfied, do one of three things: fix it, replace it, or burn it *after* you've bought it back.

4. Never overpromise; always overperform: Build credibility and trust by never promising anything you can't deliver. If you're uncertain about your ability to deliver on a promise, underpromise. That way if you make your original goal, you'll build up positive credibility with your customer.

5. Never worry about the bottom line: If you sell a lot of product and make

Tasca on Business

Something Bob Sr. used to say all the time was, "Remember, in the car business, there are bears, there are bulls, and there are pigs. It's okay to be a bear. If you want to be conservative, that's fine. If you want to be a bull and be a little aggressive that's fine too, but never, *never* be a pig."

The Big Hat Story

As told by Bob Tasca Jr.

In 1958, my father attended a Ford Product Development meeting in New York City. He was just 32 years old at the time, and in just a few short years, Tasca Ford Sales had become one of the top-ten largest-volume Ford Dealers in the New England Sales Region. Charlie Beacham was Assistant General Manager of Ford Division and he was impressed by the way my father handled himself as a young man at this meeting, and *nobody* got along with anybody at that meeting. So my father suggested that everyone be seated in alphabetical order.

After the meeting, Charlie took my dad out shopping. He said, "Kid, you did a hell of a job in there, and I want to buy you a hat." Since my father always wore hats he agreed. Charlie said, "A new hat will give you a little [more] style. You'll look a bit older and people will respect you more."

Two or three years later, same meeting, same Ford executive, same results. Dad had done a good job and Charlie took him out to buy him another hat. He said, "Kid, I want to teach you something. The hat's the same size. Whoever you are, and no matter how successful you become, don't get a big head." My father was always the same. The hat was always the same size.

Carl Tasca said, "Our father used to say, 'People make money; money doesn't make people.' Money never motivated him. He would say, 'When I make a decision will I be better off five years from now?' One thing about the old man, he never shot from the hip, but once he made the decision to do something, end of story! He had tremendous conviction and determination, which is what the late Carroll Shelby said about him when we went to dinner with Shelby a couple of years before he passed."

Bob Sr. appears (third row center) in this photograph taken of the "graduating class" at Ford Merchandising School, circa 1958–1959.

a lot of people happy, the bottom line will take care of itself.

6. Always treat every customer as custom: Start out with their needs, not your needs. Make the deal suit the taker, not the maker. Always factor in what it will cost them. If you're not sure how to treat them, treat them as though they were your parents.

7. Always give every customer the same fair deal: Menu-Price everything. If you sell the same product to ten people this month, make sure that each one pays the same price. Otherwise, you'll gouge some of your customers to make up profits you lost on the others.

8. Always take care of your customer at the absolute lowest level of management: Every co-worker is authorized to satisfy the customer, carte blanche. My co-workers know that if they don't satisfy the customer, I will, and the cost will be charged back to them, because they didn't do it. The higher up in management you go, the more it costs to satisfy the customer.

9. Always try to fix it right the first time: You won't always succeed but nothing irritates a customer more than having to return over and over again for the same problem. We tell a customer who's been back several times and still unhappy that we'll replace the vehicle. Anything to make him happy.

10. Accept getting beaten sometimes: When you totally commit to satisfying the customer, you become vulnerable. Some customers will beat you and take advantage of you. You can't let that get you down. You need to move ahead and keep making the commitment and pay the price."

By the close of the 1960s, Tasca Ford Sales was selling more than 7,000 new and used cars and trucks annually. The agency underwent a huge expansion program, effectively doubling its size with the addition of a third floor and a new office wing that was completed in early 1961. Tasca Ford Sales seemed poised and ready to face the new decade firmly established as the second-largest Ford dealer in the world. Less than two miles down the street from 777 (and in very close proximity to where Tasca's short-lived 57 Taunton Avenue dealership had been), a new billboard proudly proclaimed "Tasca Ford Sales, 777 Taunton Avenue, One Bigger [a nameless reference to Chicago, Illinois, Jim Moran Ford] None Better!"

Chapter Two: Building the Foundation of an Automotive Empire

TASCA

"Win on Sunday, Sell on Monday!"

Bob Tasca Sr. may have been a Ford man by profession but above and beyond everything else in life he was first and foremost a family man. As you can imagine, having a daughter and three car-crazy young boys running loose around the Tasca household could at times become a little hectic.

"About 85 percent of the time the boys were well-grounded kids and a real pleasure to have around," commented Josephine Tasca. "It was the other 15 percent of the time when you needed to worry as they could become little hellions."

When Bobby II and Carl were no more than four or five years old, their father decided that he would lift some of the burden off Josephine by bringing the boys to work with him. After all, that is how he got started in the car business, and it hadn't hurt him any. Imagine what a great reality-TV series that might have made had there been such things back in the day.

Carl says, "Bobby and I used to get picked up from parochial school, I'm talking about second or third grade, by the parts driver and go right to the

Tasca Ford Sales' initial entry into drag racing was with the sponsorship of customer Gordon Carlson's 1962 406-ci 405-hp Galaxie 500 4-speed car. Depending on the way the car was set up (Stock or Super Stock) it ran 13.4s to 13.5s at more than 105 mph.

The Tasca Ford Legacy

CHAPTER Three

dealership and clean cars. Every day! We did that for maybe eight or nine years. We used to put on our old work clothes and clean one car right after another. Once my youngest brother David was old enough he joined us. He started out emptying wastebaskets, cleaning ashtrays, sweeping the floors, and doing all sorts of odd jobs. Then, like both Bobby and me, he graduated to cleaning cars.

"We all started from the bottom and worked our way up. The weekends were known as the 'B Shift,' as in 'B' here when we open, and 'B' here when we close! One day I went to see my father, 'Dad, I'm tired of cleaning cars. When can I come into the front office?'

"He said, 'Well, I'll tell you what. When you clean them [cars] to my satisfaction, maybe then you can come into the front office!' He was very, very fussy."

But that is not to imply that Bob Sr. was a hardened taskmaster. In an ongoing attempt to keep his sons from getting underfoot at the dealership Bob decided to take the boys out to the Southern New England Timing Association–sanctioned Charleston (Rhode Island) Drag Strip (a converted World War II–era U.S. Naval landing strip turned drag strip) for a little quality time together. To say that the racing bug bit Bob Sr. *hard* would be an understatement; he absolutely loved it.

Those may have been the days of whitewall tires, no hubcaps, and shoe-polish lettering, but it had 90 percent of the makings of one of the best-known stock-body Ford drag racing teams in the history of the sport.

Chapter Three: "Win on Sunday, Sell on Monday!"   37

The Tasca Mechanics Hall of Fame

In its formative years, Tasca Ford featured an all-star cast of mechanics who proved to be the very best in the business.

Dean Gregson

In 1950, a young man named Dean Gregson, the son of New England Indian motorcycle dealer "Colonel" W. H. Gregson (Wigwam Sports Center), walked into Tasca's Ferncrest Motors Hudson dealership. At the time, neither Bob Sr. nor Dean Gregson realized that this was the beginning of a lifelong friendship, not to mention a *very* profitable business alliance.

"I was attending St. Pius Catholic School in Providence and had three paper routes: one in the morning, one at night, and one on Sunday. The drop-off point was almost diagonally across the street from Ferncrest Motors, so I frequently used to visit with Bob Tasca Sr. and talk about cars. Even back in those days Bob showed a keen interest in all things high performance, and had sold a number of 'hot' Hudsons to customers living in the Rhode Island/Massachusetts area.

"By 1955, I was in my late teens, married with a young family, and needed to find a job. I had sold a couple of used cars for a used-car dealer up in Masonville, Rhode Island. My biggest sale? A 1950 Ford sold to one of the teachers at LaSalle Academy. I remember the Sales Manager put a $50 bill in my hand. 'Wow! *Fifty dollars?* Can you imagine how much buying power $50 represented back in 1955?"

Later that year, Gregson hired on as a junior salesman at Howard & Lewis, which was a big Ford dealer in the New England area. It had been through a series of ownership changes and re-organizations in management, and not necessarily all of them for the better.

"There were a number of senior management at Howard & Lewis who were into the whole 'dodge' thing. I remember selling a car to a nice couple from Smith's Hill, Rhode Island, and when they came to pick it up, they [senior salesmen] tried to take the deal away from me! They said, 'Dean! You've got to go out and move $200 more.'

"I said, 'What? We made a deal.'

"To which they replied, 'Yeah, but we didn't get as much for their trade-in as we thought that we would, so now you've got to push them another $200.'

"I was absolutely furious! I said, 'You go tell them that you don't want to honor the deal! I don't want to represent you. I don't want to do business with you. I quit.' And walked out."

For a time, Gregson tried to stay as far away from the car business as he could and worked for Clint Gustafson in Greenville, Rhode Island, cutting lawns, painting houses, building stone walls, and doing all sorts of odd jobs.

"One day in 1956, I said to hell with it! I had seen Bob Tasca's newspaper ads so I drove over to East Providence [at 57 Taunton Avenue] and talked to Tasca Ford's Sales Manager Carmen Perrotti. Unfortunately, Mr. Perrotti didn't seem all that interested in talking with me because I was so young. After the interview, I was talking to a former classmate of mine who worked there named Andy Fiore about what had just happened.

"Just then Mr. Tasca came along. I said, 'Mr. Tasca, you probably don't remember me. I was a paper boy across the street from Ferncrest Motors.'

"He said, 'Sure, I remember you.'

"I said, 'Mr. Tasca, I just came down from Greenville and I told Mr. Perrotti that I would like to go to work for you selling cars, but he said that he didn't need anybody.'

"Mr. Tasca said, 'I'll tell you what. I want you to talk to our General Manager Mr. Bill Corvese who's on his way in from Woonsocket. You talk to him, and I'll talk to Mr. Perrotti.'

"Bill Corvese came over and said, 'I understand Mr. Tasca wanted you to talk to me.'

"I said, 'Yes sir,' and told him who I was. I told him who my father was, and that our family had a sub-dealership for Jones Chrysler-Plymouth in Woonsocket.

"The next thing I know, Mr. Corvese says, 'Mr. Gregson! If you can talk to our customers the same way you talk to me, you got the job.'

"I thanked him and said, 'When can I start?'

"He said, 'Right now!'" And so began Dean Gregson's 27-year association with the Tasca Automotive Group as its High Performance Sales Manager, a job that Dean took quite seriously.

On occasion, Gregson took a demonstrator out to Charleston Drag Strip just to see what it would do. That way he was able to give the customer a much more informed answer if asked about how well a particular car performed. However, Dean's real calling was road racing.

"I like road racing, I like autocross; to hell with 12 seconds. Let me get in a car and run flat out for a half hour, an hour. That was my cup of tea."

In 1965, Ford Motor Company sponsored a trip to California for Gregson to attend the Carroll Shelby Driving School. Once there, Gregson got to drive Mark Donahue's Shelby GT350 at Willow Springs Raceway, Rosamond, California, along with Jerry Titus, Ken Miles, and Bill Hauch. At the time, Dean was selling a lot of Shelbys at Tasca's and had ordered a Shelby GT350 to go road racing in the SCCA B/Production class. But when SFMR101 came in, Bob Sr. (for whatever reason) didn't want to support the project.

That led to a brief disagreement and the re-assignment of the car and Gregson to Worcester, Massachusetts's Harr Motor Company. However, the Harr Motor Company association didn't last long. After just 122 days, Gregson had grown tired of the long drive from Pawtucket to Wooster every day, and at the behest of Tasca's Roy Burchfield and Joe Connetti, he returned to the Tasca fold. As a reward of sorts, Dean was able to purchase an all-aluminum right-hand-drive Ford Cortina factory race car for $1.00. The car was obviously sponsored by Tasca, which just so happened to also be a Lotus-Cortina distributor.

"The Lotus Cortina was a great car. I could eat up Corvettes and Mustangs at tracks like Briar Motor Sport Park (Loudon, New Hampshire) and Watkins Glen (New York) with no problem. I could put the car up on two wheels. I could put it down on four wheels. I could have it up on one wheel. I could use the front wheels for brakes to go around a corner. It was just a very fast car!"

After selling the Cortina, Gregson bought a Mustang coupe and converted it into an A/Sedan racer. Then, with the SCCA's 1969 introduction of its Trans-Am class, Dean converted the coupe into a T/A car running on 289 power. That car was fairly successful but it all came to an abrupt end at Thompson, Connecticut, when a 427 Corvette slammed the door shut on Gregson going into a corner and sent him flying out into the boonies.

Ford then arranged for Dean to pick up a Mach-1 body from its Metuchen, New Jersey, assembly plant. The car was delivered to Glocester, Rhode Island, car builder Hank Fournier and converted to Boss 302 trim. Just 55 days later Gregson was back in competition at a Trans-Am race in St. Jovite, Canada.

Dean's semi-professional racing career more or less came to a close the same time Ford's Total Performance Era" did, but it had been a great 14-year run.

"There's not a place in the world where a young salesman with an automotive background could get a better education. There's not a university in the world that can give you that. In fact, we had people from Brown University with business degrees try to become salespeople. They were very, very knowledgeable people, but they couldn't get 'it' from their head to their fingers to close the deal. They also didn't have a background for the love of an automobile like Mr. Tasca did.

"Because of the Bopper, I knew camshaft, rear end, spring ratios; all that stuff was talked about and taught to me every day. I guess you could say I was born a Tasca man, and I'll die a Tasca man."

John Healey

John Healey became the best known of the group and gained national prominence as "wrench" for the team Tasca, Lawton, and Healey. Today, John is retired, but is a frequently sought "technical historian" of Ford's "Total Performance Era" rank and file. In fact John, Bob Sr., and Bill Lawton were all inducted into the 1995 edition *Super Stock* Drag Racing Hall of Fame.

Like many of his contemporaries, John Healey did a little street racing back in the day running a 1947 Chevrolet coupe, first with a modified GMC straight-six truck engine, and later updated with a 265-ci small-block Chevrolet. After the 1947 got rear-ended in a towing accident, John transplanted the drivetrain into a 1950 Chevrolet that he ran in C/Gas. Not surprisingly, the 1950 also happened to be his street car. "I used to street race that car at night, and my wife drove it during the day."

Around 1958, John was working two jobs to support his growing family. During the day, he worked as a line mechanic at County Motors in Barrington, Rhode Island. Then he worked the night shift at 777 Taunton Avenue doing the very same thing. Somewhere around July 1959 John quit his job at County Motors, and went to work full time at Tasca's.

John's racing exploits with Bob Sr. and Lawton are well documented throughout this entire book. After Bob pulled

The Tasca Mechanics Hall of Fame CONTINUED

the plug on his racing programs, Healey signed on as crew chief for the Western Region Ford Drag Team of the late Ed Terry and Dick Wood (July 1969) and remained there until cessation of the program in late 1971. After sitting out the remainder of his Ford contract, John briefly worked at the newly opened Tasca Lincoln-Mercury store as a line mechanic then returned to County Motors for a brief time.

In 1972, John put together a deal with Steven Besch (Besch & Healey) and ran a Wolverine-chassis Ford Pinto in NHRA Pro Stock running in the 9.20s at more than 152 mph. From there (1975) it was on to driving a Don Hardy–built 1970 Mustang Pro Stock car raced in conjunction with Harvey Cohen and John Downey.

Next up, John campaigned a late-model Ford Thunderbird Pro Stock car during alternating seasons with different partners and different sponsorships. In the interim, John worked for Gary Brown and Warren Johnson. In the late 1970s, Healey retired from drag racing and became involved in a number of non-car-related projects, including his other passion, carpentry.

Today, John alternates between Rhode Island and Florida, and enjoys spending time with his 13 grandchildren and 2 great-grandchildren.

"Mr. Tasca gave me a great start in motorsports when he took Billy and me underneath his wing. He was not only my employer; he was my lifelong friend."

Ralph Poirier

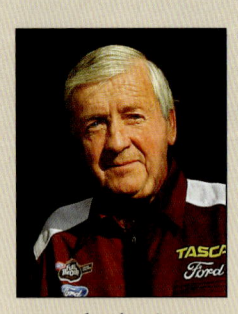

Back in the day, Ralph Poirier was a local boy who was known to have a very, very fast 1953 Studebaker street car. "I had put a brand-new J2 Oldsmobile Rocket V-8 engine in that car straight out of the box. That car was crazy fast. I used to blow the doors off fuel-injected Corvettes on a regular basis."

Ralph credits John Healey, whom he had met at Pawtucket Vocational High School, for helping him get his job at Tasca's in August 1960. At the time, Ralph was doing double duty driving a truck and working in a gas station. He started as a line mechanic but was chosen to work on the first two Tasca drag racing programs. However, Ralph was more into doing his own thing. He and part-time Tasca mechanic "Smokey Joe" Slocum built a 1937 Chevrolet running a Hilborn-injected Oldsmobile engine in B/Gas and set a short-lived record at Charleston Drag Strip at 11.00/132.00. That was around 1964.

After raising three children, drag racing became a second-generation thing when Ralph's oldest son Ralph Jr. acquired a 1975 Mustang II Ghia coupe with a 302 small-block Ford V-8 engine. While attending finance classes at Arizona State, Ralph Jr. raced the Mustang at Chandler, Arizona's Firebird Raceway and Palmdale, California's Antelope Valley Raceway. Upon his return to Rhode Island he and Ralph Sr. began playing around with the little Mustang II in earnest.

"In four years, we turned that car from a 14.4 to a 9.4, running in the 146-mph bracket." In the process, Ralph Jr. had Boston's Chick Rignolo fully tube the chassis, and he built a normally aspirated single-4-barrel [SVO] 302 small-block running a Jim's Transmission C4. Ultimately, that car ran 8.50/150. Ralph Jr.'s follow-up car was a Jerry Bickel-chassis Mustang, which ran an 8.29/165.00 on Ralph Sr.'s 65th birthday, again using a normally aspirated Ford small-block.

"Bobby Trufano and I were the first ones to take Bobby III to the drag races at Englishtown, New Jersey. That started Bobby III on the road to being a race car driver. First I built him a 1992 5.0L Mustang LX Mercury. Then he began driving his father's late-model S/C-S/G-Capri running a 440-inch Ford engine equipped with a set of John Healey cylinder heads. That car ran 8.20s naturally aspirated and a best of 7.76 on nitrous. When Bobby III decided to build a Top Alcohol funny car I worked on it. We went to 13 national events; the worst he qualified was fourth. We were runner-up in the Top Alcohol Funny Car class at Indy two years running, and we set the Low E.T. record for TA/FC at 5.45 seconds. That record lasted for three straight years; nobody ran quicker."

After Bobby III parked the Top Alcohol car and went nitro funny car racing, Ralph Sr. became involved in Carl Tasca's new-generation Cobra Jet Mustang drag racing program. "Basically what I do is suspension, gears, and clutch. The best that car has run is a 7.72/179.00!

"Bob Tasca Sr. always tried to coach me into doing the best job you possibly could at all times. When I started

40 The TASCA Ford Legacy

racing my own car with my son, he was terrific. He supported my racing activities and got me free engine parts. He got me crankshafts, cylinder heads, anything that was in the Ford Motorsport catalogue. He also bought me slicks and anything else that I needed to move along. For a guy who started out as a gas station mechanic Bob nurtured me along. He was truly 'Boss #1!'"

"Smokey Joe" Slocum

In the early 1960s, John Healey, Bill "Chicken Fat" Loomis, and Ralph Poirier worked upstairs in the Service Department at Tasca Ford. Joe Slocum worked downstairs in the Used Car Department. They were four of the greatest mechanical minds in the automobile business, all under one roof.

Joe Slocum's motto was, "Do the job right the first time." In fact he was so good at what he did that once Tasca became hands-on with Ford Motor Company's Total Performance Program, quite a few big names including Holman-Moody (H-M), Bud Moore Engineering, Penske, and Shelby American all wanted to hire Joe away.

An automotive technician for more than 14 years, Slocum not only worked at Tasca, he eventually became one of the factory reps for Ford's New England Region in the late 1960s. For a time he also worked on Mario Andretti's Formula One team. As previously mentioned, "Smokey Joe" Slocum and Ralph Poirier had run a B/Gas 1937 Chevrolet coupe in their earlier days, but when it came to contemporary forms of motorsports, Joe Slocum's real passion was road racing. He worked with Tasca High Performance Manager Dean Gregson as Engine Builder and Crew Chief on Gregson's Trans-Am Mustang race cars.

"The late Fran Hernandez was with us at the Loudon, New Hampshire, Trans-Am race and Smokey said, 'You know, Mr. Fernandez, if you fly cut the pistons this way, and did the valves that way, you could pick up five to eight extra horsepower.'

"Fran says, 'Say that again, Joe?' Hernandez went back to Ford, and they did exactly what Joe said to do on one of their [Boss 302] Trans-Am engines, put it on a dyno, and damned if they didn't pick up six to eight extra horsepower. He was quite a talent!"

Bill Gilbert

Bill Gilbert didn't join the Tasca organization until mid-1963, but by then, he already possessed a wealth of knowledge and experience racing outboard motor boats and midget race cars. When Bill was in the U.S. Navy, he worked on diesel engines. Upon returning to civilian life (1963) he went to work as a mechanic at West Warwick, Rhode Island's Caldwell Ford. However, once he found out that Tasca Ford Sales was paying their mechanics $2.50 per hour flat rate (as opposed to $1.35 per hour from his current employer) he applied for a job. "I didn't know anything about flat rating, but I was sure that I would learn quickly."

Initially, Bill began working nights at Tasca Ford, learning the ropes. At the time (1963) Bob Sr. was driving a 406 Tri-Power Ford Thunderbird but seemed to be having trouble with it. "He came over to me, and said, 'How about taking a look at my car and see what's wrong with it.' He seemed to be in a real hurry, and needed help." A quick diagnosis revealed a pinched intake gasket that Billy fixed in short order.

After that, things sort of evolved, and Bob involved Bill in an increasingly large number of Ford engineering projects beginning the following year (1964) with Tasca's increased hands-on role in Ford Total Performance racing programs.

"Bob used to say, 'You're getting a million-dollar education with all those hours you are spending on the phone with Ford,'" and he was right."

Projects of note included the Tasca Birds (1 and 2), Tasca 505 Mustang, Tasca TGT Fairlane, pre–Cobra Jet era Tasca "KR-8" Mustang, and, of course, the infamous Tasca "Street Boss" Mustang. In the early 1970s, Bill Gilbert made the transition from Ford to Lincoln-Mercury after 777 was sold and the family founded Tasca Lincoln-Mercury in Seekonk, Massachusetts. He became Service Manager, then Service Director before leaving and going into the hardwood floor installation and refinishing business with his son in 1987. Bill returned to the Tasca fold in 1994; he currently works at the Tasca Automotive Group's Cranston, Rhode Island mega-dealership.

As Bill recently summed things up, "Working at Tasca's has been a phenomenal experience for me. Bob Tasca Sr. was my mentor. It was such a pleasure coming to work every day. I was able to play in the Bob Tasca candy shop but not have to pay for the candy."

Bob Sr. returned to East Providence all fired up and ready to go drag racing. This was, after all, something he and his kids could not only relate to ("it's mainstream" he later said) it was also something that he could use to promote his business and create traffic in his showroom. For a little over a decade, Tasca, Ford Sales, Inc. specialized in the sale of high-performance Ford muscle cars, and I'm talking tons of them!

"Win on Sunday," the Early Beginnings

Tasca Ford Sales's first serious drag racing effort began shortly after that fateful day when Bob Sr. and his sons took in their first drag race at Charleston Drag Strip. In late 1961, Tasca's general manager, Roy Burchfield, sold a Cinnamon Red 1962 406-ci/405-hp Ford Galaxie 500 4-speed car (one of the first high-performance models actually sold out of the Tasca dealership) to John Healey's grade school chum from West Barrington, Rhode Island, by the name of Gordon Carlson. Carlson began drag racing his new Galaxie straight off the showroom floor, but was struggling against the local Chevrolets, Dodges, Pontiacs, and Plymouths. With Carlson having much of the mechanical work done on his car at Tasca's (just as he had done with his previous car, a Ford Starliner), and being good friends with John Healey, what occurred next was bound to happen.

Healey remembers, "I was working as a line mechanic at the time and there were no race cars at Tasca. During a conversation among Gordon Carlson, Mr. Tasca, and me, Mr. Tasca asked Gordon what he needed for his car to be competitive. 'You can get me a new set of tires,' Carlson laughingly replied. Now I want to tell you that Gordon Carlson could afford his own tires but he and his whole family had bought quite a few cars from Mr. Tasca so Bob Sr. decided to sponsor Gordon's car."

Bob Sr. summoned employees Dean Gregson, Ralph Poirier, Henry "Wimpy" Tameleo, John Pagano, and of course Healey to his office and said, "We've got a project here. We're going to try souping up this car, and then we're going to go drag racing with it."

Tasca authorized the order of some high-performance FE engine parts from the factory while John Healey worked on Carlson's Galaxie after hours using John Pagano's garage, which was located a couple miles northwest of the dealership in Rumford, Rhode Island. Even in those early days of no hubcaps, whitewall tires, and shoe-polish lettering, the "Team Tasca" professionalism stood out at the local drag races.

"I remember Mr. Tasca saying that since all his line mechanics wore blue uniforms, his race team had to be different; we had to wear a different color! We actually got a uniform company out of Fall River, Massachusetts, to do up these classy-looking white uniforms with the words 'Tasca Ford Satisfies' embroidered across the back.

"Mr. Tasca said to me, 'Hey, Healey, I got you a white coat.'"

"I said, 'Well, boss, you can leave it hung up in my locker.' Imagine! White uniforms at the drag races?"

In its initial outings, the newly formed Tasca (Ford) Racing Team did quite well, winning the Stock Eliminator trophy at Charleston Drag Strip, recording a best of 13.40/105.5 mph. The team also won a Super Stock Eliminator trophy at Charleston Drag Strip, recording a best of 13.54/105.00.

"We used a photo of Gordon Carlson's Galaxie in one of the first ads that we ran out of the newly established Tasca Ford High Performance Department in the Southern New England area," said Dean Gregson.

However, the alliance between Tasca and Carlson soon ran its course. Bob wanted to convert Carlson's Galaxie into a full-time race car. On the other hand, Gordon wanted the car to remain his daily driver. Tasca turned to Dean Gregson and said, "You know what, Dean? We've got to run our own car!"

Enter Bill Lawton

Back in the day, a young Rhode Island–born Irish kid named Bill Lawton, a piano mover by trade (Lawton Movers) and natural-born racer, was a staunch Chevrolet man who drove his

Tasca High Performance manager Dean Gregson used this Charleston Dragway winner's circle photo in one of the first ads for the Tasca High Performance Service Department in the New England area. From left to right are Dean Gregson, Gordon "Swede" Carlson, John Healey, and Ralph Poirier.

Bill Lawton.

Honduras Maroon 1962 Chevrolet 409 4-speed convertible into the Charleston Drag Strip winner's circle week in and week out. Of course, being one of the local "hitters" gave Bill Lawton bragging rights, and when it came to extolling the, virtues of Chevrolet's 409-ci/409-hp W-Series Turbo Fire big-block V-8 engine nobody could walk the walk and talk the talk like Bill Lawton.

As Bob Sr. later commented in an October 1992 interview for *Mustang Illustrated*, "Lawton broke my back night after night funning my kids and bragging to my customers that Fords were trash [Lawton's favorite line was, "Fix or Repair Daily"] and that Chevy was the car! He did this for about three or four weeks in a row. It got to the point where I finally grew tired of it."

Taunting on Taunton Avenue

What Bill Lawton did next proved to be a real game changer and, without a shadow of a doubt, the proverbial straw that broke Bob Tasca's back. One afternoon while the Bopper was working in his newly completed second-story corner office at 777, Bill Lawton had the audacity to do a series of burnouts with his 409 right in front of the dealership! Now stories vary, but the version I most often hear is that Bob Sr. stormed downstairs, walked briskly outside, and slammed his hand down on Lawton's hood, gaining Bill's immediate and undivided attention. "Willie, you can either come to work for me and drive my cars or I'll make sure you will never win another race!'"

Once Bill Lawton joined the team the pace really began to quicken. Tasca Ford's new 1962 Galaxie Club Sedan with solid lifter cam, G-Code 406-ci/405-hp Tri-Power FE big-block and 4-speed ran a career best of 13.16/106.14.

Chapter Three: "Win on Sunday, Sell on Monday!" 43

Speaking of 409s, Bill Lawton puts a car length on one at Charleston Drag Strip. Says mechanic John Healey, "In 1962, we were just getting our feet wet. Basically, we ran locally at Charleston where, to my recollection, we won Stock Eliminator honors over Bruce McLane's 413 Plymouth!"

Shortly thereafter an astonished (and somewhat humiliated) Bill Lawton drove away. What he didn't know was that Bob Tasca had already ordered a 1962 Galaxie 406 Club Sedan Super Stock car through Ford. The lighter-weight no-frills Galaxie featured an 11.4:1 compression, solid lifter cam, G-Code "Thunderbird 406 High Performance (FE) Engine" package equipped with the factory Tri-Power 6V aluminum intake, and three Holley 2100 2-barrel carburetors. These engines were power rated at 405 hp at 5,800 rpm and 448 ft-lbs of torque at 3,500 rpm.

Also available was the newly introduced Ford big-block version of the BorgWarner T-10 4-speed transmission and a number of optional 9-inch Posi-Traction gear ratios ranging from 4.10:1 to 5.83:1.

Tasca's new Galaxie *could* be a formidable competitor in local Super Stock competition given the correct preparation and driver.

As it turned out, John Healey was able to perform both of those duties with equal aplomb. "John was not only a talented wrench man, he was also one hell of a race car driver," commented Bob Sr. during an October 1992 interview for *Mustang Illustrated*.

In John Healey's words: "Mr. Tasca said, 'The job's yours if you want it.'

"I said, 'Oh yeah, boss? How much more an hour?' He just looked at me and laughed because I worked flat rate with no guarantee. We worked long

This is "Healey's Corner." Well, not really, but you get the general idea. Note the reference on the door to Bill "Go-Go" Lawton. The sign on the wall reads "We Must Serve Well to Prosper, We Must Prosper to Serve Well."

44   The Tasca Ford Legacy

What's interesting about this classic starting-line launch photo is the flagman. This was the "pre–Christmas tree era" when flagmen still started races.

Back in the day, Tasca Ford also sponsored the 1957 Ford B/Gas car belonging to the team of brothers Bobby and Ernie Audette.

hours on that car, and it was a real learning curve. He gave me my first start in motorsports, and I'll never forget him for that!"

John Healey drove Tasca's newly christened "Go Getter" Ford Galaxie Super Stock car in time trials only, where the car ran an impressive 13.36/90.00! Of course, Bill Lawton was also at Charleston Drag Strip that day and witnessed the Tasca Ford Super Stock Galaxie's debut. Lawton's best run with his 409 had been a 13.60, so after hearing what the Bopper's new toy had run, he became a little more than just inquisitive.

When Billy wandered over to Tasca's pits to see what all the fuss was about, Bob Sr. was poised and ready! "So you think that Chevrolet of yours is fast? Why don't you drive a good car and we'll see what happens."

"Billy being Billy, shifting the way he did [in that regard, Bill Lawton was later compared to 4-speed impresario (the late) Ronnie Sox], got into the car and made a great run," commented Dean Gregson.

"After the run, Lawton got out, handed the keys to Tasca, and commented, 'The clutch is slipping. Fix it.'"

Years later, however, Lawton commented in a video-taped interview prior to his untimely passing, "My 409 was a real sled compared to that thing!"

So now Bill Lawton's sold on Ford power, and the next thing Bob Tasca says is, "How would you like to race that car for the rest of the year?" And that's exactly what Bill Lawton did, as John Healey recalls.

"In 1962 we were just getting our feet wet. Basically, we ran the car locally at Charleston Drag Strip where we won (to my recollection) at least one race [August 5, 1962] taking Top Stock Eliminator honors with a 13.19 over Bruce McLane's 413 Plymouth with a career best of 13.16/106.14. We also went to Indy for the first time that year. We did fair, but nothing like with our later cars; we really didn't get our act together until about mid-1963. Back in those days we were limited to a 7-inch tire so with that much horsepower, you really had to feather the clutch."

Bob Tasca now had himself a genuine, for-real, drag-racing team. He was quoted in Ford's May–June 1962 issue of *Ford Crest News* magazine as saying, "Teenagers have brought in their parents to the tune of forty-one sales in our first six weeks in racing."

This is generally the time when most Ford historians and the whole Tasca family agree that Bob Tasca coined the phrase, "Win on Sunday, Sell on Monday!"

Tasca Ford's 1962 Galaxie Lightweight

Through his connections with Ford Motor Company (and most specifically, Charles. E. "Charlie" Gray Jr.) Bob Tasca had gotten wind of the midsummer release of a fleet of eleven 1962 Ford Galaxie Club Sedans ("lightweights") being built. These hybrids had been authorized by Ford's Stock Vehicles Department

Tasca also raced one of the 1962 Galaxie lightweights in A/FX with driver Bobby Price rowing the tiller. Price was the only driver apart from Billy Lawton to have ever driven a Tasca-owned race car.

Chapter Three: "Win on Sunday, Sell on Monday!" 45

under the supervision of John Cowley, Charles E. Gray Jr., and Drag Racing Team Coordinator and test driver Richard H. "Dick" Brannan. They were prototyped through Ford's Experimental Garage, or "X-Garage" as it was known. Actual vehicle assembly took place at the Wayne, Michigan, Ford Assembly Plant at the tail end of the 1961 model year. In fact these plain-vanilla Galaxie Club Sedans were the last 10 cars off the line, and were immediately shipped to Ford's X-Garage for final preparation.

The 11.4:1-compression 406-ci G-code Thunderbird Special V-8 (FE) engines used in these lightweights were power rated at 405 hp at 5,800 rpm registering 448 ft-lbs at 3,500 rpm. Tri-Power (featuring three Holley 2,100-cfm carburetors) was another special feature, along with aluminum-cased BorgWarner 4-speed transmissions and 9-inch Ford Traction Lok rear ends with Lincoln aluminum alloy brake drums.

Other features included a severely lightened frame; sound-deadener delete; thinner-gauge window glass; fiberglass hood, front fenders, doors, and deck lid; aluminum inner fender panels; aluminum front and rear bumpers and bumper brackets; armrest and carpet delete; heater and radio delete; lightweight front bucket seats; and a relocated trunk-mount battery. In all more than 800 pounds had been pared off each car in an attempt to make them competitive with the Chevrolets, Pontiacs, and Mopars in NHRA's upper-echelon Super Stock Eliminator classes.

Tasca Ford was part of a select group of key players (the "Ford Drag Council") to campaign these "dollar cars," along with Phil "Daddy Warbucks" Bonner, Jerry Harvey, Les Ritchey, "Gas" Ronda, Bob Ford–Len Richter, the Ed Martin Ford Team, Jim Price, Jerry Alderman–Alderman Ford Sales, and of course, Dick Brannan himself. The newly christened *Orbiter-1* with driver Bobby Price handling the reins (the only other soul to drive for Tasca other than Lawton) was capable of elapsed times in the low 12s at more than 112 mph. However, before any serious drag racing took place, NHRA re-factored the Galaxie lightweights into A/Factory Experimental (A/FX), citing their relatively small number (remember, NHRA required that 100 cars be built to be legal for their stock and super stock classes) and their weight-saving components as non-production items, for S/S, anyway.

Challenger II: Bigger Engine Meets Small(er) Car

In 1962, Super Stock Eliminator racing may have become *the* product showcase and revenue generator for Detroit's Big Three, but Factory Experimental proved to be the "what if" category where carmakers were able to think outside the box and come up with some really awesome drag racing machines. Tasca Ford's Rangoon Red 1962 406 Ford Fairlane A/FX car was certainly proof of that. It was the brainchild of Ford Special Vehicles and subcontractor (the late) Andy Hotten from Dearborn Steel Tubing (DST). This particular car is considered by many to be an early forerunner of the infamous 1964 Fairlane Thunderbolt.

Hotten had taken a stock 1962 Ford Fairlane 500, complete with working radio and full interior, and made a series of radical modifications to the engine compartment and firewall area to accommodate the gargantuan 390 FE big-block. A set of full-size Galaxie front springs and shocks were substituted in place of the lighter OEM Fairlane springs and shocks. The floorpan and front section of the transmission tunnel had to be modified to clear those massive FE cylinder heads and bellhousing. DST then fabricated a set of engine and transmission mounts prior to installing the 406 Tri-Power solid-lifter-cam big-block FE engine and BorgWarner T-10 4-speed transmission.

One of the biggest challenges was the exhaust; the factory cast-iron exhaust manifolds simply did not clear, so a set of Hedman Hedders were modified and used. Other items included a specially modified generator, Ford Galaxie radiator for cooling, and relocating the battery to the trunk. A 9-inch Ford Traction Lok rear differential and heavily modified (narrowed) 9-inch Ford axle housing rode on a set of de-arched Fairlane rear

Dollar Cars

This is Ford Motor Company's official definition of a "dollar car" as interpreted by Ford Motor Company Communications Western Region official John Clinard:

"In cases where we [Ford] want a car showcased for the company [for example, at the SEMA Show, or in an important magazine] Ford's marketing/promotional budget would be tapped to pay for the car and it would be sold to the responsible individual or firm for one dollar. In effect, the expenditure equates to advertising. The exposure achieved by the dollar car is equated to the same money spent on advertising.

"Why sell the car and not give it away for free? It is necessary to take 'consideration' (one dollar) for the car to legally transfer title to a new owner. The vehicle then becomes the responsibility of the new owner, including compliance with emissions and safety requirements. In some cases, such transactions specify 'for off-road use only' if we [Ford] know the car will be heavily modified and no longer in compliance. The practice of a dollar car is done much, much less today than in the past."

This particular Marty Schorr photo shows a rather unique induction system, which John Healey tried on the A/FX car in order to increase airflow and horsepower.

Nonetheless, Healey had made a number of running changes to the exhaust, fuel system, and front and rear suspensions, which really made *Challenger II* come alive. In an attempt to get the car to hook up better, John swapped out the BorgWarner T-10 4-speed transmission with a big-block FMX 3-speed automatic. With that done, *Challenger II* began running in the 12.70-second range at more than 115 mph, which by comparison to the performance numbers being generated by similarly equipped A/FX cars seemed closely competitive.

However, at the U.S. Nationals, Charlie Gray and company decided that perhaps Ford didn't need another car essentially competing against their Galaxie lightweights and themselves in A/FX, so the Fairlane was entered in the A/Gas class. Unfortunately, the car didn't fare all that well against faster cars such as Norm Hall's trophy-winning 1939 Willys, which ran a best of 12.06. The exact fate of *Challenger II* is unclear. Some say the car was crushed. There is, however, a replica of the car making the rounds.

The name *Challenger II* was assumed to have come from the fact that "Challenger" was the actual name given to the optional 221- and 260-ci high-performance small-block Ford V-8 engine family made available in Fairlanes that year. With the shoehorning in of a 390 FE big-block, the name *Challenger II* certainly made sense. Then, too, it could have just been the fact that the entire project itself was a real "challenge." You decide.

springs. A set of Traction Master Traction bars were also used, along with M&H Racemaster slicks for increased "bite."

Except for a Thunderbird hood scoop and a set of Cal Custom chrome-plated wheels, the exterior of *Challenger II* looked surprisingly stock because it was, as Dean Gregson recalls.

"One day the Bopper said to me, 'You've got to drive Josephine and me to New York. Pack an overnight bag because Ford's going to take us out to dinner at the Four Seasons Restaurant. Then you're going to meet up with a guy in Hershey, Pennsylvania, change dealer plates, and bring back the car he's driving!'

"I drove to Hershey [Dean recalled the whole town smelled of chocolate] and met an engineer from Ford who handed me the keys to a red two-door Fairlane 500 with a Ford 406 Tri-Power and 4-speed! At the time, the car had a 'street' gear in it, and I actually drove the car home on the Pennsylvania Turnpike!

"I remember some guy in a Corvette pulled up. I was moving along at a pretty good clip when I saw him coming up in the rearview mirror. I casually slipped the car into third gear. When he pulled up alongside me, I nailed it, shifted into fourth, and blew him off like he was standing still. About ten or fifteen minutes down the road, I pulled into the service area at the entrance of the Jersey Turnpike. The guy jumps out of his car and says, 'What the hell have you got in that thing?'

"I said, 'Oh, just a little old Ford V-8!' I never did tell him that it was a 406 with three deuces on it. That was really funny!"

Suddenly, Team Tasca was showing up at the drag races with *three* cars. While Bill Lawton concentrated on driving the team's 1962 Galaxie S/S, Bobby Price was driving Tasca's 1962 Galaxie A/FX lightweight and the Fairlane. On occasion, John Healey or Dean Gregson also made "test and tune" time runs in the cars, John Healey recalls.

"That car [Fairlane] was not popular. It was a real pain-in-the-ass to work on because with the 406 in it, the shock towers weren't moved or anything. I mean, it was a real tight fit."

Chapter Three: "Win on Sunday, Sell on Monday!" 47

Tasca also intermittently raced this 406-powered Rangoon Red 1962 Fairlane 500 in A/FX dubbed *Challenger II*. The car was built by Ford Special Vehicles and DST's Andy Hotten and is considered the forerunner of the Ford Thunderbolt.

Here's another classic photo of the Southern New England Timing Association (SNETA) starter flagging off a Tasca car in 1962. The 406-engine 4-speed car was capable of running 12.70s at 115.00.

48   The Tasca Ford Legacy

Here's a fairly rare color photo of the Tasca Fairlane at rest in the pits. Note Tasca's 1962 Galaxie A/FX car in the background.

TCB with the TSEs

If you're wondering what "TCB" stands for then by all means read on! As early as 1960, Bob Tasca realized that not everybody could afford to buy the top-of-the-line Ford car or truck regardless of product offering, yet customers still wanted to be viewed by their contemporaries as driving something more than just utilitarian transportation. Keeping in mind the catch phrase, "You Are What You Drive," Tasca created the "Tasca Special Edition" cars, which was pure marketing genius.

Bob took a base-level car or truck (1960 Ford Falcon, 1961 Ford Econoline van, and 1963 Ford Custom 300 sedan were some of the earliest examples) and "glammed them up" with whitewall tires, fancy hubcaps, a little extra chrome trim, perhaps a vinyl top, and changed the interior a bit to sell it as a special-edition vehicle only available through Tasca Ford Sales; a "TSE." As such, Tasca was "Taking Care of Business" (TCB) by creating a market for a product that, until the moment it rolled off the transporter, technically didn't exist. In the process, the dealership realized an enhanced profit margin, not to mention moving more products.

Bob later referred to it as "Betting on the Come," which is gambling parlance that means "placing a bet on the outcome, a bet on what you believe you can make happen in the future." In reference to the "Tasca-ization" of the 1963 Ford Custom sedans, longtime Tasca friend and racing associate (the late) John Pagano related the story about how Bob Tasca bet on the come by buying a fleet of *600* plain-Jane Ford Custom 300s and transformed them into the Tasca "T63." It sold for less money but looked just as good as the top-of-the-line Ford Galaxie 500.

"Back in 1963, Bob Tasca Sr. got a call from Ford [New England] Regional Sales. 'Bob, we have a 600-car fleet order here that the buyer just canceled. How many can we put you down for?' Fleet cars were what they called 'strippers'; they had the least amount of creature comforts as possible. No retail customer would buy one unless he couldn't afford anything else. Bob told the regional Ford guy, 'You poll the other New England Ford dealers, and what they won't take, I will.'

"Regional calls back a week later. Bob asked, 'How many [cars] do you have left?'

"'Six hundred,' came the reply.

"'All right, I'll take [all of] them.'

"Now even though Tasca Ford sales were about 7,000 cars a year at the time, 600 cars that were a mistake and wouldn't sell retail represented a huge gamble. How were we going to sell another 600 units beyond what we already had on the lot?

"Bob knew they wouldn't sell as is. He also knew that many of his customers craved something a little different, something unique. So he set about doing what he called 'waking up the car.'

"He found among Ford Motor Company's parts inventories bits and pieces that would make the 600 strippers look different, such as an anodized aluminum side trim piece from an Econoline van. Those were the days when Americans accepted, and even loved, lots of chrome accent pieces. When Bob got done, the former stripper cars looked

> *I said, 'Oh, just a little old Ford V-8!' I never did tell him that it was a 406 with three deuces on it. That was really funny!*

like a totally new car line from Ford. Bob promoted the T63 available only at Tasca Ford. They sold like hotcakes!"

Presentation is another thing that Bob knew would sell even the most mundane of cars. Longtime Tasca family friend Bill Kolb Jr. was a successful drag racer (the John Healey engine "Little Yellow Wagon" wheelstander), high-performance car salesman (Larsen Ford, Gotham Ford, and White Plains Ford), the owner of his own Ford agency (Bill Kolb Jr. Ford, formerly known as "Faulkner Ford"), and current Subaru franchisee.

"We go all the way back to 1961 when I first started selling cars. I really admired the man for his ingenuity. For example, he would take an unusually colored car, like a Rose Dust–colored Thunderbird, and would put that car in his showroom on a turntable. About five feet all the way around it were these bright yellow flowers. You

Chapter Three: "Win on Sunday, Sell on Monday!"

The Tasca-Shelby Connection

Over the years, many people have asked Bob Tasca how it was that he came to meet with Carroll Shelby, a Leesburg, Texas, chicken farmer-turned-international driving champion and the father of the 260/289 and 427 Cobra roadsters, the Shelby Daytona Coupe, and the Shelby GT350 and Shelby GT500 Mustangs. Carroll Shelby had an idea. After successfully racing in both the United States and Europe for several years, and winning prestigious races such as the 24 Heures du Mans, Shelby (named *Sports Illustrated* "Sports Car Driver of the Year" in 1956) wanted to marry a lightweight European body, the A.C. Bristol "Ace," with a good-handling suspension and American V-8 power. The end result was the original 260-ci Ford small-block engine leaf-spring front-suspension Cobra roadster CSX 2000. It was created in February 1962 at Dean Moon's Santa Fe Springs, California, speed emporium, and publicly debuted April 1962 at the New York Auto Show.

Once that was accomplished, Shelby wanted to take his creation and go racing. However, to homologate the Cobra with the SCCA, Shelby first had to produce 100 cars. Now this was in the earliest days of Shelby American (established in August 1962), before Ford threw its huge financial machine behind the project as well as Shelby establishing anything that even remotely resembled a manufacturing facility. As a stopgap, Shelby said that he could assemble "kits" containing all the necessary bits and pieces and then drop ship them to participating dealers and they could put them together and sell them.

The only problem was that Shelby didn't have any dealers to speak of but Ford certainly had plenty of them. Would tapping into Ford's vast dealer network provide the answer? Ford wasn't too awfully hot on the idea, doubting that its dealers would be all that interested either. Finally, Ford's Lee Iacocca suggested that they gather a number of the company's top performance-minded dealers and Shelby could make a sink-or-swim presentation.

Bob Tasca Sr. happened to be one of those dealers standing in the room that day while Carroll Shelby gave his sales pitch. At the end of the presentation Shelby asked, "So what do you think?" It was so quiet you could hear a pin drop. Nobody said a word! Bob Sr. looked around the room and nobody offered to buy one of these cars so he raised his hand and said, "I'll take all of them!" That started the ball rolling.

Another dealer spoke up. "Well, he can't have all of them, right? That would be unfair. If we wanted to buy five or six, we could buy five or six, right?"

Bob said, "Anyone who wants to buy them, fine, but this man needs to sell all 100 of these cars, and I'm saying to all of you if you guys don't buy them, I'll buy them."

Before you knew it, the room was abuzz and Ford agreed to back the project. That was something Carroll Shelby never forgot, and a lifelong friendship between Carroll Shelby and Bob Tasca Sr. was cemented. Carroll Shelby later commented, "Bob Tasca had tremendous conviction and determination. Had it not been for him, I probably would not have become involved with Ford. Not that I possibly couldn't have done it all by myself, but he definitely was a huge contributing factor in making it happen."

The Shelby American Automobile Club (SAAC) actually lists only two such dealers having made a commitment at that auspicious meeting. Pittsburgh, Pennsylvania's Ed Hugus' European Cars (officially listed as Shelby's first distributor) purchased seven cars: CSX 2001, 2003, 2004, 2153, 2340, 2450, and 2472. Tasca Ford initially bought four cars: CSX 2024, 2028, 2029, and 2034. Tasca's John Healey assembled and prepared those early-production Cobra roadsters with the help of Tasca line mechanic (the late) Roger Roy.

Healey recalls, "Mr. Tasca came to me one day in 1962 and said, 'You're going to have a new project.' He told me what it was and said that he wanted me to get together with the Service Manager and Service Director and get one of the guys to work with me from the shop. I already knew

Cobra creator Carroll Shelby made several visits to Tasca Ford. In 1965, Shelby rolled up with the Cobra Caravan and put on a technical seminar. One of the social high points of the evening appeared to be the race between Carroll and Bob Sr. on a slot car track that had been set up in the Tasca service department. That's John Healey to the left of Bob.

whom I wanted to get. We had a World War II vet working for us, and his name was Roger Roy. He and I put the first three Cobras together. The car came in a crate. The motors came in a crate. The front suspension and rear end came in a crate, and we had to put them together. They were just one big kit car!"

When it came to the early Cobras, Bob Sr. held an entirely different opinion. He once told Bill Gilbert, "Take this little acorn and park it outside. Leave the keys in it and the engine running and maybe somebody will steal it!" Being a portly man of 6 feet, 1 inch "with a 57-inch waist and weighing about 275 pounds, Bob Sr. could not fit comfortably inside the tightly cramped interior of a 289 Cobra roadster. As it's been pointed out before, Bob Tasca had very little use for anything he couldn't drive and enjoy. But that didn't mean he wouldn't sell them. The actual sales figures for the 289 and the 427 Cobras are listed on page 127.

Chapter Three: "Win on Sunday, Sell on Monday!" 51

A Tasca technician attends to a 1962 Ford Galaxie customer car in the Service Department. Tasca's motto "May we service you?" (at practically any time of the day or night) is one of the things that helped vault the East Providence, Rhode Island, dealer to number two in sales nationally.

Here's a view of the Tasca Service Department. Note the Tasca S/S Galaxie in the background. They called this Healey's Corner and a lot of championship-winning Ford race cars were maintained and prepared in that area over the years.

would look at that Rose Dust car with all these pretty flowers all around it and you would think it was the most beautiful car you ever saw. I don't know of another dealer in the country who would stock that color car but Bob would have 25 of them in stock, ready to go when customers fell in love with the one on the showroom floor. That was one of the things that really fascinated me about his ability to market different things."

Badges?
We Don't Need No Stinking Badges!

Tasca Ford's famous chrome-plated block-letter badge (which inspired the cover art of this book) was designed in the late 1950s by Bob Tasca Sr. It not only signified to other motorists that the particular Ford that just passed them came from the second-largest Ford Dealership in the nation. The Tasca Ford badge also went on to become a highly collectible "prize" with Ford restorers and memorabilia collectors; it was even (at one time) listed in the Ford Racing catalogue! Tasca family friend and jeweler "Uncle Gene" Sormanti was responsible for casting up the actual chrome-plated "Tasca Ford" emblem, which was made by the tens of thousands.

John Healey remembers mounting countless numbers of those emblems on the rear deck lids or taillight panels of Ford cars sold through the East Providence, Rhode Island, Ford agency. "Once we found the exact mounting location for the emblem, we would carefully scribe the paint using the tips of the mounting pins. We would rock them back and forth, leaving a scratch mark in the paint. Then we would use an 11/64-inch drill bit and expansion nuts to secure the emblem in place.

"Of course, we couldn't help but wonder if, for whatever reason, a customer didn't want to have a Tasca Ford emblem mounted to their car. Yes, that

This family photo taken of Tasca technicians reflects well on Tasca's motto of customer satisfaction and high degree of professionalism.

Tasca is taking care of business in his newly completed upstairs corner office. The window at Bob's back afforded him an excellent view of the "A-1 Useful Cars" lot to the left. To the right is where Tasca first heard, and then witnessed, the now infamous (and humorous) "Bill Lawton Burnout Incident on Taunton Avenue."

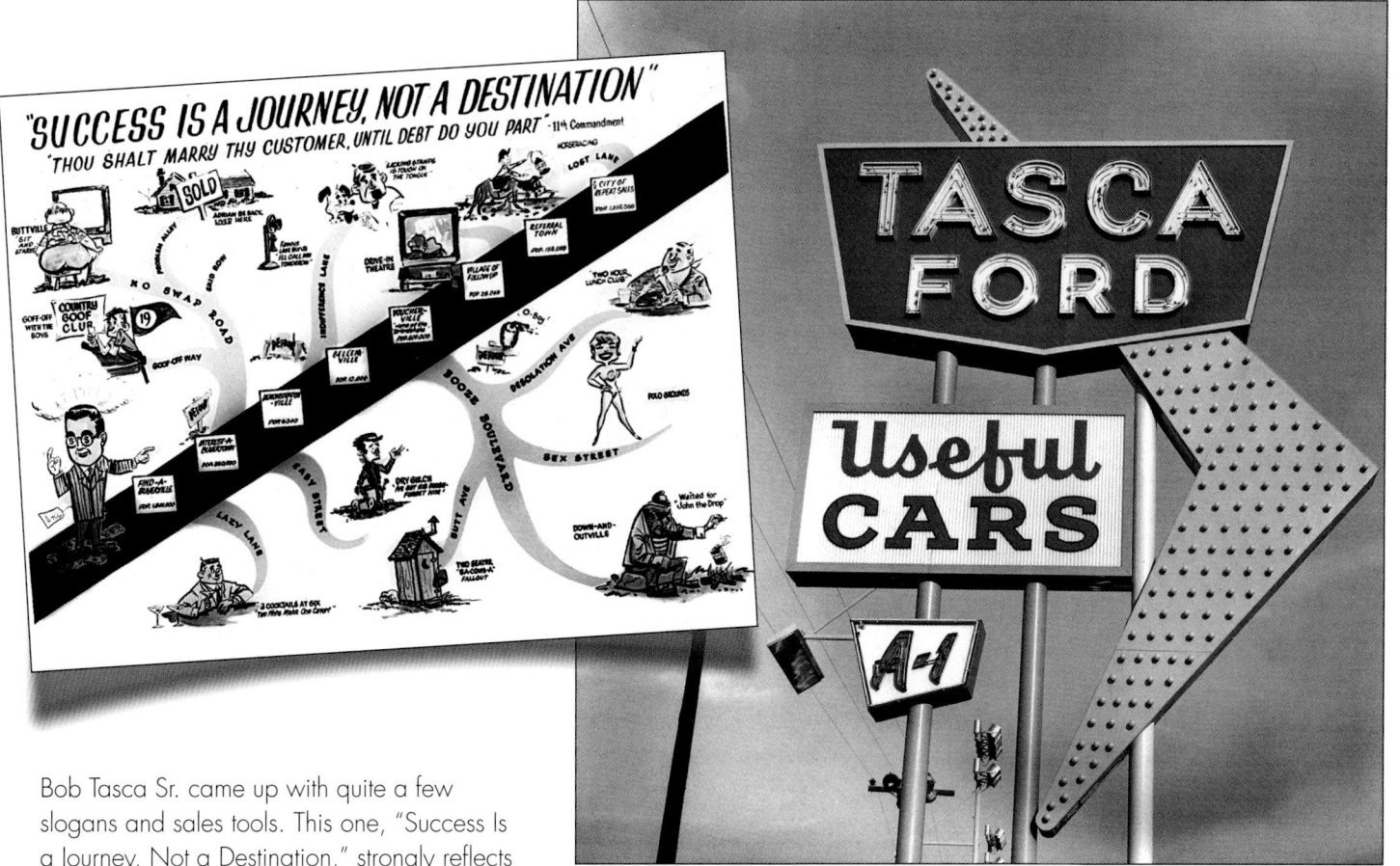

Bob Tasca Sr. came up with quite a few slogans and sales tools. This one, "Success Is a Journey, Not a Destination," strongly reflects Tasca's desire to become the number-one Ford dealer in the nation.

Here's a close-up look at Tasca Ford's famous "A-1 Useful Cars" sign, the word "useful" being a clever interpretation of FoMoCo's "A-1 Used Cars" sign.

Chapter Three: "Win on Sunday, Sell on Monday!"

(also) happened a number of times, so it was off to the body shop to have the holes filled and get a little paint touch-up!"

Galaxie Lightweight or Frankenstein Ford?

In 1963, Ford Special Vehicles "married" their newly introduced solid lifter cam, medium-riser 427 FE-Series pushrod V-8 engine (which in 2x4 configuration produced a whopping 425 hp at 6,000 rpm and 480 ft-lbs at 3,700 rpm) to their equally new NASCAR-inspired 1963½ Ford Galaxie 500 fastback body. The end result was the 1963½ Galaxie 500 XL lightweight. A grand total of 200 cars were built. They were purebred race cars by design, and Ford Special Vehicles affixed a tag to the inside of the glove compartment specifically stating so.

Features included a lightweight boxed-frame design chassis, the aforementioned 427 FE-Series 8V/V-8 engine with solid lifter cam, cross-drilled mains, 427 crank, 427 H-beam connecting rods, forged-aluminum pistons, a set of big-valve FE medium-riser cylinder heads, a 2x4 Holley-equipped aluminum intake, RC Industries/NHRA–approved aluminum flywheel, and cast-iron factory headers. Also included were a BorgWarner T-10 aluminum case 4-speed transmission and 9-inch Traction Lok live rear axle.

These cars featured fiberglass hoods, fiberglass doors (on some cars), fiberglass trunk lids, fiberglass front fenders and inner fender aprons, thin-gauge window glass, aluminum front and rear bumper and bumper brackets, a pair of Bostrum lightweight bucket seats, rubber floor mat, and hood support rod.

Production delete items included heater, body sealer, sound deadener, clock, radio, door window anti-rattlers, trunk lid torsion bar assembly, rear seals to wheelhouse, anti-squeak insulators, trunk mat, carpet, arm rests, quarter ashtrays, spare wheel and tire, spare-wheel mounting hardware, jack and lug wrench, dome lamp, courtesy light, single horn, and hood hinge spring delete.

But why the "1963½" designation? Re-tooling delays at Ford's Pico Rivera, California, and Norfolk, Virginia, Assembly Plants had pushed the production version release date for the Galaxie 500 XL fastback up to late spring. That made the "1/2" designation a first for Ford from a model year standpoint. Initially, this production delay posed something of a problem to Ford Special Vehicles Drag Racing Program Coordinator and test driver Dick Brannan.

However, in pure Frankenstein tradition, Ford's "Experimental Garage" took a 1963½ Galaxie fastback "body in white," bolted it up to the highly modified "framework" from Brannan's 1962 Galaxie lightweight, then transplanted a new "heart" in the form of a 427-ci 425-hp 8V FE engine with aluminum-cased BorgWarner T-10 transmission.

This unholy "marriage" of parts and pieces was given the number 832 and it became the official test mule for the 1963½ Galaxie lightweight program. Other X-Garage re-bodies included Phil Bonner (who actually ended up with two cars after losing the first in a towing accident), Ed Martin Ford, Len Richter–Bob Ford, and Tasca Ford. In a logistical attempt to save time and money, Les Ritchey's and Gas Ronda's cars were re-bodied by X-Garage employee Bill Holbrook at Long Beach, California's Bill Stroppe & Associates. The remainder of the 200 1963½ Galaxie lightweights were assembled at Ford's Norfolk, Virginia, Assembly Plant.

As Ford's Bill Holbrook recalled, "Dick [Brannan] was the first one to re-body his 1962 Galaxie Lightweight ,and I converted that car over to a 1963½ right there in our garage. Then of course we converted three more of them there as well and one of those cars was Tasca's. Ronda's and Ritchey's cars were re-bodied out in Signal Hill, California. I had bodies in white from the Los Angeles Ford [Pico Rivera] Assembly Plant sent over to Bill Stroppe's. We did the 1271 Process Sheets and so forth going down the production line, keeping them from spraying the Dum-Dum and stuff.

"While we were converting the cars at Bill Stroppe & Associates, someone said, 'Do you suppose you could slip those bodies back an inch and not mount them on the original holes?' I said that I didn't know how well that would work but we would give it a try. I'll tell you that was the biggest damned can of worms I've ever gotten into in my life. If you stop and think about it, the steering column, the shift linkage that fastened to the transmission and stuff, now everything is not in the same position. Wires, you name it.

"The one thing I do remember is that I just cut the hand-brake cables off and stuck them in a frame hole. It was the biggest mess I've ever gotten into. What normally took me about two or three days to do took me a week to put the damned cars back together. And that was with help. God Bless Bill Stroppe for that!

"Bodies were in white, and the two cars we were changing out? One was red and one was blue. I took the VIN plates off the cars and moved them. Somehow when I got everything done, I had the blue car where there should have been a red car and I had a red car where there should have been a blue one with switching the chassis and all. That was kind of funny. Some of the magazine writers have commented on that quite a bit."

Dick Brannan's car proved to be the fastest and quickest of the bunch, setting the first NHRA National E.T. Record for a Ford Super Stock car at 12.02 on July 13, 1963, at York U.S. 30 Dragway, York, Pennsylvania. However, Tasca's Galaxie lightweight eventually ran even quicker, recording 12.0s at both Charleston and Connecticut Dragways with a top-end charge of 117.00 and 117.94, respectively. Simultaneously, Tasca's

Tasca's new 1963½ Galaxie 500 lightweight Super Stock car was the car that helped the team really begin picking up momentum. This classic photo taken at Charleston Drag Strip shows Lawton squaring off against none other than Dave Strickler's *Old Reliable IV*, a 1963 Chevrolet Impala lightweight running the ultra-rare Z11 427 and 4-speed transmission.

Here's a different angle of Tasca's 1963½ Galaxie 500 lightweight defeating one of the local Mopar racers. In reality, the Tasca Ford Galaxie lightweight was one of the original handful of re-bodied 1962 406 Ford A/FX cars. Once updated with new sheet metal and 427 Ford power, the car became a holy terror.

Chapter Three: "Win on Sunday, Sell on Monday!" 55

Tasca takes on the Carrano Brothers' 1957 Chevrolet C/Gas convertible during time trials at Charleston Drag Strip. Guess who won?

Here's Team Tasca after a local win at Charleston Drag Strip with their 1963½ 427/425-hp Galaxie Super Stock. Left to right are mechanic Henry "Wimpy" Tameleo, mechanic Jon Pagano, chief wrench John Healey, driver Bill Lawton, and High Performance Manager Dean Gregson. Note the advertisement in the rear window.

To the winner goes the spoils. Bob Sr. (left) and Billy Lawton (right) congratulate each other while John Healey looks on. Bob's widow, Josephine, still has all of these early trophies in the trophy room at their home.

56   The Tasca Ford Legacy

This vintage Tasca ad indicated that when it came to buying a high-performance Ford, Tasca was *the* place. Now how many dealers do you know that carried 427 Super Stock Galaxies with a fiberglass fastback roof?

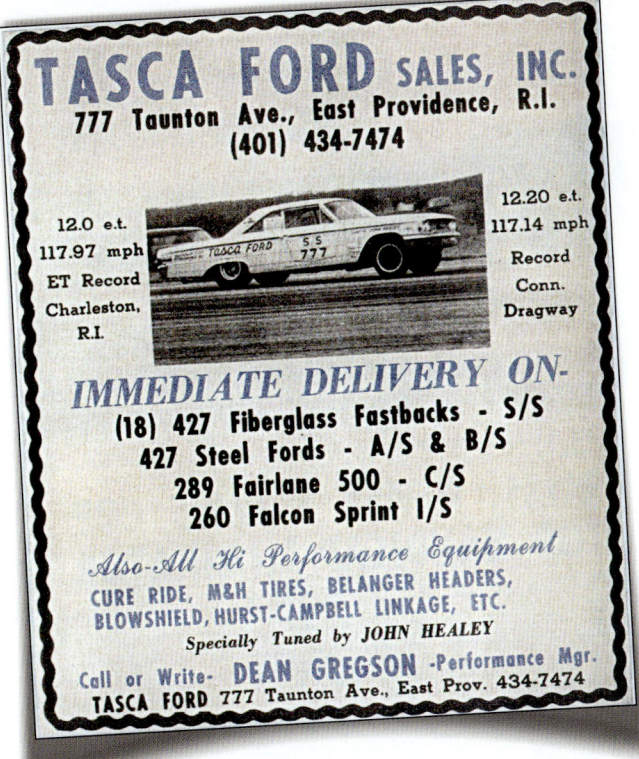

John Healey was also helping H-M and Ford develop their 427 medium-riser racing engine program.

According to Dean Gregson, "Prior to the mid-1963 creation of the 427 Side Oiler engine, Ford and H-M were having oiling problems with their medium-riser engines. It was John Healey who told them how to cross-drill the mains and drill out the cranks so that they wouldn't lose the bottom ends."

Sell on Monday

"So, 1963 comes along and we're running the 1963½ Galaxie lightweight, aluminum bumpers, no heater, no radio, no nothing," says Dean Gregson. "I ordered *fifty* of them that year; that's one-fourth of Ford's total Galaxie lightweight production. Now you would think it would be pretty hard selling these cars in the dead of winter with no heaters and all, but hey, it is what it is, know what I mean? Guys were coming from all over the eastern seaboard to buy them."

Tasca's drag racing program was also beginning to attract its fair share of attention publicity-wise.

Telling It Like It Is

By the early 1960s, the Tasca name was well known by Henry Ford II, Lee Iacocca, and virtually every CEO of Ford Motor Company ever since. By mid-1963, upward of 60 percent of the vehicles sold each month (including trucks) and 40 percent of Tasca Ford's total sales were high-performance Ford muscle cars. Now that Bob Tasca Sr. was the number-two top volume Ford dealer in the country it gave him plenty of clout, which he used at both Ford Motor Company dealers meetings and assembly plant tours.

"Now I don't know the mathematics of it," says Bob Jr. "But he [Tasca Sr.] had it all figured out ahead of time [early 1960s]. He didn't like the fact that a Chevrolet was worth a substantial bit more than a Ford in re-sale value after two years. I don't know the numbers, but my father had done the math. He said, 'Listen, you [Ford] owe the dealers $560 million. That's what you owe us!'

"The guy from Ford says, 'Are you out of your mind?'

"Actually, I think Mr. Ford was in that meeting.

"The guy says, 'How did you come to that conclusion?'

"My father says, 'Well, you charge us the same when the cars are new, right? But in two years, their car [GM] is worth x-amount more. I did the math, and when you multiply that out, that's what you owe us.'

"The guy says, 'What do you expect us to do, write a check to all our dealers?'

"My father said, 'No; put the money in product.'

"That day, Ford committed to invest a huge sum of money on Ford Product Development, and they still do. That's a true story!"

Bob Sr. was also big on powertrain technology. He felt that the big difference between Ford and General Motors was that the number-one market share holder, Chevrolet, built small engines that breathed and made lots of horsepower at higher RPM levels. A 327 Chevrolet small-block outperformed the pants off a Ford 390 FE on any day. Conversely, he felt that Ford made big engines for trucks that didn't breathe very well, and they put them in cars. He wasn't at all happy about it, and was often quoted as saying, "The way Ford used to set up their engines was like taking a racing dog and putting a muzzle on its snout and a cork up its ass, and then expect it to run!"

"My father had a big meeting with all the Ford engineering executives. I think Charlie Patterson was one of the top engineers at the time. My father was criticizing Ford's motors, saying 'I'm mad as hell. I'm mad as hell!'

"Henry Ford II was at that meeting, so the executives sitting around my father were kicking him under the table.

"Henry Ford II said, 'No, let him talk. Let him talk. I want to listen to what he has to say.'

"My father said, 'Mr. Ford, you better change the name of your company.'

"Henry says, 'You mean I can't call it Ford Motor Company anymore?'

"My father replied, 'You got to call it "the Ford Company." Why? Because you don't make a motor that's worth a shit! You got to take the "motor" out of Ford Motor Company!'"

Like it, or not, Henry Ford II knew

Tasca Flashback

By Martyn L. Schorr, former High-Performance Cars *magazine editor/publisher*

The first time I met Bob Tasca was late in 1963. I was doing a story for Magnum-Royal Publications' *High-Performance Cars* magazine. The article was about Tasca Ford's racing operation, specifically the number 777 Super/Stock 427 (1963½) Galaxie. I had driven a pre-production 427 Galaxie fastback in Europe during the 1963½ Ford Total Performance press program along with a 289/271-hp Fairlane and a 260 Falcon Sprint in and around Monaco. Impressive cars; incredible driving along part of the legendary Rallye Monte Carlo route in the Maritime Alps.

Spending a couple of days with Bob Tasca Sr.'s driver, Bill Lawton, team mechanic John Healey, and High Performance Sales Manager Dean Gregson proved to be an eye-opening experience. Who would've ever thought that a Ford dealership in the smallest state in our country, Rhode Island, could possibly be one of Ford's top high-performance dealers as well as field drag racing cars that left their marks nationally?

I met Bob Tasca for the first time not behind a desk but in the shop with John Healey, helping him install a dual-quad 427 race engine. There he was, plaid jacket, tie, expensive shoes, and a pipe in his mouth, going over the engine on a hoist with Healey! That's when I learned that Bob was a totally hands-on car guy, as comfortable in the shop hanging with the mechanics and pulling an engine as he was with Henry Ford in the Big Glass House in Dearborn.

I would learn by my second visit the next year that Bob Tasca was incredibly connected with Ford, more so than traditional Ford dealers. He had built personal relationships with engineers, managers of competition projects, and key players at the Dearborn, Michigan, and Kingman, Arizona, Ford Proving Grounds.

Tasca put together a boutique cast for his racing team, much like a producer does when choosing cast members for a high-profile TV program. He had the right mechanic, driver, mechanic support, and sales dynamo who knew how to capitalize on the team's success. He also had factory support at the highest level. The Tasca operation was the ultimate expression of the Total Performance program: Win on Sunday, Sell on Monday!

After the Super/Stock 1963½ Galaxies came one of the factory 427 Fairlane Thunderbolts and, of course, a series of hot Mustangs kept Tasca Ford in the limelight for close to a decade. John Healey was the "wrench" and (the late) Bill Lawton drove these cars to numerous national records and kept Tasca Ford in the NHRA record books.

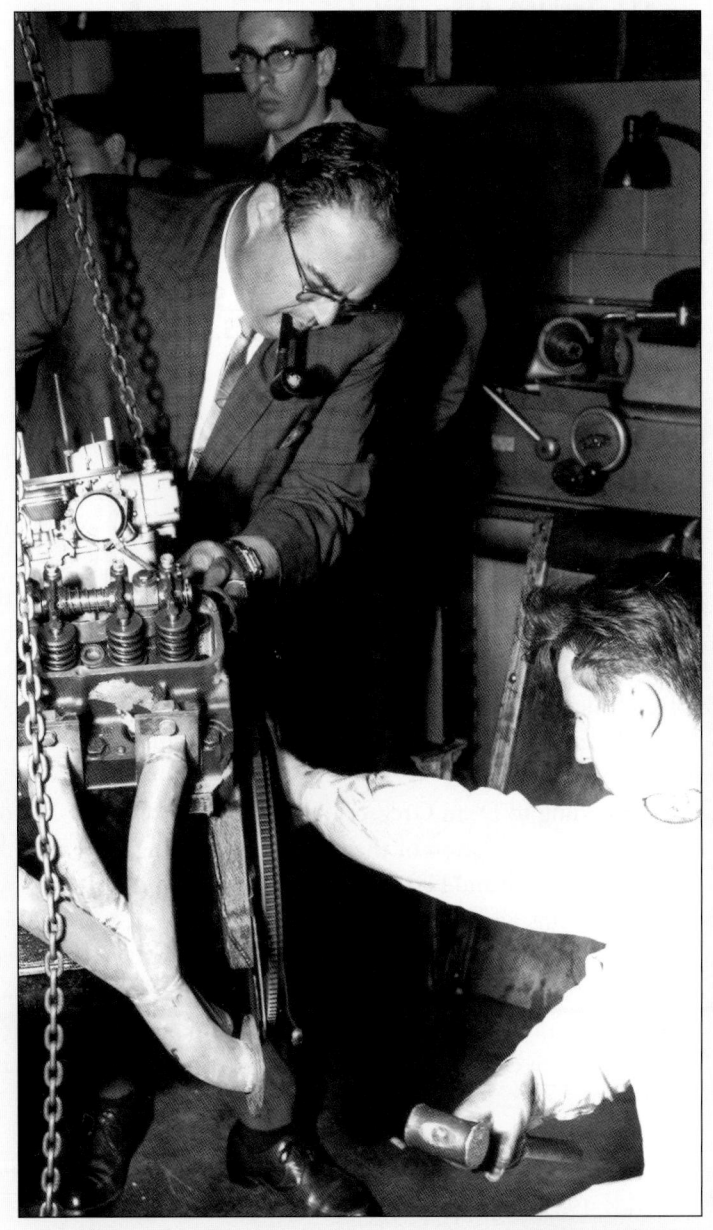

According to former *High-Performance Cars* magazine editor Martyn L. "Marty" Schorr, "There he was, plaid jacket, tie, expensive shoes, and a pipe in his mouth, going over the (427 FE) engine on a hoist with Healey!" (Photo Courtesy Martyn L. Schorr)

Bob Tasca continued advising Henry Ford II on performance projects and has of course been credited for the 428 Cobra Jet Mustangs and KR [King of the Road] iterations. Bob Tasca loved winning, both in drag racing and the sales race, and [that] was reflected in his dealership's reputation in the hobby and industry. I feel very fortunate to have known him as well as the guys who built and raced his cars.

Me Incorporated

Bob Tasca Sr. worked long and hard to become the country's second-largest Ford dealer and one of the most famous high-performance Ford agencies in the land. In early 1963, Bob sat down and wrote a paper called "Me Incorporated." It is a personal and professional declaration to both family and business associates that he was in the car business for the long haul. Come hell or high water, he would make it successful!

> Sure, I'm a salesman, and have been for years. I'm proud of my profession, and wouldn't trade it for any other.
>
> Do I get tired working for somebody else, did you say? Wouldn't I like to run my own business and be my own boss?
>
> Why man, I am my own boss. I have my own business. I'm "'Me Incorporated!'" Maybe you think that sounds crazy, but it's the truth.
>
> Whether you are the head of a corporation or a peanut vendor, the principals are the same. You invest so much; that's your capitol. You sell so much; that's your volume. It costs so much to produce and operate. The difference between what you take in and what you put out is what you make.
>
> If your business is large and includes stockholders, you call it dividends. If your business is small and closely controlled, you simply call it net profit. In my business it is called commissions.
>
> Here's how I run Me Incorporated: My capital is my brain, my energy, my ability, and my time. The company gives me plenty of opportunity to put my capital to work. I'm in business to produce sales. The more productive I am, the more efficiently and the more thoroughly I work my territory and the less motion I allow, the more volume I get and the greater my net profit.
>
> My company has analyzed my territory on the basis of former sales, my ability, natural growth, and the possibilities of my field of operation. If I produce the maximum quota set, my dividends, or my commissions, for the whole year increase. That's what I've got my eye on right now and I can't afford not to do it.
>
> I run myself like a hardboiled president of a money-making company. I supervise my habits, my health, my manner of working, and my expenses. I take the results of each day's work home and go over them like an efficiency expert, cold bloodedly, impersonally, without any alibi because 'Me Incorporated' is in the business to make money.
>
> I'm tougher on me than any other boss could possibly be. You see, I can't put anything over on myself. I could think up a plausible "Why not?" that might get by with anyone else, but I know. I can fool all of the people some of the time and some of the people all the time, but I cannot fool myself any of the time!
>
> And what is more, if I have had a bad month—and miss the extra commission at the end of the year—my stockholders want to know why. Although I may hold the controlling shares, my wife and youngsters have big blocks of stock.
>
> Call it a game if you like—but if you've got anything in you at all, there is nobody better able to bring it out than yourself, and when I say '"Good-bye"' to the wife and youngsters in the morning, I know they are depending on my earning dividends, and that pushes me harder all the time in the confidence they have in 'Me Incorporated.'
>
> Bob Tasca

According to Tasca's High Performance Sales Manager Dean Gregson, Tasca sold 25 percent a total run of 200 1963½ 427 FE engine Galaxie fastback lightweights. We're talking about 50 cars here, folks!

that Bob Tasca knew exactly what he was talking about and affectionately called him "the Critic." High praise indeed especially since Bob devoted his time, his boundless energy, and his efforts for free. He never accepted a check from Ford in spite of all he did. Having such a tuned-in executive on his staff was a huge benefit to the company as a whole: Ford, Lincoln-Mercury Division, or what have you.

In 1963, Henry Ford II offered Bob Tasca a seven-figure annual salary to become General Manager of Ford Division. Bob politely replied, "Thank you, Mr. Ford, but no thank you. I've never wanted anything more than to just have a successful family business and I have that. I prefer to be the one to sign the front of the check, and not the back!"

Zimmy-1

In 1963 Frank E. "Zimmy" Zimmerman was the Sales Manager for Ford Motor Company and was also charged with the responsibility of overseeing Ford's Special Vehicles Department. One weekend Frank invited Bob Tasca and his family to spend some leisure time at his lake house with Zimmerman and his family. Once safely away from corporate "ears," Frank Zimmerman confided to Bob that he didn't know much of anything about racing, and would Mr. Tasca agree to help him? That was the beginning of another long and fruitful association between Bob Sr. and Ford Motor Company's upper management.

Zimmy-1 was a Ming Green 1963 Ford Fairlane 500 initially equipped with a 406 FE medium-riser engine named in honor of Frank Zimmerman. The A/FX one-off was a multi-department project between Ford's Special Vehicles under the supervision of Charlie Gray, sub-contractor DST, and Bill Gay at Ford's Engine & Foundry Department (E&F). It served as the "test mule" for the 1964 Ford Thunderbolt Super Stock cars.

John Healey recalls, "Tasca never owned that car. That was Ford's car. It was the mule car for the 1964 Ford Thunderbolt program. I mean it was a carbon copy of the 1964 Ford Thunderbolt. The car was assigned to the X-Garage under the supervision of Charlie Gray, although the bill of sale, or window sticker, actually listed the name of a private party

60   The TASCA FORD LEGACY

who 'owned' the car. That was the way Ford set things up. That car spent a lot of time going back and forth between Dearborn and East Providence."

In its earliest of days, *Zimmy-1* received a 427 FE medium-riser engine transplant. Its bulbous scooped hood was also replaced with what many think to be the prototype "clover leaf" hood design that was originally used on the 1964 T-Bolts.

Bill Humphries drove *Zimmy-1* at the 1963 U.S. Nationals, where the car lost out in the eliminator against Don Kimball's 1963 Z11 Chevrolet due to a missed shift caused by fouled transmission linkage. Nonetheless, low-13-second runs were normal. Bill Lawton also drove *Zimmy-1* near the season's end and set the NHRA A/FX MPH class record at 121.29 during a Connecticut Dragway/NHRA Northeast Division One Points Meet before it was shipped back to Dearborn. *Zimmy-1*'s ultimate fate is unclear. As a prototype, the car was most likely dissected and crushed.

Tasca Bird-1

"Exclusivity." That was a word Bob Tasca Sr. liked despite being in the kind of business being that largely depended on sales volume to survive. As such, he created a number of special one-offs. One of his earliest examples was "*Tasca Bird-1.*"

According to former *High-Performance Cars* editor Martyn L. Schorr, "When I visited Tasca Ford in 1964, Bob tossed me the keys to his unique candy apple red Thunderbird customized by the Alexander Brothers in Detroit. Larry and Mike Alexander applied the 26-coat candy red lacquer paint that literally glowed in the sunlight. It wasn't the paint, unique grille treatment, reshaped hood, and fenders, or Cibie rectangular headlights that grabbed me. First my eyes went to unique 'Tasca 427' emblems. Then the exhaust note grabbed me. Neither normally associated with production Thunderbirds. That is, unless your name is Bob Tasca.

"According to the Big Bopper, '"I have some connections at the [Ford] Assembly Plant and I had a 427 engine with 390 markings appear while my car was on the line. Nobody seemed to notice that it was bolted up to a high-RPM Cruise-O-Matic, the automatic transmission that would be available the following year on the factory drag cars.'

> " By the early 1960s, the Tasca name was well known by Henry Ford II, Lee Iacocca, and virtually every CEO of Ford Motor Company ever since. "

"When Bob's T-Bird arrived at Tasca Ford, John Healey pulled the engine, blueprinted it, and put it back in the car. The results? A mild single-4-barrel version of the 427 race engine used in the Ford drag cars. It was quick, had incredible mid-range performance, an exhaust note to die for, and more luxury interior appointments than any factory T-Bird, much less the top-of-the-line Lincoln.

"Bob later told me, 'It'll hit 60 mph in 6 seconds flat and top out at around 135 mph and, thanks to European suspension parts, out-handle any T-Bird or other luxury car on the road.'"

Lightning Strikes! Tasca Ford's 1964 T-Bolt

There is absolutely no doubt that Tasca Ford's 1962 and 1963 experiments, working in conjunction with Charles E. Gray Jr., Vern Tinsler, and Dick Brannan at Ford Special Vehicles Department and sub-contractor Andy Hotten from DST (stuffing a big engine into a medium-size car like the Ford Fairlane), was the progenitor of the 1964 Ford Fairlane Thunderbolt. However, although Tasca was a "team player," it was left up to Ford Special Vehicles and DST to further develop the concept for the following year. Bob Tasca had a dealership to run.

According to Ford Special Vehicles Drag Racing Program Manager Dick Brannan in an interview for the July and September 2011 issues of *Drag Racer* magazine, "In 1964, we went to the 427 Fairlane. Danny Jones, who also had worked on the Indy car program, had a big hand in the development of that car. He is the guy who ultimately designed the famous T-Bolt Traction Bars [as part of Thunderbolt's "leapfrog suspension system"] used on these cars.

"These cars were ordered through Ford Special Vehicle's employee Vern Tinsler. They were shipped to DST, an outside contractor for special projects like this one. Mr. James 'Hammer' Mason was the Project Manager at DST and was a tremendous help to me as we improved and developed these cars prior to delivering them to our teams.

"We decided on the name Thunderbolt, taken from the World War II fighter plane [Republic Aviation designed and built P-47] as we would also do later in the year for the Mustang [North American Aviation–designed and –built P-51]. At first, the NHRA wouldn't approve the Thunderbolt for Super Stock racing, demanding that we build fifty automatic cars and fifty 4-speed cars to qualify as 'legal' Super Stock cars.

Chapter Three: "Win on Sunday, Sell on Monday!"

Zimmy-1 was a Ming Green, 1963 Ford Fairlane 500 that (although owned by Ford) was a joint project between FoMoCo Special Vehicles Department, DST, and Tasca Ford. The car originally started out being powered by a Ford 406 and 4-speed but quickly graduated to a 427 medium-riser engine. It was driven by Ford's Bill Holbrook at Indy in 1963, as well as by Bill Lawton who set an NHRA MPH record (121.29) during an NHRA Division One Points Meet at Connecticut Dragway. This car was a virtual blueprint for the 1964 Ford Fairlane Thunderbolt project.

"We agreed to those minimum numbers but we didn't say that we would stop at 100 cars; we just said that we would build 100 units. I believe the final total, which is a contested figure by my records, indicates that we built a total of 127 1964 Ford Thunderbolts."

Hot Rod Reports on the Latest (Detroit) Hot Rod

In the February 1964 issue of *Hot Rod*, Publisher (the late) Ray Brock wrote a glowing four-plus-page report about this new breed of Super Stock car titled *Draggin' Bolt*. It dissected the Butch Leal–driven Mickey Thompson Ford Thunderbolt (Leal's car was the more successful of the two Mickey Thompson T-Bolts) saying, "As turned out by Ford, these Thunderbolts are ready to run. They have special traction devices, wide-base wheels with drag slicks on the rear, tuned headers, fresh air intakes for the carburetors, and almost anything else that will give a low elapsed time and maximum speed.

"The 427 [high-riser] engine is the top of the line with 13:1 compression, long-duration camshaft, high-RPM valvesprings, and dual 4-barrel carburetion. It is designed for short bursts and wide open throttle . . .

"All the knowledge Ford has gained from high-speed racing on the stock car circuits has been incorporated in this high-performance 427 . . .

"This could conceivably be the car to watch for 1964 in the Super Stock [Eliminator] class. At the [U.S.] Nationals

Follow Me!

The popular French phrase *"Suivez Moi,"* or "Follow me" was first used on the back of *Zimmy II*, indicating that like the Ford Dealership itself, Team Tasca had no intention of finishing second to anybody!

Testing Tempers at the Dearborn Test Track

As told by Bob Tasca Jr. and Carl A. Tasca

Bobby II begins: In the early 1960s, my father was working on the prototype Ford Thunderbolt [*Zimmy-1*] and Ford gave him a Lincoln to drive while he was in Dearborn. Carl and I had to be ten or eleven years old. Guess what we were doing that night while the Bopper was out hobnobbing it with the Ford executives? Driving his Lincoln around the test track!

Someone from track security said, "What are those kids doing out on the test track?" Then someone else said, "Those are Bob Tasca's kids." So the first guy says, "Oh," and that was all there was to it! You couldn't do that today. I'm at the test track a lot, and security there is so tight. But Carl and I drove Dad's Lincoln all over the Dearborn Test Track and I don't know whether he knew we were even doing it.

Carl interjects: Oh, he knew! He used to ask us, "What did you do today?" But he already knew the answer. We used to think he had eyes in the back of his head. It never did any good to lie to him. It was better to tell the truth and have him chew you out, or give you some menial job to do as punishment. Lying only made things worse. You would stand there, and he would just keep grilling you.

next summer there could be some Fords in there battling against the Dodges and Plymouths for Top Stock honors."

Now it wasn't that Ray Brock had a crystal ball or anything like that, he just knew his Fords *and* he knew his drivers!

By all standards, Tasca Ford's Thunderbolt *Zimmy II* was one of the prettiest Thunderbolts running in the eliminator with its Vintage Burgundy and Cadillac Gold paint scheme and chrome-plated Mickey Thompson "Rader" five-spoke steel wheels, let alone one of the fastest and quickest of the breed. Tasca, Lawton, and Healey set both ends of the NHRA S/S World

Tasca Bird-1 was low and sleek with its candy apple red paint, bar-tube grille, Cibie rectangular headlights, Lincoln MKII turbine wheel covers, and thin-stripe whitewall tires.

Tasca Bird-1 was designed by Tasca Ford, executed by the Alexander Brothers (Larry and Mike) of Detroit, and powered by a John Healey–blueprinted 427 medium-riser engine originally installed per Bob Sr.'s request right on the assembly line. Talk about having horsepower!

The Case of the Driverless Ford

Josephine Tasca tells a funny story about seeing a new Ford driving across the lot without a driver, or did it? "One Sunday the kids and I brought my husband's dinner down to the dealership. He was always working on something, day or night. I looked out the window of Bob's office, and here's this car driving around the dealership all by itself!

"I said 'Oh My God, there's nobody behind the wheel!'

"Come to find out, it was Carl! I think he was nine or ten years old; he couldn't even see over the steering wheel but that didn't seem to matter. We ran out and stopped him because we thought he was going to drive out onto Taunton Avenue.

"That was typical of Carl."

Chapter Three: "Win on Sunday, Sell on Monday!"

Quick Enough to Outrun the RCMP

As told by Bob Tasca Jr. and Carl A. Tasca

Bobby II begins: Our father was driving the 427-powered *Tasca Bird-1* home from Detroit one night, so he cuts through Canada at Sioux St. Marie, where he encountered a situation with a Royal Canadian Mounted Police officer. I think he was driving over the Ambassador Bridge. His T-Bird had been customized by the Alexander Brothers and it was painted candy apple red with a 427 medium-riser engine in it that Ford said wouldn't fit. He had a friend at the factory drop in the 427 engine on the assembly line. In those days you could do that.

Anyhow, the trooper was following him. I think he had a Chrysler. Our father turned in to make a pit stop and gas up. The trooper looked at the T-Bird and says, "Pretty nice! What's it got underneath the hood?"

Our father says, "Oh, it's got a pretty good motor under the hood; it runs pretty good."

The trooper says, "You think it can outrun my Chrysler?"

Now our father's wondering, "Is this guy trying to set me up? Is he going to try to put me in jail?"

So Dad says to him, "Well, trooper, let me say this to you. When we leave here now, I'll follow you. When you're running wide open, you put your left blinker on, and I'll drive by you."

And he did! True story. You can't make that stuff up!

Carl chimes in: Speaking of making pit stops, whenever we drove to Detroit, we would usually drive at night, and our father would drive nonstop. You want to go to the bathroom? You went to the bathroom when the Bopper went to the bathroom. He would always say, "You can hold it to the next exit." The only problem was you would usually see a sign that said, "Next exit 45 miles."

As to how Bob Tasca Sr. became known as the Big Bopper, the story goes that one day he drove *Tasca Bird-1* into Connecticut Dragway and owner/announcer Frank Maratta says, "Here comes the Big Bopper, Bob Tasca Sr.!" This dynamic man, a man who seemed bigger than life, was given the colorful nickname that day that lasted him the rest of his life.

Regarding the actual fate of *Tasca Bird-1*, according to Bobby II and Carl, the Bopper and Josephine were having dinner at Tavern on the Green in Manhattan, New York. The late Sammy Davis Jr. was also there that night, and fell in love with the car and just had to have it. Of course, Bob Sr. was more than happy to oblige Davis. So today, the whereabouts of *Tasca Bird-1* is unknown. However, there are some publicity photos floating around entertainment industry archives of Davis posing with his prized car.

Record at Connecticut Dragway during an NHRA Division One Points Meet on September 20, 1964, at 11.69/126.05. Healey still has the certificate. They also won the 1964 North East Division Super Stock Eliminator Championship that same year.

Bob Tasca later said, "My expertise was more suspension than engine." John Healey was the only one allowed to work on the engine.

"I would say, 'The engine's fine, John. Lock the hood!' I felt that if we could put the power to the pavement running the right transmission and rear axle ratios, we could make the car

This January 7, 1963, advertisement from Tasca says a lot because there is a lot to say. Note the lower right-hand reference to the 1963 Cobra, billed as the "World's Fastest Production Sports Car." They were right!

64 The Tasca Ford Legacy

launch better. During the course of development, we also fooled around with spring rates, front end geometry, and [in conjunction with M&H Tires' Marvin Rifchin] we developed better tires!"

Retired Atco Dragway mouthpiece and veteran NHRA National Event announcer Bob Frey commented, "As a kid growing up in the famous 'match race era,' one of my earliest memories of going to the drag races was in 1964 when I went to Vineland Dragway in Southern New Jersey. The attraction was the 'Stockers Bonanza,' an event that featured all the top Super Stock cars of the day. As reported in the *National Dragster*, 'Bill Lawton, driving the maroon missile from Rhode Island, beat a field of a dozen top stars to take home the $4,500 top prize.' When it was all over, Lawton had the bucks, and Tasca Ford had all the glory."

Ford Engineer Bill Holbrook provided this Joe Farkas photograph (Joe was one of Ford's official photographers) taken at the November 1963 Ford Thunderbolt preview at the Dearborn Test Track. Pictured left to right are Homer Perry, Don Martin, Ford Special Vehicles Drag Racing Program Manager Richard H. "Dick" Brannan, Dave Evans, Ford Special Vehicles' John Cowley, Paul Harvey, Ford Engineer Bill Holbrook "Doc" Gould, Bill Lawton, Emil Loeffler, Les Ritchey, Ed Terry, John Healey, Danny Jones, Bob Rice, Jacques Passano, Larry "Butch" Leal, Mickey Thompson, Charlie Gray Jr., and Bill Innes. Eight cars were at the presentation (all painted maroon) and to avoid any favoritism, Ford Drag Council members drew their prospective car by pulling a number out of a hat. Tasca got car number 8.

The Tasca Ford Thunderbolt (here at Indy in 1964) was not only the fastest and quickest T-Bolt in the nation, setting both ends of the record at 11.69/126.05 during a Connecticut Dragway NHRA Division One Points Meet. It was also the prettiest with its Vintage Burgundy and Cadillac Gold top and Mickey Thompson "Radar" wheels.

After getting skunked by Al "Lawman" Eckstrand's 2-percent A/FX Plymouth during a match race at New Jersey's Island Dragway, Bob ordered the T-Bolt parked and put it on a weight-saving diet, equipping the car with what Bill Lawton later referred to as an "A/FX Kit."

Now running as a legal A/FX car, and doing quite well at it (clocking 11.5s to 11.6s) Tasca Ford put the hurt to the likes of Dave Strickler (now running a Dodge), Bob "Flying Carpet" Harrop, Bill "Yankee Peddler" Flynn, and of course, Al "Lawman" Eckstrand.

Chapter Three: "Win on Sunday, Sell on Monday!" 65

"You know, back in those days being a member of the Ford Drag Council, we were expected to share our information with fellow team members," said Bill Lawton. "But racers being racers, you always held a couple of tenths back."

As John Healey put it, "Back in those days, if we got in a local paper it was okay. If we were mentioned in a magazine, that was great. Getting in *Drag News* or *National Dragster;* now that was *really* big!"

Dick Brannan best summed up the year 1964 with this: "The Thunderbolt was one of the greatest Super Stock cars ever built, winning major events and today commanding large sums at collector car auctions. That year, we won the NHRA Winternationals [Gas Ronda/Downtown Ford], we won Indy [Butch Leal/Mickey Thompson], we set both ends of the class record [Bill Lawton/Tasca Ford], we won the Hot Rod Magazine Championship Drag Races [Gas Ronda/Russ Davis Ford], and we won the NHRA Super Stock Eliminator World Championship [Gas Ronda/Russ Davis Ford]. That was a very, very successful program."

> "We decided on the name Thunderbolt, taken from the World War II fighter plane."

Roll Out Racin'

As previously mentioned, West Covina, California's Gaspar "Gas" Ronda won the 1964 NHRA Super Stock World Championship driving his Russ Davis Ford–sponsored 1964 Ford Thunderbolt. He tells of an interesting encounter he had with Bob Tasca Sr. at one of the NHRA national events.

"Cliff Brien [Ronda's Chief Mechanic] and I had the Fairlane up on jack stands and were adjusting the rear control arms to enhance traction. At the time, Cliff used a combination of regular grease with something else on the front spindles, which increased rollout. Anyway, you could spin that front wheel forever it seemed; it would just keep spinning and spinning.

"At first, he [Tasca] didn't know we were doing anything special. Once he got

The Thunderbolt Teardrop Hood Caper

As told by Butch "The California Flash" Leal, former Ford Thunderbolt pilot and 1964/1965 NHRA U.S. Nationals S/S Eliminator Champion

In November 1963, Mickey Thompson and I were in Dearborn at the Ford Thunderbolt preview. Gas Ronda and I were running around together and they had told us about these cars so Gas says, "Hey, let's try to sneak in and take a look at 'em!"

I said, "Let's do it!" You know me, I wanted to look too. I was really excited. So Gas and I snuck in and got a look and lo and behold, seven of them were sitting there but only one of them with the reverse teardrop hood scoop we all eventually used. The other six had what I would call a "four-leaf clover" hood and it was the ugliest thing I've ever seen! When you stop and think about it now, an original one of those hoods would be priceless to a hardcore Thunderbolt collector.

Anyhow, we got to talking and both Gas and I agreed how much better looking the teardrop hood was. We went to the dog-and-pony show Ford had later that evening with Henry Ford II, Charlie Gray, Bob Tasca, Dick Brannan; everybody was there. They [Ford] had said, "We've got this new reverse teardrop hood. You're all going to get one," blah, blah, blah!

To keep things on the up and up, everybody would draw a number out of a hat. The T-Bolt that had the good hood was car number 6. That didn't mean it was the sixth car built; Ford had just numbered the cars 1 to 8.

When it's my turn, I draw number 7, and Gas drew number 6. From the look on his face I could see that he was all excited. Mickey [Thompson] saw my excitement disappear after I drew number 7. I just put my head down and didn't say anything but Mickey noticed. A couple of minutes later he asked, "What's wrong?"

I said, "Well, boss, Gas Ronda and I snuck in there earlier and got a good look at the cars, and number 6 had the good hood."

He said, "And you drew number 7?"

I said, "Yup!" That was all that was said. The next morning we're going to go out to the Dearborn Test Track, and run the cars for everybody. Lo and behold, number 7 had the good hood on it! Gas was obviously really, really upset. But Bob Tasca, who drew number 8, didn't like it too much either. He knew Gas and the two of them had been with Ford quite a few years before Mickey and I ever became involved. But that's really the true story.

My new T-Bolt ran really good and I actually outran everybody for top speed that day. They didn't have any E.T. clocks; the road that they were all parked on in that photo (taken by Ford Motor Company photographer Joe Farkas) was actually the race track! I remember they gave me a little trophy and a watch, which I still have.

Tasca also tire tested for Watertown, Massachusetts, neighbor, M&H Tires, and helped develop the 8-inch drag slick that helped even the playing field in both the A/FX class and in match racing.

wind of it, he walked over to my front wheel and without saying a word, spun it. That wheel kept turning and turning! He ran me down right away and said, 'Gas! What have you guys got in these wheels to make them turn so freely? I spun one of them and it seems like it kept going for about fifteen minutes!' That was just one of the things the man was good at. He noticed the details."

A Moral Compass in a Sea of, Well . . .

Bob Tasca was a man of faith, and it was apparent to all who met him that he was straight-laced and all business. On one of Team Tasca's visits to the U.S. Nationals at Indianapolis (around 1964) it was very late at night; Bob Sr., Bob Jr., Carl, David, and John Pagano were all walking to their hotel rooms. As they came out of the elevator, two doors opened and two women ran bare-ass naked out of each room laughing wildly. They passed each other in the middle of the hallway and ran into the opposite room.

As the doors slammed shut, Bob turned to John and said, "Pagano, we're not staying here!"

John said, "Mr. Tasca, it's U.S. Nationals weekend. There's not a vacant hotel room for 150 miles."

Bob looked at John and said, "*Find one.*" And John did.

Bob didn't feel that this place was a very good environment for his young and impressionable sons, and he wasn't going to put up with it for another minute!

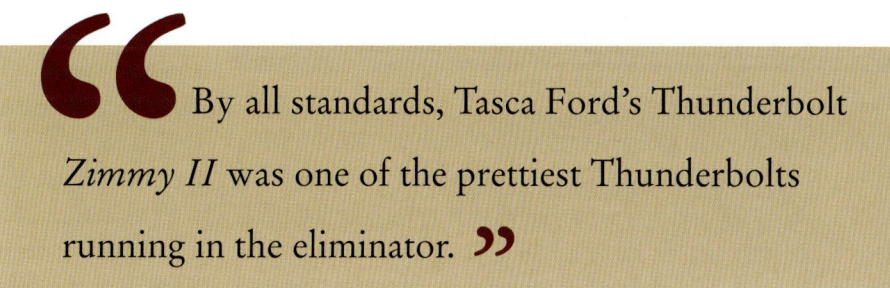

> "By all standards, Tasca Ford's Thunderbolt *Zimmy II* was one of the prettiest Thunderbolts running in the eliminator."

Game On!

Bob Tasca never went to the drag races thinking he was going to get lucky and win. He was always there to do nothing but win. Of course, he didn't always win but he always went fully prepared. On one occasion, a guy came up to him and asked, "Well, Mr. Tasca, do you think you're going to get lucky today?" Tasca turned to the man and said, "Well, I'm not just here to get a sunburn."

"When it came to standing on the starting line, our father had a real presence," said Carl Tasca.

"He used to stand there with his pipe in his mouth and watch his cars run," younger brother David added.

"My father was always humble [at the races], whether he lost or won. But when he lost he went back to work to make his car better. He didn't want to shake the hand that won; he wanted to shake the hand that lost. He was a very passionate man. He wanted to be the best at everything, and that's what he taught us!"

All things considered, as an NHRA-legal Super Stock car, the Tasca Ford Thunderbolt was nearly unbeatable. However, by mid-1964, the face of stock-bodied drag racing was rapidly changing and "Team Tasca" was forced to change with it.

"We made a verbal contract with Plymouth driver Al 'Lawman' Eckstrand to run a match race up at Island Dragway in New Jersey," said Dean

Chapter Three: "Win on Sunday, Sell on Monday!" 67

Gregson. "It was Super Stock 'A' against Super Stock A/Automatic. Now the Bopper didn't go but John Healey, Billy Lawton, Henry 'Wimpy' Tamalio, John Pagano, and I went and we got our asses kicked. Eckstrand had brought one of those 2-percent A/FX cars with the altered body. It was *not* a legal NHRA Super Stock car; it was an A/FX car!

"The next day I got called upstairs with Mr. Healey. Mr. Lawton had also come by and we got our asses chewed out! We were told point blank by Bob Tasca that he got a call from so-and-so at Kar Kraft [telling him] that we got beat by a car with the wheels offset front and back. [He told] us to park the Thunderbolt, take off every piece that can be taken off the car (hood, fenders, trunk, doors, window glass; everything), and do not move the car again until he tells us.

"The Bopper had had it. You want to play with the Bopper? Out comes the Thunderbolt Lightweight Kit, Plexiglas windows, fiberglass hood, fiberglass doors, fiberglass fenders, and fiberglass trunk lid. We moved the wheels forward and installed 10-inch slicks, so now we can race NHRA A/FX."

"Once we got our little [A/FX] kit installed things got much better," commented Bill Lawton. "We took the car to Sanford, Maine, and were running 10.5s and 10.6s, which was unheard of at the time. That's when we 'built' the graveyard on the rear deck lid and started painting on headstones of Chrysler racers: Bobby Harrop's *Flying Carpet* Dodge, Bill Flynn's *Yankee Peddler* Dodge, Al 'Lawman' Eckstrand's Plymouth, and all the others."

Being a car salesman first and foremost, Bob Tasca never kept any of his old race cars. When he was done with them, he was *done* with them! At the close of the 1964 season, Bob sold *Zimmy II* to George "Cork" Marshalko, aka "Mr. Automatic." As with many factory-built race cars from that era, the ex-Tasca T-Bolt was transformed into a full-on "run what ya' brung" southern-style match racer by early 1966. In the process it lost most of its "born with" identity.

Basically, the car was cut into two pieces with the removal of the entire front frame clip along with the entire floorpan; only the basic body structure, or shell, remained. Its rear wheels were also radically moved forward some 12 inches with accompanying sheet-metal modifications and a complete tube frame was then installed underneath. According to the official Ford Thunderbolt website the original front-end clip (complete with factory-original "leapfrog" front suspension) was sold to a party in Canada, and was lost to the ages.

Marshalko actually kept the car until 1985, when Lyons, New York, Ford muscle car restorer Randy Delisio (Delisio's Performance and Restoration, 7544 Route 31, Lyons, New York) purchased its remains and restored it to its original as-raced condition as an NHRA-legal S/S car.

Today, the car is owned by New Hampshire resident Steve Ames, owner of Marlborough, New Hampshire's Ames Performance Engineering.

Go Karts R US

As told by Bob Tasca Jr.

Carl and I used to have a Thunderbird Go Kart with a single-stroke Briggs & Stratton engine, but it just wasn't fast enough. Hmm! Wonder where we got that from? At the time, we lived in Barrington, Rhode Island, and one day we took a trip with John [Healey] to Ed Lindskog's Machine Shop in Lexington, Massachusetts, to get some balancing work done.

Ed had a sideline selling West Bend gasoline engines and the top-of-the-line engine was something like $70! We didn't have $70, so we went to the Bopper and said, "Dad, you know there's an engine that we want to buy that costs $70."

One of his big things was that he would always ask, "What are you going to accomplish?"

I didn't know what the word "accomplish" meant. So I say, "We want to make it faster, Dad."

So he says, "All right [looking out his office window at the car lot below]; I'll tell you what. The lot looks a little tacky. Let's see what you can do, then come back and see me."

We swept and washed and detailed every car, and we're talking about close to 500 of them, using only our hands and a rubber hose. The dealership had no car wash at the time. We were it. I mean, we absolutely killed ourselves! It took us almost three days. I looked at my brother, Carl, and said, "You know, Carl, we got screwed on this deal. I think the old man got the best of us. I mean, we worked like animals!"

Anyway, we bought our new engine and put it in our Go Kart. I remember John [Healey] made a custom exhaust for it, and stuffed it with steel wool and a screen at the end of it so that it would be a little quieter. I'll never forget it. We were buzzing around my father's back lot and Carl (who always tried to get me into trouble) said, "Why don't you take it out on the track?"

We used to have a jogging track at East Providence High School. So there I was. I had no throttle and was just running the engine from the back with one hand on the carburetor linkage, and driving with the other. I mean, totally against the law. Now I don't hear anything but the sound of that engine, and I'm running hot laps. Suddenly I look up and there are cop cars and flashing red lights everywhere, and away I go.

My Uncle Ernie had to bail me out on that one.

Tasca's T-Bolt Lives to Race Another Day

During the research for this book, I had a conversation with Randy Delisio, Thunderbolt restorer.

Author: How did you find the Tasca Ford 1964 Ford Thunderbolt?

Randy: Well, as you know, I've restored quite a few Thunderbolts. I had restored a Thunderbolt for another customer and I had indicated to him that I was in fact looking for a Thunderbolt myself, one that had some history. I had become aware that the Tasca Ford Thunderbolt still existed because another acquaintance of mine (who worked for Ford Motor Company and was also a Ford Thunderbolt enthusiast) let it slip one day that he knew where the Tasca Ford Thunderbolt was. He actually had had the opportunity to look at the car. He wouldn't divulge where the car was because he had hopes that he was going to buy the car himself.

In the meantime, I had restored a Thunderbolt for another customer, Dennis Kolodziej, and we had chatted about it. His car made it into a magazine, I don't recall what magazine it was, but anyways, he got a phone call one day from a guy who claimed that he owned the Tasca Ford Thunderbolt. The guy indicated that he was interested in selling the car. Dennis was out in Ohio on a search venture, and somehow came across the car and actually went and looked at it.

Anyway, he and [Bob] Truvano wanted to buy the car but they but couldn't get together with the seller on a price. He called me up and said, "If you're still interested in a Thunderbolt, I got a call from a person who says

In late 1964, the Tasca Ford Thunderbolt was sold to racer George "Cork" Marshalko and raced under the "Mr. Automatic" banner. Typical of the time, Cork seriously altered the wheelbase, and installed a tubular subframe with a straight front axle. In essence, the car was cut in half. (Photos Courtesy Randy Delisio)

he owns the Tasca Ford car." He told me where the car was located and I said that kind of makes sense because I kind of gathered that much from my conversation with Dennis.

Dennis said, "If you're interested in buying the car, I'll give you the guy's phone number, but it's going to cost you!" Well, I don't mind paying for information. I ended up giving him a 427 side-oiler high-riser engine for the information on where to find the Tasca car. I called up that number and had a talk with the person: George "Cork" Marshalko. After talking to him, I was pretty convinced that this was the real deal.

He told me what he wanted for the car and what condition it was in. So right then and there, I committed to buy the car. I said, "I'm going to head out," so I did. I got the truck and trailer and headed for Toledo, Ohio, did the deal, and brought it home."

Author: So what was the post-Tasca history of the T-Bolt?

Randy: He [Marshalko] bought the car from Tasca and it was sponsored through Grundee's Ford in Toledo, Ohio. Actually, when Cork first started campaigning the car, it was still burgundy. But after awhile (like everybody else in those days) he started cutting the car up because he was going to make it better. He wanted to keep up with the Mopars like everybody did back in those days. In actuality what he did was end up destroying the car. It was so unsafe, and so unpredictable!

Author: I heard not much of the original car was left.

Randy: Yes! The front end was gone. The engine was gone. When I got the car (I have pictures of it someplace)

Chapter Three: "Win on Sunday, Sell on Monday!" 69

Tasca's T-Bolt Lives to Race Another Day CONTINUED

In 1991, Lyons, New York muscle car restoration specialist Randy Delisio learned of the whereabouts of the ex-Tasca Ford Thunderbolt (Marshalko still owned it) and purchased the remains. A total of three Fairlanes (two T-Bolts and one street car) were needed to put the car back together. (Photo Courtesy Randy Delisio)

This is the restored Tasca Fairlane prior to paint. Virtually no expense was spared in this lengthy, well-researched, and expertly executed one-year restoration. (Photo Courtesy Randy Delisio)

Here is the Tasca Ford Thunderbolt restored to its original Super Stock specification. The 'Bolt is currently owned by New Hampshire muscle car collector Steve Ames.

Author: So what else were you able to identify?

Randy: I took the rear end out of the car and had it sandblasted and cleaned. I found arrows that were trick-punched into the traction arms. On one side, the arrow was going up and on the other side the arrow was going down. I contacted John Healey, introduced myself, and told him what I had. Of course, John wasn't as much a skeptic as the Tascas had been once I told him what I was finding on the car.

I told him about the arrows that were trick-punched onto the traction arms; that (partially) convinced him that "Boy, this guy has got that car." That was something that nobody else would have put on a Thunderbolt, or would even have knowledge of. It was the little things that were actually the convincing factors that yes, I do have the original car.

it looked like a gypsy circus wagon. The car was painted red, white, and blue. It was just ugly! But from the transmission back, the car was still original. It still had the original transmission. It still had the original shifter. The rear end, traction bars, the axle housing, and center section were all original.

At least he altered the wheelbase correctly by cutting the floorpan out of the original car and moved it forward [12 inches] so the car still retained the original Thunderbolt crossmember for the traction arms. That was one of the key components to identify when I first approached the Tascas and told them that I had the car. At first, they were in total disbelief. They didn't think that I had the car.

Two of the Thunderbolt's most distinguishing features are its teardrop hood and ram air intake using the car's inner headlights for the openings. Also note the lightweight aluminum front bumper.

Author: What year was that?
Randy: That was 1990 or 1991. I would have to go back and look, but I think it was 1991. I started shortly after I purchased the car. I can't remember the exact date but it was very shortly after I got it because I don't let the grass grow under anything.

Author: So you had to replace both the entire front structure *and* part of the floorpan?
Randy: Okay, I'll describe to you how I restored that car. The car still had the original dashboard on it. That was untouched. They didn't get into that. I can't remember if the firewall was there or not. In fact, the firewall *was* gone. It's been so long, I just have instant recall on some facts. The car (also) still had the original doors on it but the trunk was gone. Somebody had replaced it with an aluminum trunk lid. That's actually what I started with as far as the original Tasca structure.

Now, once I took the fiberglass doors off the car, on the inside, scratched into the fiberglass was the word "Tasca." They also had a five-digit number, "21635," on them as well. Both doors had that but I never found out what that five-digit number was. But the doors did have the name scratched right into the fiberglass, and I took a picture of that.

I had also mentioned that it had the original dashboard. On the dash was a plaque that said "New York State Champion ESTA Safety Code, 1964." In 1964, Mike Gray in the Reynolds Ford Thunderbolt raced Tasca at Cicero, New York's ESTA Safety Park for the state championship, and Tasca won. I've got pictures of that race where they were racing each other on the final. Ironically, I ended up buying Reynolds' Ford Thunderbolt, which I also restored, so I had owned both cars that raced each other for that championship in 1964.

Author: That's great!
Randy: Yes, it was. At any rate, to get back to the Tasca Ford car, I didn't really start with a lot. I started stripping the paint off and as you know, their team colors were Vintage Burgundy with a gold roof. Well, I was stripping some of that circus paint off the roof of the car and came down to the gold paint. In fact, I even saved some of that original paint that I scraped off the roof and saved it in a container, more evidence that the car was the Tasca Ford Thunderbolt.

That gold paint on the roof was actually a Cadillac Gold color. It was not a Ford color. It was a color that they liked, and it ended up being a Cadillac

Coming or going, these cars make a bold visual statement. Note Team Tasca's famous French slogan lettered on the rear deck lid *Suivez Moi!* or "Follow Me!" And many did!

Chapter Three: "Win on Sunday, Sell on Monday!"   71

Tasca's T-Bolt Lives to Race Another Day CONTINUED

Powering the Tasca T-bolt is a period-correct, date-code-correct 427 Ford FE block with high-riser heads, the correct "XE" experimental 2x4 intake, and "C3" date-coded 780-cfm Holley 4-barrel carburetors, numbers 9510CV and 9510CU. When it comes to authenticity, Delisio totally nailed it.

When I restored the car, I had bought a rust-free Fairlane donor car from someplace. You know how the Fairlane 500s have that wide stainless-steel molding that runs down the quarter panel? I cut the car right through the center of the mounting holes that hold that molding in place, and I cut the Tasca car the opposite way.

I cut one car high on the holes and the other car low on the holes. I also split the body sections at the taillight panel. I even changed the rocker panels. I drove all the spot-welds out on the doorjambs. In essence, I put this donor floorpan underneath of what remained of the Tasca body. I actually made a jig to bolt the quarter panels through the square holes that the molding clips fit into.

I made a steel bar that ran the full length of the quarter panel and actually bolted the quarter panel together; it held the corners perfectly straight. Then they were welded back together. When I did my finish work, the seams were undetectable. That's how I repaired the main body structure itself.

I also had the remains of a genuine Thunderbolt that was beyond saving. I kept the firewall and engine compartment, which I grafted onto the Tasca Fairlane. That was an original DST-modified front end assembly.

Author: So basically, you could say that pieces from two additional Fairlanes [Thunderbolt and non-Thunderbolt] were required to put together a totally original car; namely, the Tasca Fairlane Thunderbolt.

color. [They most likely bought it at next door's Lorber Cadillac, Dick Lorber owner, now East Providence Nissan, and soon to come under the Tasca Automotive Group banner.]

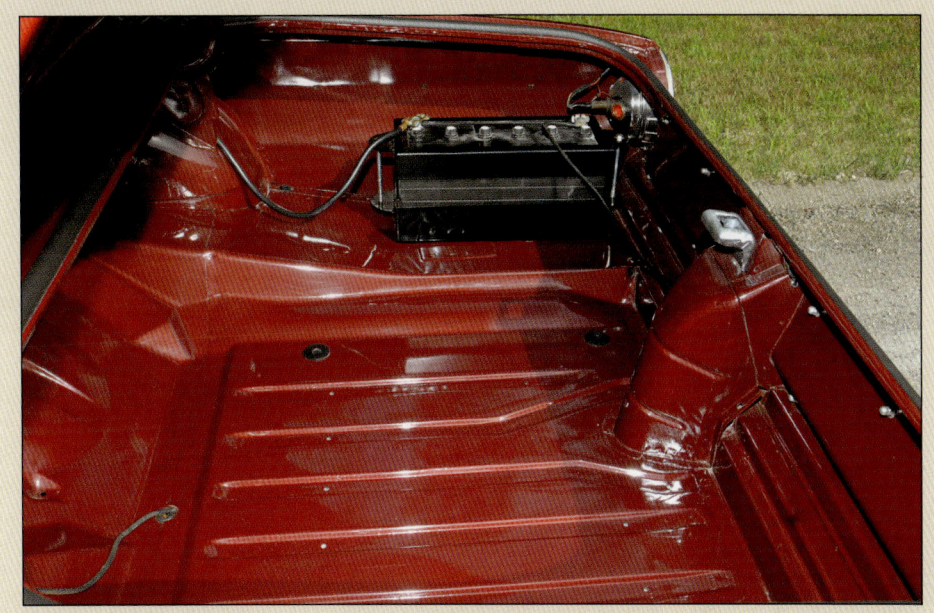

The trunk area in the Tasca Fairlane is pretty basic and features the correct trunk-mounted Diesel truck battery.

Retired Tasca Ford Crew Chief John Healey proudly holds his original copy of the NHRA "Certificate of Performance" for setting both ends of the Super Stock class record at 11.69/126.05 on September 20, 1964, at Connecticut Dragway. It's signed by NHRA Competition Director (the late) Jack Hart.

Randy: That's correct! It's a pretty difficult job to change an entire front clip on a Fairlane body, unlike on a Mustang, which I've done numerous times and is almost a piece of cake. On a Fairlane it gets a little more complicated. Because of the way the torque boxes are incorporated into the frame structure it's a much more difficult process to cut things apart in that area and install a new substructure on it. But it's still doable; it's just more work than some other cars.

What I do, and did with this car, is before I started cutting the first parts car apart for the floorpan, I took a steel I-beam structure that I built years ago; it's a very rigid platform. I built a jig on this I-beam structure that actually cradles the chassis. Then I level it so it's perfectly square on all four corners.

Then I weld the floorpan. I also jig the front frame rails. When I had the floorpan welded back into the Tasca Ford car, the body was already in the jig because I had the floorpan in my jig to keep all of the alignments square. When I installed the engine compartment onto the body, I just slipped it into my fixture that held the front frame rails off the donor car. That way I was assured that all my dimensions were going to be 100-percent correct and the structure was going to be square. In essence I built a big jig to hold all the key mounting points on the floorpan.

Author: Okay, so how long did it take you to totally restore the Tasca Fairlane?

Randy: I probably worked on it for a year. Like I said, I don't let the grass grow underneath a project. When I start on something I pretty much work on it in all my spare time.

Author: I take it you already had the 427 high-riser engine, or did you put one together with parts that you had on the shelf?

Randy: Well, the engine's a whole other story. Coming up with the correct block wasn't extremely hard because it was just basically a low-riser 427 block. I had several 427 blocks including the correct date code one for that car. I had the cast-iron crankshaft and the other key components for that engine (things a lot of people have no knowledge of). Those cars use 63 date code high-riser heads. The majority of date-coded high-riser heads floating around today are all 1964s because in 1963, the 427 high-risers technically didn't exist. They [Ford] were still experimenting with them, so they used 1963 high-riser heads.

The intake manifold was an experimental [XE] intake man-

Chapter Three: "Win on Sunday, Sell on Monday!"   73

Tasca's T-Bolt Lives to Race Another Day CONTINUED

You can just picture Bill "Go-Go" Lawton sitting behind the wheel waiting to make yet another 11-second pass! Another Thunderbolt feature was the removable passenger seat when match racing.

ifold for a 427 high-riser. I had the correct intake manifold for that car. The carburetors were 1963 "C3" date-coded 780-cfm [Holley] 4-barrel high-riser carburetors, 9510CV and 9510CU. Most of the Holley carburetors are "C4" carburetors, but these were "C3s."

Another component was the radiator. I had the original [Ford] Thunderbolt aluminum radiator in that car. It didn't come that way from the factory but any of these components could have been installed on this car. I'm not so sure that Tasca didn't run an aluminum radiator on that car because they were available to all the race teams.

Throughout my career, I've been involved in so many cars; [Thunderbolt] parts come along. Cars would come along; I had some cars come with extra parts that weren't needed in the restoration. I always ended up buying and acquiring these parts throughout the restoration that weren't needed. That's how I came across a lot of these parts for that car. They would come in on other jobs, and they weren't necessarily needed. That's how I came up with some of this very rare stuff. The engine on that car is 100-percent Ford correct. I've got Ford data on how the first 11 high-risercars were built for the Thunderbolt program. I followed that to a "T."

Author: When was the car's official debut date? I seem to remember that you took it to one of the Shelby Club Conventions, didn't you?

Randy: Yes, I did. I had it at the Shelby Convention in Watkins Glen, New York. I think that was in 1992. If I'm not mistaken, that was the first big outing I took the car to. I didn't take the car up to Rhode Island until 1995. When I was restoring the car, I called Tasca L-M and asked to speak to Bob Tasca himself. I introduced myself and told him the story about how I had gotten the car. His first reaction was, "You can't have that car. I sent it back to Ford and it was crushed."

Author: I'm sure Mr. Tasca was briefly mistaken and referring to *Zimmy-1*, the 1963 Fairlane instead.

Randy: I said, "I'm sorry to disagree with you Mr. Tasca, but that's not the way it is." The more we talked about it, the more Mr. Tasca started to come around and became convinced that I knew what I was talking about. I spoke with him several times. I also talked with John Healey, who was really instrumental in making some inroads for me. Of course, John is a dear friend of the Tasca family and he became 100-percent convinced that what I had was *the* car.

At the time when I first approached Bob Tasca with what I had, they no longer had their Ford dealership. They were in the Lincoln-Mercury business. Then when Tasca had the grand re-opening of "777" and that

74   The Tasca Ford Legacy

Here's the underside of the Tasca Fairlane. Note the DS&T fabricated cross brace and traction bars and 9-inch Ford rear end. There's even the correct token rear muffler to make class.

T-Bolts all used what was known as a "leapfrog" suspension: 90/10 shocks, 6-cylinder front springs, minimal-diameter front stabilizer bar, drum brakes. Also note the technically correct three-piece headers, 8-quart deep-sump oil pan, and Rotunda oil filter.

dealership in 1994, I agreed to bring the car for their grand re-opening. It turned out to be a reunion with the original Tasca Racing team as Mr. Tasca, Bill Lawton, and John Healey were all there. I pulled up to the place, went in, and introduced myself to Mr. Tasca, and so forth.

Then we went outside, and when I pulled the car out of my trailer, he broke down and cried like a baby. He could not believe what he was seeing. After I showed him the car, I showed him all the pictures I had of the restoration and so forth where it had the words "Tasca" scribed inside the doors, the NSTA Safety Park plaque on the dash where they had won the New York State Championship, the whole thing. He was absolutely elated. He was convinced that was the car. Mr. Tasca was a great person!

I would have to classify that grand re-opening event in 1996 as a "magical weekend," as the Tasca Ford name had kind of been dormant for a long, long time. I think that having the car at that show was instrumental in making Mr. Tasca [who was beginning to experience serious health problems at the time] acknowledge that life goes on.

I had some real heart-to-heart talks with him. As a matter of fact, he took me to his home and gave my daughter one of his prize German Shepherd pups. I'm serious! He treated me like family. He really respected what I had done for the "Tasca" name and showed his appreciation. It's things like that that most people only dream about but haven't been able to experience.

Author: You know, that was the ultimate compliment with him: giving you one of his dogs. I've talked to a number of other people, former John Force Racing Crew Chief Austin Coil, for example, who were given dogs by Mr. Tasca. That was the ultimate compliment.

Randy: That's right. They were his pride and joy.

Author: When did you sell the Tasca Fairlane?

Randy: I think it was in 1997. I sold the car to Steve Ames, who still owns it to this very day. He had the car at the York Nostalgia Reunion the same year that they inducted the Bopper into their Hall of Fame. I've got quite a few pictures of the car under construction. I haven't had them out in awhile, but I've still got them. Besides that, I gave Steve quite a few pictures when I sold him the car, and some of them are originals. I've also got all of my negatives.

Bob, I could go on for hours on this subject but I don't know how much you're looking for, or how much information you need. I'm not like a lot of people who hoard this stuff. I don't mind sharing information because it brings drag racing history to life. That's what this is all about. I get great pleasure out of doing this, and the enjoyment people get out of seeing this stuff all over again.

It's the (427) Cammer Power Hour!

By the close of the 1964 season, Ford realized that the competition was going to get a *lot* tougher the following year. Rumor had it that some very "funny" things were going on over at Chrysler Racing, and Ford needed something new and revolutionary to maintain the upper hand.

Initially, Ford experimented with installing one of the 427 high-riser engines from the T-Bolt program into the shorter-wheelbase Ford Falcon by way of a test mule built by DST. Dick Brannan tested and ran it in competition on a limited basis (running as well as 11.28/128.79) in anticipation of installing the same powertrain into the midyear (April 17, 1964) "Mustang" for 1965. The Falcon and the Mustang shared the same unit-body platform.

Dick Brannan, former Ford Special Vehicles Drag Racing Program Manager, tells the story of how those cars actually came to be. "We thought that with the Hi Rise 427 Falcon program we had a basic platform designed (and tested) and could go ahead and build a fleet of fifty 427 high-riser-powered Mustang 2+2s for the upcoming season designed for Super Stock class racing. Then when NASCAR outlawed the 427 SOHC engine (which weighed 75 pounds more than the 427 high-riser) in the fall of 1964 (for which it had originally been designed), it freed up all the 427 SOHCs that Ford Engine & Foundry had on hand. So we decided not to build the fifty 427 high-rise Mustangs; we revised that number down to twelve 427 SOHC A/FX Mustangs instead.

"Again, Ford Special Vehicles chose T-Bolt program builder's DST to build two 427 SOHC Mustang development mules, one red and one white. The red 427 SOHC Mustang (number one) was driven by Brannan himself. He was not only responsible for project development, he reported race results and worked with the secretaries at Ford helping translate ongoing reports into language that could be understood by important people within the company who were involved in the day-to-day operation.

"We shipped the red car out to Pomona the day after Christmas, December 1964, and Charlie Gray and I started testing. Then we found out that we *might* not have enough 427 SOHC engines ready for installation after all. Connie Kalitta had become involved with our department, driving a 427 Ford SOHC AA/FD (*Bounty Hunter*), and needed spare engines to develop for this completely new program.

To further complicate matters, DST couldn't guarantee delivery of the remaining cars in time for the Winternationals at Pomona. My boss, Charlie Gray, contacted H-M to see if they could commit to our timetable. Once they said yes, we had the white development car, which was still back in Dearborn, shipped down to Charlotte, North Carolina, where Holman-Moody could copy it and build the remaining ten cars."

H-M's John Wanderer (today a lawyer in Las Vegas) was dubbed "Project Engineer" of the A/FX Mustang program. Ten small-block V-8 Mustang 2+2s were shipped directly to H-M from the Metuchen, New Jersey, Ford Assembly Plant. Along with the ten cars, Wanderer and his crew received all the blueprints. The front suspension and quarter elliptic springs were designed by Ford. Ten or eleven sets of front suspension parts were also shipped.

Ford Special Vehicles/DST had also done extensive testing on the Vern Tinsler–designed (rear) lift bars, their length, and attachment points to the Mustang platform. Numerous other parts still needed fabricating. To clear those massive Cammer cylinder heads, the steering boxes (gleaned from an Australian Ford Falcon) were mounted to the outside of the driver-side front rail. The headers were also built right there at H-M.

Once all the necessary components were gathered or fabricated, a mini-assembly line was set up and the respective cars knocked out. Simultaneously, H-M made a series of jigs and later built additional cars as well as sold "A/FX Mustang Kits."

Because Ford didn't have enough 427 Cammer engines, only five of the remaining ten Mustang A/FX-ers (at 3,300 pounds) initially ran the 427 SOHC engine: Gas Ronda/Russ Davis Ford, Bill Lawton/Tasca Ford, Phil Bonner/Archway Ford, plus the two original DST cars with Len Richter/Bob Ford and Dick Brannan driving the Stark/Hickey Ford Mustang. The remaining A/FX Mustangs, although constructed to accept the 427 SOHC engine, left H-M with the 427 high-risers (at 3,230 pounds). They were converted early in the 1965 season when more "SOHC engines" became readily available. As confirmed by John Healey, Tasca Ford got the very first H-M–built Mustang A/FX car.

"We picked that car up at H-M, and drove straight from Charlotte to Pomona. I remember Dick Brannan asking, 'You didn't set that car up yet, did you?' I said no because all those engines were originally NASCAR engines. We

> "Being a car salesman first and foremost, Bob Tasca never kept any of his old race cars. When he was done with them, he was *done* with them!"

The Tasca Ford Legacy

This is the late-1964 new space-age computer-designed (a first for Ford Engine Engineering) 12.1:1-compression NASCAR 427 SOHC engine, or Ford's "90-day wonder." Unfortunately it was banned for super speedway competition by the association but it proved to be perfectly suited for Ford's upcoming A/FX Mustang 2+2 project. They were capable of winding up to 7,800 rpm and, when equipped with a 2x4 Holley-equipped intake, produced in excess of 650 to 700 hp.

This is one of two original DST-constructed 427 Mustang 2+2 mule cars originally prototyped for NHRA's Super Stock class and to be powered by Ford's 427 high-riser engine. Fifty of these cars were slated to be built. However, with NASCAR outlawing the SOHC engine for Super Speedway competition, Ford rapidly shifted gears and commissioned H-M to build ten more cars using this engineering mule as a rolling blueprint. (Photo Courtesy Dick Brannan)

Tasca Ford received the first H-M–built 1965 427 SOHC A/FX Mustang and drove straight to Pomona from Charlotte, North Carolina. They proceeded to win the Top Stock Eliminator at the NHTRA Winternationals and beat Jim Thornton and the Ramchargers Dodge on the final.

Chapter Three: "Win on Sunday, Sell on Monday!" 77

Immediately after Pomona, Ford requested that Tasca attend the 1965 running of the Daytona 500 and participate in the parade lap of the race. I guess Ford wanted to show NASCAR what they did with all those surplus engines! Shown left to right are Dean Gregson, John Healey, Bill Lawton, and Bob Tasca Sr.

changed out the cams and did a bunch of other things and then went testing at both Pomona and Irwindale.

We painted the car so that it would match the old 1964 car. It was supposed to have been painted Cadillac Gold on the top, like the Fairlane, but it ended up being painted another shade of gold, and it didn't have the same brilliance. I said to Mr. Tasca, 'Well, what do you think? It doesn't match the old one,' He said. 'Leave it alone; it's different. We'll repaint it once we get it back home.'

But that never happened after Tasca, Lawton, and Healey went out and won Factory Stock Eliminator at the first race of the NHRA season, the Winternationals at Pomona, California. There just wasn't enough time, as Bill Lawton succinctly commented: "From that day on, that car won *everything*!"

"That was truly one of the greatest races I've ever witnessed," said Bob Tasca Sr. "At the time, Bill Lawton was probably the sharpest guy around out of the gate. Of course, he had a good set of wheels under him. I never gave him anything to drive that he was ever ashamed of."

For Bob Jr., Carl, and David Tasca, Lawton's big win was the thrill of a lifetime. "To stand next to our father at the 1965 NHRA Winternationals when Billy won A/FX; I'll never forget it as long as I live. We were like kids in a candy store hanging around all those race car drivers working on their cars. In the first round we drew 'Dyno Don' and his 427 SOHC Mercury Comet. Bill was complaining, 'Jeez, why do I have to race the fastest guy in the first round?'

"My father says, 'Get in the car and do what you know how to do, and that's win the race!' Lawton beat Nicholson, he beat Roger Lindamood in *Color Me Gone* [Dodge], he beat Tommy Grove in *Melrose Missile* [Plymouth], and he beat Jim Thornton in the "Ramchargers" [Dodge] on the final. He beat all the top guys and ran a 10.50/128.20."

The NHRA house organ *National Dragster* wrote, "The mighty grip of the Mopars was broken, Ford picked the Mustang to lead their 1965 racing efforts and Bill Lawton and Tasca Ford's performance indicates that they are ready for many (more) trips to the winner's circle."

78   The Tasca Ford Legacy

Gas Ronda, fellow Thunderbolt teammate and then reigning NHRA Super Stock Eliminator World Points Champion, later commented, "Bill Lawton's shining moment with the Tasca Ford A/FX Mustang had to be at the 1965 NHRA Winternationals, where he took home all the marbles. His car beat mine in eliminations. I called Mr. Tasca to congratulate him and said, 'My congratulations, Mr. Tasca. Your brain beat me again!'"

Pomona Proved to be the "Pits," Literally!

David Tasca won't forget Pomona either, but for an entirely different reason.

"My father used to stand by the tower most of the time and I would stand alongside him and watch the races. It was a Saturday, and he was with the Ford people most of the day. My brothers Bobby and Carl were told to watch me. When 'Dyno Don' Nicholson fired up his car, my brothers ran over to his pit, and just left me standing there. I was four or five years old at the time. I'm standing in the middle of this parking lot with thousands of people and cars all around me and I didn't know what to do.

"Finally someone from the NHRA took me up to the tower. Luckily I had a Tasca Ford jacket on, so they paged my father and he came and got me. Was he ever mad at Bobby and Carl because they were told to watch me! I spent the rest of the day with my father. I never left his side.

"Then once my mom found out, she wasn't happy at all.

"You know what's kind of funny? In 2010 I went back to Pomona to watch Bobby III race. It was 35 years later; I'm at the same track [which has been thoroughly modernized], and I got lost all over again."

Letting Off Steam

Bill Holbrook, retired FoMoCo Special Vehicles technician, related, "Tasca stayed at the Cloud 9 Motel

> "To further complicate matters, DST couldn't guarantee delivery of the remaining cars in time for the Winternationals at Pomona."

in Covina, California. The restaurant located on the premises had a stream running inside with all kinds of flora and fauna around it. It connected to a pool and a little waterfall outside. Lawton and Healey had gone down to the local dollar store and bought a big bottle of bubble bath, which they poured into the fountain. They had to close the restaurant because there were bubbles all over the place. Of course, nobody would tell them who had done it."

Once in the public limelight, members of the Tasca Racing Team emerged as distinctive personalities on a national scale, and life was never quite the same. For example, just a week after Tasca's Factory Stock Eliminator win at the NHRA Winternationals at Pomona, Henry Ford II requested Team Tasca's presence at the Daytona 500, Daytona Beach, Florida. The 2,474-mile cross-country drive

Later that summer Tasca, Healey, and Lawton won the first annual *Super Stock* Magazine Nationals held at York U.S. 30 Dragway. This is the famous Jim Kelly photo that appeared on the cover of the second issue of *SS&DI*. (Photo Courtesy Dick Towers, Match Race Madness)

Ever wonder what kind of rig Tasca used to transport the 1965 Mustang A/FX car? How about this matching 1965 Ford F-100 pickup?

Chapter Three: "Win on Sunday, Sell on Monday!" 79

Bob Tasca Sr., Ford Special Vehicles Drag Racing Program Manager Richard H. "Dick" Brannan, and John Healey talk shop while waiting in the tech line at the U.S. Nationals at Indy.

Sitting behind the wheel of the Tasca Mustang at Pomona is 14-year-old Bob Jr. He tells an interesting story about his brother Carl and himself driving 777 around 777 Taunton Avenue and getting onto the gas just a little too hard. "That thing took off and it scared the hell out of me!"

Bill Lawton bangs third gear while competing at the U.S. Nationals at Indy. Ford wanted to know exactly how much RPM was lost through the gears, so that summer the Tasca Ford Mustang was installed on a dyno at Ford's Engine Engineering labs. Lawton made a run, and the RPM drop between shifts proved to be infinitesimal.

80   The Tasca Ford Legacy

culminated with a hero's welcome as well as participation in an all-Ford parade lap before the start of the "Great American Race." In attendance were Bob Tasca Sr. and family, Bill Lawton, John Healey, and Dean Gregson.

The Tasca Ford Mustang A/FX proved to be one of the strongest-running and most-consistent 427 Cammer cars in the country. In the spring of 1965, the team won the NHRA Northeast Division One (NED) Grand Opener at Cecil County (Maryland) against "Dyno Don" Nicholson's 427 Cammer Comet Cyclone.

In June 1965, Tasca, Lawton, and Healey were runner-up to none other than Ronnie Sox in Top Stock at the inaugural NHRA Spring nationals, Bristol, Tennessee. On August 7 the team was again in the final at the First Annual Super Stock & Drag Illustrated Nationals (aka, the "Woodstock of Drag Racing"). This time they were in the winner's circle after winning the 3,200-pound class beating Melvin Yow's Dodge, then besting Cecil Yother in the *Melrose Missile* AWB Plymouth [or "Cuckoo Clock Cars" as Bill Lawton called them] for all the marbles. They clocked a 10.62/129.87 to Yother's final-round red-light run of 10.74.

As Tasca's Bill Gilbert put it, "That was quite a weekend. We had blown the motor in the car the week before, and John didn't have enough time to build a new one. Dick Brannan sent us a 427 Cammer short-block to use that was kind of worn out. The thing was like a bug sprayer. You could see the oil coming out of the headers. Every run the car ran slower, and Billy drove it harder and it stayed together. The only thing we changed was the clutch before the final round.

"To make matters worse (as if changing a clutch wasn't bad enough), they [York U.S. 30] had erected a snow fence to help control the crowd. Well, by midnight the crowd had trampled the fence near the shutoff area, so when Billy drove back up the return road to the starting line he ran over the fence and flattened both slicks. We borrowed Dick Brannan's slicks and ran the final at 3:40 in the morning; what a night that was!"

Exactly how consistent was Bill Lawton with a 4-speed? Well, Ford wanted to know. That summer they installed the Tasca Ford A/FX Mustang onto a "Drag Dyno" installed at the Dearborn Engine Engineering labs, and Lawton made a series of runs through the gears. The loss of RPM between gear changes was found to be infinitesimal at best.

Al "Batman" Joniec told me, "We were all at the 1965 NHRA U.S. Nationals in Indianapolis. At that race, I had to replace all the rod bearings in my new SOHC engine after every single run, due to a heat-treating problem with the connecting rods, which Ford finally identified. I believe we replaced a total of 32 rod bearings over two days' time. We borrowed rod bearings from them [Tasca] and everyone else I could find just to stay in the race.

"I clearly remember Bill Lawton looking over the railing of the motel we all stayed at while he drank beer, pointing his finger, heckling us, genuinely having a good time. I miss his horrible smile and sense of humor.

"I'm not sure how it happened, but we raced each other in the first run of eliminations. I won fair and square. My guys told me that Bob Sr. threw an ice chest into the air in pure frustration and yelled, 'That damned Joniec,' but he came over later to congratulate me!"

David Tasca remembers, "We used to drive that car [1965 A/FX Mustang] around the lot all the time. Carl and I would take turns. It's my turn this time; it was your turn last time. That was our favorite car. I remember Carl and I used to clean it downstairs at the old 777 Taunton Avenue dealership. One time, I was driving the car out of the wash stall, I think I was 14 years old, and I got on the gas a little too hard. "Rum-bah!" That thing took off and scared the hell out of me!

"'I remember another time Billy Lawton drove that car from the Air Porter Inn Motel to Indianapolis Raceway Park. I mean, right out on the open highway, open exhaust and all. The cops were totally cool; they would let us.

> " I'll never forget it as long as I live. We were like kids in a candy store hanging around all those race car drivers working on their cars. "

"Ford also had a shop rented near the race track. That's where all the Ford racers would work on their cars. One day we said, 'Billy, you've got to jump on it.' Lawton went through first and second gear and part of third. The car accelerated so hard that Carl got thrown into the back; I mean, what a thrill that was!"

Tasca's John Healey wasn't comfortable working around large crowds, whether it was at the drag strip or in the shop but he always had time for the Tasca boys as David Tasca fondly recalls. "I used to spy on Johnny as he worked. Sometimes he would hang me up on the engine hoist by my belt when I was being a real pain. Yeah, Healey used to do that but he would always take me down before my father would walk in. I used to love watching Johnny work."

Chapter Three: "Win on Sunday, Sell on Monday!"

Tasca was rightly proud of their most recent accomplishments for 1965: they won both the Winternationals at Pomona and the Super Stock Nationals at York. They also took the runner-up spot at Bristol.

Radar, Radar, I Got Your Car!

In early 1965, Dean Gregson and Tasca Assistant Service Manager Manny Carter got a call from Bob Tasca saying, "We're going to New York's La Guardia Airport to pick up something. Grab a couple of dealer plates, and we'll jump into my LTD and head for New York."

Gregson relates, "Carroll Shelby had shipped us two Wimbledon White Shelby GT350 Mustangs by air. Now we're on our way back to Providence, and guess what happens? The Bopper goes through a radar trap with me following close behind. Of course, me being the closest, I get pulled over by the police. Now Bob's a millionaire, and I'm supporting two families, a wife and a child, and guess who gets the ticket? Me!"

With Bob Tasca's increasing success on the race track, it was no wonder that 777 Taunton Avenue had become a high-performance Mecca of sorts during the mid-1960s. In the summer of 1965, Carroll Shelby and his "Cobra Caravan" paid a visit to Tasca Ford with Shelby as the featured guest during one of the dealership's highly acclaimed high-performance seminars. Shelby rolled up with a couple of Cobras, a GT40, a Cobra Daytona Coupe, and a Shelby GT350 Mustang.

Carl Tasca added, "We closed the place down to the public that night and threw this big shindig, which included a lengthy Q&A session, lots of door prizes, and even slot car racing. It was quite a night."

Stripes or No Stripes?

According to SAAC GT350 Registrar and board member Howard Padre, "Since Tasca Ford didn't have their own body shop, most of their work was done at nearby Seekonk Auto Body located about a half mile south and a little east of Tasca. When Tasca received one of the early Shelbys and the customer wanted Le Mans stripes, Seekonk Auto Body did the work. The body shop ran two shifts a day and, for a while, three, until the owner got burned out and cut it back to two. The shop was owned by SAAC member Ed Veader's father.

"A young Ed would sit in class dreaming about going to his father's shop after school to shuffle cars back and forth to Tasca's. It was a good day indeed whenever he got to pick up or deliver a Tasca-sold Shelby GT350."

The Tasca "Mystery" Mustang Match Racer

By late 1965, Ford Special Vehicles had built a number of altered-wheelbase 427 SOHC Mustang drag cars, which were driven by Drag Racing Program Manager/Test Driver Dick Brannan. A couple of these cars were equipped

82   The Tasca Ford Legacy

The Tasca Ford Bowani Mustang Lives!

The ex-Tasca Ford 1965 427 A/FX Mustang lives! The car was sold to NASCAR great Bondy Long and Carson Hyman at the end of the 1965 season without the 427 SOHC engine. The car was outfitted with a 2x4 427 high-riser engine, straight axle, repainted candy blue, and was renamed *Bowani*. In 1968, the car was leased to Sam Auxier Jr. and match raced in NHRA Division One running 10s at 135.00. This is how the car (which is slated for restoration) looks today.

Camden, South Carolina's Bondy Long was a well-known NASCAR team owner (1963–1968). He raced under Ford sponsorship and his team was known as Bowani Racing, an acronym for the three Long brothers' first names Bondy, Walter, and Nicky. Racers under contract to Long included Larry Frank, Bobby Isaac, James Hylton, A. J. Foyt, Marvin Panch, Bobby Allison, Mario Andretti, and Ned Jarrett, the latter of whom won Bondy the 1965 NASCAR Gran National Championship.

Bondy Long and drag racer Carson Hyman were buddies. Bondy may have been an oval-track enthusiast, but he also had an interest in drag racing cars. The Bowani 1965 match race Mustang 2+2 was and is the former NHRA Winternationals–winning Tasca Ford A/FX car delivered to H-M by John Healey. It was minus the 427 SOHC engine (which the team used in their new long-wheelbase *Mystery 9* Mustang match racer) immediately after the 1965 NHRA World Finals in October at Tulsa, Oklahoma. In its place, an H-M 427 high-riser engine with dual carburetors was installed. Bondy and Carson Hyman also installed a straight front axle, and repainted the car candy blue.

Long and Hyman also raced a stretch-nose 1966 Mustang, which eventually replaced the 1965 as their full-time hot rod. In early 1968, Sam Auxier Jr. worked out a percentage deal with Long and Hyman to match race *Bowani* at UDRA, AHRA, and NHRA drag strips throughout the Northeast; it ran in the low 10s at 135.00 mph. Auxier's biggest win that year was the 1968 Cars Magazine Championships at Cecil County, Maryland, where Sam defeated Bill "Grumpy" Jenkins' 1968 big-block Camaro to win the NAAR Ultra Stock final.

Upon completion of Sammy's record-setting UDRA Ultra Stock 1969 Mustang, *Bowani* was returned to its owners. After that, very little was heard of the ex-Tasca Ford Mustang. The story goes that the car was converted into a Super Gasser but rarely raced. Then some 15 years ago, noted factory muscle car/drag race car collector Mike Guffey purchased the Mustang. About five years ago he sold it to collector Todd Warren. Since then, the car has been authenticated by both John Healey and Sam Auxier Jr. and is slated for future restoration using muscle car collector Nick Smith's restored Gas Ronda 1965 427 SOHC Mustang A/FX car for technical reference as both the Tasca and Ronda cars were built out of the same batch.

Tasca University Dean Mike Perlini comments, "Back in the day, Billy [Lawton] beat everyone with that old Mustang. Remember those stamped-steel Mustang dashboards? One time, Lawton missed a shift and dented the dashboard with his fist. That was some pretty heavy-gauge metal back then. I guess in order to do a technically correct restoration you would have to leave that dent in there."

with C-6 automatic transmissions and fuel injection instead of carburetors and 4-speeds for testing the effects of nitromethane in anticipation of what would be coming during the following season. The outcome of that extensive testing program indicated that the shorter-wheelbase Mustangs (Ford experimental with a number of different wheelbase lengths) didn't handle nearly as well as they should.

With the increased power produced by the introduction of nitro, the shape of the Mustang body produced lift on the top end, resulting in a horrific crash of one of the cars during testing at Martin, Michigan. Dick Brannan sustained injuries including four compression fractures to four of his backbone vertebrae. He walked away from the incident all the wiser. After that, Ford started working on various front and rear spoiler configurations and a standardized wheelbase; 112 inches in length proved to be the ideal.

Tasca was the second-largest Ford dealer in the United States (with Chicago, Illinois' Jim Moran Ford being number one) and played an advisory role in almost every Total Performance program being developed at Ford. It was only natural that he was privy to what was going on with the Ford Drag Council cars. As such, Tasca received the first H-M–built, 112-inch-wheelbase, "long-nose" Mustang match racer.

However, Bob participated in that program with some degree of reluctance. "John Cowley and Charlie Gray were the impresarios at Ford and they wanted me to build a funny car, but I had no reason at all to build a funny car. I didn't like funny cars from the very beginning because you can't sell funny cars. As far as I was concerned, Ford Motor Company should only have been involved in racing if racing sells cars and parts. That's the whole reason why you get into racing. My motto was, 'Win on Sunday, Sell on Monday!' Now really, how many

> " I used to spy on Johnny as he worked. Sometimes he would hang me up on the engine hoist by my belt when I was being a real pain. "

*Mystery 9*s am I going to sell off my showroom floor?"

The *Mystery 9* Match Race Mustang program happened nonetheless and proved to be an instant hit with drag racing fans. In the late summer of 1965, Ford shipped an all-steel Mustang 2+2 shell (aka, a "Body in White") down to H-M for conversion. With the rear wheels moved forward 10 inches and the front end extended 16 inches over stock, the car boasted an engine set back 15½ inches, meaning that driver Bill Lawton also sat back farther in the car. The weight transfer factor was something like 60/40.

Of course, this meant fabricating an entirely new chassis. H-M began with a set of 2x2-inch main rails. Inside they installed a six-point NASCAR-style tubular roll cage with the runners extending to the rearmost pickup points on the chassis. Up front, a set of upper frame rails were tied into the forward hoop of the roll cage at the cowl, extending forward and joining up at the most forward pickup point on the lower main rail. Extensive triangulation was done as well, producing a sturdy space-age frame design.

The front suspension on the *Mystery 9* was originally a Ford upper A-arm/lower trailing arm although early in the 1966 racing season most racers changed to tubular front axles, Mustang drum brake front spindles, and a conventional Mustang steering box. A similar version of the 1964 Thunderbolt/1965 Mustang A/FX trailing arm/torque arm rear-leaf suspension was used in conjunction with twin coil-over shocks and a 4.56:1-geared Ford 9-inch rear end.

On the outside, the *Mystery 9*'s extended front fenders were actually made by splicing two sets of A/FX Mustang fiberglass front fenders together. The hood required three separate hood pieces. Lightweight Plexiglas windows were also employed, along with minimal use of aluminum interior paneling. Although no two cars were the same (Gas Ronda's car had an all-fiberglass body), the Tasca *Mystery 9* served as the basic blueprint for the 1966 Ford Drag Council program.

People have often wondered, after a series of three different "Zimmy" cars, why Tasca's stretch-wheelbase 1966 Match Race Mustang was called the *Mystery 9*. The answer: Once it was built and having never raced this kind of car before, it was a "mystery" to everyone involved as to how well the car would actually perform! Tasca Ford's *Mystery 9* was featured in a number of "buff books" from that era including the January 1967 issue of *Super Stock & Drag Illustrated*, which reported that *Mystery 9* had been built by a crew of 10 H-M technicians in two weeks! *Mystery 9* was also featured in the April 1966 issue of *Car Craft*, and the June 1966 issue of *Drag Strip*.

According to John Healey, "Here again that was something Charlie Gray and Dick Brannan from the Ford Drag Council wanted us to do. They put that whole program together. In its first incarnation that car was pretty ugly. It had a huge hood scoop on it that said "Mystery 9." My name was misspelled on the car ["Healy"] and in the article as well, which appeared in *Super Stock & Drag Illustrated*.

In late 1965, Tasca Ford fielded the first 112-inch-wheelbase long-nose Mustang match racer working in conjunction with Charlie Gray, John Cowley, and Dick Brannan from Ford Special Vehicles, and constructor H-M. This original publicity photo was taken by (the late) Don Hunter on the runway at the Charlotte, North Carolina, airport, which fronted H-M's property.

"I can't remember where we tested the car but the first pass on it was a 10.27/141.06. Then once Billy got used to it, and we got things ironed out a bit, it went 9.89/140.00 and 9.82/141.76. We used the same [600 hp] motor from the old 1965 A/FX car because we only had one motor. Hard to believe, isn't it? Honest to God, we had one motor because there were no spare pieces around."

Mystery 9 debuted with twin carburetors and a 4-speed. With the addition of a set of Hilborn fuel injectors, *Mystery 9* ran as quick as 9.78/140.00 one month later [February 11–13, 1966] during the AHRA Winter Nationals at Irwindale Raceway, defeating Gas Ronda's similarly equipped 1966 Mustang match racer in the final."

After their successful West Coast debut, Tasca, Lawton, and Healey ventured to the NASCAR Winternationals in Deland, Florida, where the team won the Grand National Stock title. Probably the most impressive thing about the early version of *Mystery 9* and its string of victories was the fact that Bill Lawton actually drove that car with a 4-speed. Imagine "what a handful of car" that must have been!

Mystery 8, the Second Incarnation

On February 9, 1966, P. F. Manley from Ford Stock Vehicles wrote a memo to Ford Division General Accounting Office employee W. J. Wells (with

H-M technicians fire up *Mystery 9* for the first time at their shop.

Chapter Three: "Win on Sunday, Sell on Monday!" 85

The Tasca 505 Mustang

The Tasca 505 Mustang was so named because of its more than mildly warmed-over 505-hp 289 engine. It was mildly restyled by the Alexander Brothers and featured pearl white paint, Cibie square halogen headlights, a bar tube grille, specially built Hurst wheels, and a full custom interior, prompting *American Rodding* magazine to award the car the "Perfect Performance Car of the Year," presented to Bob Tasca Sr. (right) by Executive Editor Lyle K. Engel (left).

All throughout the 1960s, Bob Tasca Sr. was highly instrumental in the building of close to a half dozen "one-off" show cars, which remained recognizably Ford. Each exhibited an independent and progressive look to what might have been, or, from a car dealer's perspective, what yet might be. Bob Tasca's "505," a stylized 1965 Mustang 2+2, was the epitome of this kind of out-of-the-box thinking, and is by far the Big Bopper's best-known show car. Engineered completely by Tasca, the 505 Mustang was as much (if not more) "go" as it was "show."

The proverbial "steak" in this equation, a John Healey–engineered and –built Hi Po 289 engine, had been stroked to 325 ci. As you might guess, the 289 block had to be "massaged" to accept the 3.25-inch stroker crank. The lower skirts on the block had to be hand scalloped to clear the connecting rods that were also incorporated into the build, as well as fly-cutting the pistons. The engine featured a 271-hp Mustang solid-lifter camshaft (courtesy Ford E&F's Poppa "Sully" Sullivan) with twin Holley 4-barrel carburetors, a hand-massaged 289 high-rise 4V intake, and a Ford/Shelby Engine Dress-Up Kit.

It Was "Totally the Bomb"

According to Bill Gilbert

At first, the engine just didn't want to run. Our reaction was, "What's going on here?" If you know Holley carburetors, then you know they have bleeds up in the top of them. I took a pair of ball-point pens and stuck them in the bleeds, and that straightened everything out. The thing simply wanted more fuel at idle.

But run it did! The Tasca 505 Mustang pumped out 505 hp at 7,600 rpm on the dyno (hence the "505" designation) and was backed by an aluminum-cased BorgWarner T-10. With Bill Lawton driving, the Tasca 505 was clocked in the low 12-second range at more than 120 mph, and registered a terminal speed of 147 mph!

And now for the "sizzle"; credit for the Tasca Mustang 505's mildly restyled exterior sheet metal and mother of pearl with blue and white striped paint goes to Detroit's famed Alexander Brothers. Custom touches included rectangular Cibie halogen headlights, a 1966-style bar-tube grill, a completely remodeled rear taillight panel creating a wall-to-wall Thunderbird sequential taillight effect, rectangular side-marker lights, Shelby GT350-style side scoops, and a set of special-order blue-center anodized Hurst five-spoke aluminum wheels with one-off custom-made Goodyear tires. The interior featured a [Frank] Caito Auto Top custom white upholstery job and white Persian rug carpeting.

Man, what we did to the inside of that car. I spent over seven weeks at Caito's working with them on that interior. We packed it with so much house insulation: the top, side quarters, door panels, under the floor mats that you

Tasca seized the opportunity of winning the *American Rodding* award to promote customer awareness proclaiming "Tasca Ford, First Again!" The Tasca *505* Mustang was likewise displayed in Tasca's *777* Taunton Avenue showroom. Note the Firebird-like snorkel hood scoops, which were a later addition. This car still exists and is in the hands of a private collector.

could drive that car down the road and it was so quiet you couldn't even hear the hum of the tires!

Tasca Ford's 505 Mustang won the *American Rodding* "Perfect Performance Car of the Year Award" for 1965. Presenting the award to Bob Tasca and Ford V.P. Donald Frey was Lyle K. Engel, Executive Editor of *American Rodding*, with the 505 parked right in front of Ford's corporate headquarters in Dearborn, Michigan, aka, "The Big Glass House."

"Back in those days that car was a real tiger," commented Bob Tasca Sr.

If You Can't Run with the Big Dogs, Stay on the Porch

According to Bill Gilbert

There used to be a burger bar across the street from Tasca Ford called the "Pink Elephant." It was the local hangout for all the Chevy boys; if you showed up with a Ford, they would all laugh you off the lot. One night Bill Lawton showed up with the 505 Mustang. He does this huge burnout across the parking lot in front of all these Chevy guys, and nobody would even start their engines up and go after him!

Did anything emerge from the Tasca 505 program that would go into production on a future Ford product? Bob Tasca thought so.

That would have been the Boss 302 Mustang. The 505 car was the guts of the whole Boss 302 Mustang program. The Boss 302 was a magnificent little car. Insurance availability and a big engine, it was quick; one hell of a unit.

Another Tasca 505 Story

According to Bill Gilbert

Being that the Tasca 505 had Cibie rectangular halogen headlights, it took a bit more time to set then correctly. We're at the old [777] Ford store. I don't know; it had to be 1:30 to 2:00 a.m. and I'm aiming and adjusting the headlights. Well, this East Providence cop comes in with his gun drawn. He must have thought someone was inside with a flashlight or something so he hollers, "Put your hands on the car!"

So Mr. Tasca says to him, "I'm Bob Tasca," and the cop says, "Yeah, and I'm Jesus Christ. Put your hands on the car!" This was one of those incidents where you had to be there.

The next day, the cop got reprimanded for what he said to Mr. Tasca and exclaimed, "Well, I didn't know who he was! I just can't walk in and say, 'How are you guys tonight, and what are you up to? I mean it's kind of out of the ordinary to be adjusting headlights at 1:30 a.m. with all the lights out and with the dealership all closed up.'"

The Tasca 505 was eventually sold to fellow Ford dealer and Ford Drag Council member Paul Harvey of Paul Harvey Ford in Indianapolis, Indiana. Son Jerry Harvey drove the car around for a while and eventually sold the Tasca 505 to the late Hoosier Bill Gilbert (no relation to Tasca's Bill Gilbert). In early 1970 Gilbert traded in the Mustang for a Ford Super Cab from Greenwood, Indiana's Perry Ford. Co-owner Dave Perry drove the Tasca 505 Mustang for a short time, prior to selling it to a private party living somewhere in the Midwest. The good news is that the Tasca 505 still exists. The bad news is that its current owner wishes to remain nameless. Bummer!

Unlike Tasca's 65 A/FX car, *Mystery 9* was a purebred racer. Note the sturdy six-point roll cage and no-nonsense steering setup. Driver Bill Lawton commented that the first time he drove *Mystery 9* it was so loud that it sounded like bombs going off inside his head!

cc: to Ford's J. L. Pfeifer) listing the sale of five "dollar cars." Tasca Ford Sales C5HM-10065-DR (*Mystery 9*) was listed along with five other factory race cars for Ford contract racers Gas Ronda, Richard Brannan, Bill Ireland, Al Joniec Jr., and Les Ritchey. "The total of $6.00 should be credited to the parties mentioned on file in this office." Now it was official. The long-wheelbase, or "stretch-nose" Mustang match racer program had come of age.

John Healey said, "In late February, we took the car back to H-M. Charlie Gray told me to get together with John Wanderer and do whatever we wanted

This is an outtake from the photo feature that originally appeared in the January 1966 issue of *Super Stock & Drag Illustrated* magazine. It was taken by future NHRA/Winston drag racing photographer (the late) Don Hunter.

88   The Tasca Ford Legacy

This picture of Bill Lawton (right) and John Healey (left) is from the *SS&DI* photo files that are now part of the Tasca Automotive Group archives. This was the very first magazine article ever to be published on the car and it helped generate an immense amount of interest in the soon-to-be-debuted stretch-wheelbase 1966 Mustang program.

with the car. We changed it around, took some weight off it, put on the newer-style hood and new doors for it, and eliminated the front brakes and that kind of stuff. We got quite a bit of weight off the car because in its first incarnation [at 2,500 pounds] *Mystery 9* was pretty heavy."

On April 14, 1966, Ford Motor Company Drag Racing Program Manager "Dick" Brannan submitted a paper called the "Tasca Report" citing the results of a three-day modification program and test session at Connecticut Dragway, April 6–8. As you can see on the report to the left, testing during the early spring proved to be a touch-and-go situation.

Tasca's Mystery Mustang match racer was extremely popular with strip promoters, and specifically at strips located throughout the Eastern Seaboard. Tasca was especially popular at two Washington, DC, area tracks: Capitol Raceway (Maryland) and Aquasco Speedway (Maryland). They were co-owned and operated by Julio Marra, who commented, "Actually, we booked Tasca, Lawton, and Healey into quite a few match races, some as early as 1963 when they were racing Bob Tasca's white 1963½ Ford Galaxie lightweight. My late wife, Betty, just thought the world of Bill Lawton, who also handled all of the bookings for the team. She really liked the way he presented himself and would book him in anytime she could. John Healey was also a super mechanic but it seemed like we never had the time to hold any long

---

Wednesday, April 6, 1966

Engine and transmission were readied for installation. Since the car had never been modified to accept the (C6) drag automatic transmission, a rear crossmember had to be fabricated and the floorpan raised to provide proper clearance.

Thursday, April 7

Installation was completed and the car was transported to the Connecticut Dragway. On arrival the car was unloaded and the oil was changed. The car was warmed up on alcohol and AG-2 spark plugs. After warm-up was completed the car was readied for the first run.

Temperature: 42 degrees F	35 degrees timing
Crosswind: 15 to 18 mph	22 and 23 camshafts
50% nitro 5% benzole	Driver: Bill Lawton
60 bypass jet	First Run: 9.27 at 150.25 mph
30A nozzles	

Winds picked up and it was unsafe to make any more full quarter-mile runs so first and second gear kickoffs were made to try to obtain the best tire pressure and weight combinations. The wind never subsided and at 4:30 pm the car was transported back to Tasca Ford.

Friday, April 8 (8:00 am)

Car was readied for return trip to the drag strip. However, due to wind and rain the trip was delayed until 11:00 am. On arrival the car was unloaded and warmed up. Car was ready for first run.

Temperature: 48 degrees F7	38 degrees timing
Crosswind: 15 to 20 mph	22 and 23 camshafts
50% nitro 5% benzole	Driver: Bill Lawton
60 bypass jet	First Run: 9.58-147.40 (let off)
30A nozzles	

Lawton felt crosswinds were too unsafe, however; said engine felt much stronger with increased timing.

Car was returned to Tasca Ford, given complete check, and readied for the race on Sunday.

Perhaps one of *Mystery 9*'s biggest wins was when it defeated fellow Ford Drag Council racer Phil "Daddy Warbucks" Bonner's 427 SOHC Falcon at the Cecil County Raceway (Cecil County, Maryland) "Factory Showdown" in August 1966.

The classic Ford-versus-Mopar battle: Bill Lawton and Ronnie Sox at Capitol Raceway. Is Billy out on Ronnie, or what? (Photo Courtesy Bob Bissell)

90   The Tasca Ford Legacy

Tasca's *Mystery 8* Mustang also won the B/XS over Dave Strickler and his *Old Reliable* Corvette (hmm, this seems like a recurring theme) at the 1967 NHRA Winternationals in Pomona, California, with an 8.69/168.22. (Photo Courtesy Steve Reyes)

This classic Jere Alhadaff photo, taken during Super Eliminator action at the 1967 NHRA Winternationals, clearly illustrates the diversity that is drag racing. As this was a full two years before NHRA instituted its highly popular Funny Car Eliminator category, the association used Super Eliminator as sort of a "dump all" category where hot cars of all classes converged.

Chapter Three: "Win on Sunday, Sell on Monday!" 91

By early 1967, the Tasca *Mystery 8* Mustang was really beginning to show its age. This particular run against Gene "Snowman" Snow's Dodge Dart almost ended in disaster when the (C-6) transmission grenaded on the top end, and the ensuing fire burned off the parachute. (Photo Courtesy Jim Kelly)

conversations with John the way we did with Bob Tasca Sr. and Billy Lawton. He was always very, very busy."

Claimed John Healey, "I didn't know it at the time, but the old man [Tasca] considered me one of the hardest workers he ever laid eyes on. Between Billy running his family business and me working on the race car, we collectively worked very, very hard at it. I was always known as one of those persons who could work two or three days straight without any sleep!"

Perhaps that's one of the reasons Tasca, Lawton, and Healey used to win 90 percent of their match races regardless of where they raced. According to Julio Marra, Tasca's *Mystery 9* participated in one of the most memorable and well attended match races in Capitol Raceway history. In 1966, Tasca, Lawton, and Healey match raced (the late) Ronnie Sox in the Sox & Martin Plymouth Barracuda (*Bacarruda*) sponsored by Greensboro, North Carolina's Gate City Motor Company.

Cracking the 8-Second Zone

Tasca Ford's *Mystery 9* officially morphed into the Tasca *Mystery 8* when Tasca, Lawton, and Healey match raced Charlie Allen and his Atlantic Dodge–sponsored Dodge Dart late June/early July 1966 at Connecticut Dragway.

"We were running three out of five," said Healey. "Unfortunately, I was having big problems with the fuel system but only because I had created them myself! In an attempt to try to make the car run faster [on 30- to 40-percent nitromethane], I replaced the 150-gph Hilborn pump with a 175-gph Hilborn pump. I had also taken the Hilborn injector manifold and made some modifications to it with a significant change in the [injector] nozzle location and how it approached the top of the [intake] valve.

These photos were taken of *Mystery 9* at the 1966 AHRA Winternationals at Irwindale Raceway in Irwindale, California. Tasca, Lawton, and Healey defeated Gas Ronda's long-nose Mustang running as fast as 9.78/140.00.

92   The Tasca Ford Legacy

The whole system was just set up to flow major volume!

"Bob Sr. kept saying, 'Give it up, Healey; it will never work.'

"I would say, 'No. I'm going to work this out,' reasoning that I could always switch things back to our old setup baring any other major developments. We would go testing and I would make a couple of passes. When it wouldn't be right, we would just take everything off and put the car back to the original setup.

"The Bopper would get mad at me, and tell me that I should pay closer attention to what he was saying. I said, 'Yeah, yeah. I understand all that, boss, but this is a pet project of mine and I'm going to make it work.'

"Well, the long and the short of it was that we were two down to Charlie Allen and the Bopper was really getting upset. All Allen had to do was beat us one more time at our home track, which would be a huge embarrassment for us. I said to Larry Metivier and John Pagano, 'You know I've been working hard on this new setup, and I'm going for it! I'll probably get fired over this but win or lose, I'm going for it.' I said to Bill, 'This might be the last time I race with you, Billy, but I've got to try to make this work. Billy sarcastically said, 'Well, it's been fun, and thanks!'

"In the meantime, I had changed the pill size from a number to a blank. That's how much fuel I put through that motor. When we fired it up, you could tell by the sound. It sounded so happy, I said, 'Oh yeah!' Senior looked over at me. I looked back at him, then Billy did his burnout. We had also changed the procedure in doing the burnout and he knew where we were going with it. Billy started out in first gear, quickly shifted to second, and when the tires really started smoking, he would shift it into high. When he backed the car up, I gave him the thumbs-up sign and he gave me the thumbs-up sign again.

"The tree counted down and he put a hole shot on Charlie Allen like you've never seen! That car just flat moved! We broke into the 8s for the very first time and I don't mean an 8.90 or something like that. It ran in the 8.60s! The top-end speed was also unbelievable! It was something like 169.00 mph! Talk about getting all choked up.

"I remember my two sons, Johnny and Billy, were there. I grabbed them and said 'Come on guys, we've got to go back to the pits and get the car ready for the next run.' By that time, I was really beginning to get a little misty.

"John Jr. said, 'What's wrong, Dad?'

"I said, 'Nothing; it's a great day!'

"When we got back to the pits, Senior came over to me and said, 'Well, you did it! I'm proud of you. You did it!' Deep down inside, he knew that I knew that this setup was going to work. That's when Frank Maratta came over and crossed out the '9' in white shoe polish and wrote an '8' on the back of the car."

The story continues with Charlie Allen coming over to Tasca, Lawton, and Healey, saying, "Well, you got me good that time. You know, Healey, you just ruined my clean sweep [referring to the Atlantic Flyer's perfect win/loss record during his 1966 national tour]."

"In the end, we beat Charlie the next three rounds. What a great night that was!"

Of course any Ford-versus-Chevy match race also brought in the crowds. Tasca, Lawton, and Healey match raced both Frank Federicci's *Shark* Corvette and Malcolm Durham's *Strip Blazer* Corvair at Capitol with equal success. The crowds just ate it up! On one particular night at Capitol Raceway, Tasca, Lawton, and Healey drew "Dandy Dick" Landy's 1966 *Landy's Dodge* Dart match racer during Round Robin competition. Landy burned out first. As he backed up, Lawton hit the loud pedal and suddenly there was a huge "bang."

John Healey later commented, "I said to myself, 'Holy Christ, what the hell was that?' I looked at Larry Metivier and said, 'Did you see that?' I'm looking up, and you see this red thing glowing in the air. It comes down and goes clink, clink, *clink* on the ground. It turned out to be the head of an intake valve that had failed. By then, Billy's backing up. The car is misfiring, and raw fuel is shooting out of the injector stack and headers.

"I'm saying, 'This is not good.' Then the rains came.

> " Claimed John Healey, "I didn't know it at the time, but the old man [Tasca] considered me one of the hardest workers he ever laid eyes on." "

"I looked at Larry and said, 'You know, we just got lucky.'

"Landy says to me, 'What the hell was that?'

"I said, 'It's an intake valve that came straight through the injector stack!'

"He says, 'How much damage did it do?' I said I wasn't sure.

"Billy said, 'What are we going to do?'

"'Pull the head off,' I said, 'and have a look at everything.'

"Back then the 427 Ford Cammer was the hardest motor to work on between rounds. It took two hours just to properly degree the cams. The intake valve was obviously missing but, surprisingly, there was not a mark on the piston. There's not even a mark on the combustion chamber, or valveseat pocket. The

Bob Tasca proudly stands among a "sea" of trophies (more than 50) won by the team of Tasca, Lawton, and Healey over the course of nine years. That's a lot of hardware!

Altered roadster *Winged Express*. Later that summer, *Mystery 8* also won the Super Stock Nationals at New York National Speedway.

All told, Tasca's Mystery Mustang was raced from the tail end of 1965 to June 1967 when Tasca, Lawton, and Healey got their first flip-top-body Logghe-chassis car.

Healey commented, "Toward the end there, you could set the car up, and it would go straight one time, and the next time it wouldn't. Bill used to say, 'Jesus Christ, Healey!'

"I would say, 'Well, Bill, this old mule's getting pretty darned tired!'"

"Tired" wasn't the word for it. Upon taking delivery of their new 1967 Logghe-chassis *Mystery 7* Mustang funny car, the original Tasca Mystery Mustang was stripped of all its pieces at Ford's Experimental Garage. When the forklift came to take what remained away to the crusher, the car broke in half! After almost two years of hard campaigning, that's how weak the car was.

Taking the Wind Out of Their Sails

"My philosophy was that if I could sell what I raced, I raced it. If I couldn't sell it, I wasn't interested in it," said Bob Tasca Sr. "I once told Mr. Ford, there's no use in going to Daytona or Indianapolis, and so forth. You see, it was easy for me to talk to Henry Ford II. He and I were very close to each other.

"I said, 'Henry, if you listen to me I can show you how to make a lot of money racing. I know you guys like the high-brow stuff and that's what attracts you. As I'm concerned, that's fine for image, but I don't put image in the bank; I

> "The tree counted down and he put a hole shot on Charlie Allen like you've never seen! That car just flat moved!"

only thing that was damaged was the injector manifold.

"I said, 'We're in luck. I have another intake manifold in the trailer that's identical to the one that's on the motor. Go get it!' Now, I had no idea why I threw it in the trailer, but I did. We put a new intake valve in the head; put everything back together just like nothing had ever happened!"

Perhaps the billing that night should have actually read, "Tasca, Lawton, Healey, and Lady Luck." With the rainout, the event was rescheduled for the following afternoon at nearby Aquasco Speedway.

Healey continued, "The management at Capitol said we had to start from scratch and requalify. We drew Landy first round and beat him. Dick was quite the racer. With his ever-present cigar and his sense of humor, I had good rapport with him. He said, 'What in the Christ do you have in that thing? How big is that motor? [Affectionately referred to as Big Bertha.]

"I said, 'It's just .015 over; it's got a 4.250 bore and a stock stroke.'

"'Bullshit!' he says.

"'Well, I'm telling you. That's *exactly* what it is!'"

Perhaps one of the Tasca Mystery Mustang's biggest wins was its August 1966 triumph over Phil Bonner's *Daddy Warbucks* 427 SOHC Ford Falcon, winning all the marbles at Cecil County Raceway's "Factory Showdown." Tasca's Mystery Mustang also won the B/XS class at Pomona in 1967 over (the late) Dave Strickler and his *Old Reliable* Corvette with an 8.69/168.22.

It then went a couple of rounds in Super Eliminator as witnessed by the famous Jere Alhadaff photo racing "Wild Willie" Borsch's AA/Fuel

94 The Tasca Ford Legacy

put dollars in the bank. I can make money drag racing because it's mainstream.'

"I got a call from Donald Frey after Ford won Le Mans in 1966. He said, 'Mr. Tasca, I just wanted to call you and let you know that we just won Le Mans.'

"I said, 'Can you hold the line for a minute? I just want to check my stock of GT40s because I haven't sold one yet.'

"Then I said, 'Good luck. How do you end up running one of those [cars] on the street?' That ended the conversation. Ford spent $16 million to beat Ferrari at Le Mans. Well, that's ego. I don't spend $16 million for ego. I sell about 100 hot cars a month, and about $6 million worth of Autolite parts a year. If you called me from California looking for a hotter cam, I would tell you how to get it, and from whom to order it. I'm not selling product for Tasca, I'm selling product for Ford," and sell Tasca did!

Contest This!

Sales contests have always been a motivational sales tool to sell more products. Every successful sales-driven corporation uses them, and Tasca Ford was no exception. Dean Gregson recalls a couple of monthly sales contests where he did exceedingly well.

"My wife, Patricia, and I had a baby girl named 'Gale,' who was born February 3, 1966. There was a big sales contest that month because of the new sales tax being installed in Massachusetts the following month. I could not work the first week as I stayed home with our daughter Kelly Ann, who was one year old then.

"So I worked the last three weeks, wrote 48 deals, delivered 40 units, and won $750 in the contest with a straight Royal Flush in the card game on the last delivery at 9 p.m., February 28, 1966, drawing the Queen of Hearts.

"You got to draw a card after each new car delivery."

Gregson was also top finisher in another contest held for the combined months of October and November in which he won a big-screen RCA Console TV worth more than $1,000 for being top salesman, having sold 40 cars during that period. Other prizes were also awarded to second- and third-place finishers, such as a refrigerator and a deep freezer.

"Raising" the Bopper's Blood Pressure

Carl A. Tasca told me a funny story about the time he and his brother Bobby arbitrarily gave themselves a raise.

"The old man's in Dearborn one week, and I decided I wanted to give myself and my brother Bobby a raise. I'm maybe 13 years old.

"A couple of days go by, and the old man comes back and calls me into his office and says, 'Uh, you guys get a raise last week?'

"So I said 'Yeah, I think it was . . .'

"'Did the minimum wage go up?' he asked.

"I said, 'No.'

"He said, 'Well, when it does go up, *then* you'll get a raise.'"

A Pep Talk from the Coach

Both Bob Tasca and Vince Lombardi were great motivators, leaders, and true champions. They were the best at their "game" and possessed a dynamic that inspired people to give nothing short of 100 percent (effort) to be a part of a championship-winning "team." However, every once in a while, even in the best of organizations, you've got to kick a few butts to keep your "players" moving in a forward and positive direction.

"My father did his best thinking during the middle of the night," commented Tricia Tasca-De Cristofaro. "He didn't sleep much. All of the beautiful sayings and quotations that he would put together, like 'Mc Incorporated,' and/or whatever his sales meeting was going to be about that next day, he usually wrote down in the middle of the night."

The following from approximately 1966–1967 titled "My 3:00 a.m. Thoughts to All Members of the Tasca Sales Organization" is one of those late-night motivational memos.

> In my lifelong desire to make Tasca Ford Sales the finest dealership in the world, I've encountered many hardships, untold difficulties, and overwhelming challenges. With the Grace of God and the unending efforts on the part of my loyal co-workers we have met and overcome them time and time again. Many of us, including myself, have sacrificed a great deal of the normal joys of life to achieve the enviable position in which we find ourselves today. Quite often it becomes apparent that some take today's tremendous position of this organization altogether too lightly. This, to me, is one of my greatest disappointments.
>
> As a specific example, I refer to near-complete breakdown on your part to pursue a planned intelligence program to further enhance your position as a leader in the field of professional salesmanship. Can it be that all the programs, promotions, and merchandising techniques together with past, present, and future planned benefits that I unhesitatingly provided you with have added up to anything other than an unprecedented advantage for us over the competition? I think not!
>
> Gentlemen, have we become too gentle (or should I say too "complacent") with all we have to be thankful for? I hope not!
>
> These thoughts would not be complete without a few choice expressions, "When we stop becoming better, we'll cease to be the best. We all have the way; if only more of us had the will. For all we have received, let's start giving!"
>
> Bob Tasca

A Typical Day in the High Performance Department

At the height of its popularity, Tasca Ford Sales High Performance Department, staffed by Bill Gilbert, Ralph Poirier, and Frank Carnevale averaged about 20 high-performance jobs per month as well as performing minor mechanical tweaks and twists for customers who couldn't afford to pay to have complete tune-up jobs done to their cars all at once.

"Most of our high-performance customers are attracted to us because of the dealership's racing reputation and the ability of our mechanics to make good cars run even better," said Tasca.

Tasca specialized in what was known as the "10-hour high-performance pre-delivery job" expertly done by Gilbert and Poirier, which cost the customer an additional $150. Included therein was a chassis tune-up (more on that in a moment), re-setting the distributor curve and timing, and optimizing carburetor jetting with necessary modifications. In other words, an optimization of the car's suspension and powertrain per factory specifications.

Next on the menu was Tasca's $300 high-performance tune-up, which consisted of suspension tuning, carburetor tuning, ignition system tuning, and a camshaft change using Ford-Autolite high-performance parts.

For $500 Tasca also blueprinted the cylinder heads by milling them to lower the cylinder volume, raised the compression ratio, "cc'd" the combustion chambers, and installed high-performance valves and valvesprings as part of a total valvetrain package.

Suspension Tuning by Tasca

As outlined in the Ford *Motorsports* magazine:
"Place the car on scales (rear wheels). Optimum reading should be +85 pounds on the right wheel. If not, proceed as follows.

1. Install extra number-2 leaf right rear spring.
2. Increase length of right rear spring hanger 1 inch.
3. Increase length of left front stabilizer bar spacer 3/4 inch.
4. Install 3/16-inch spacers under left front shock spring mount.

Before the vehicle is placed on the scales, set air pressure to 30 pounds front and 26 pounds rear. Elevate front wheels by placing board spacers under front wheel to simulate height equal to rear wheels on scales. If 85 pounds is accomplished with step 1, discount steps 2, 3, and 4.

In the final analysis, the car must be driven to determine its straight-line track ability. If the car goes straight under hardline acceleration, the mission is accomplished. If the car pulls right, increase weight on right rear wheel by continuing with steps, 2, 3, and 4 until this condition is corrected.

If the car pulls left (same circumstances) decrease weight on right rear wheel by elimination of steps 2, 3, and 4. If the car still pulls left, repeat steps 2, 3, and 4 as needed to right front suspension.

After suspension work is completed, reset the front end as follows: 3 degrees caster plus stock camber. Stock toe-in.

The Tasca 10-Second Test

According to Bill Gilbert, Tasca Ford High Performance Department technicians used to determine how fast a car could run by giving it the "10-second test." Of course this was before fully computerized measuring devices such as an accelerometer or "G-Analyst" were invented.

Tasca High Performance Center technicians Gilbert, Poirier, or Carnevale took a stopwatch and begin with a rolling start, which eliminated wheel spin. At 30 mph, they clicked the stopwatch and simultaneously floored it, and then lifted off the throttle again at exactly 10 seconds.

At the end of that measured 10 seconds they noted the speed on the speedometer. If they pegged the speedometer before 10 seconds' time had elapsed, they roughly estimated just how fast the car actually was based on the last certifiable number on the speedometer versus how many remaining seconds it took to reach that figure.

De-Bugging Henry's Hot Rod

By the mid-1960s, overall product quality in the entire automobile industry had gone into noticeable decline, Ford Motor Company notwithstanding. Bob Tasca knew that the cars he sold had "bugs" or inconsistencies in workmanship due to an ever-increasing number of shortcuts being taken on the Ford assembly line. Furthermore, Tasca understood that if a Ford was built exactly according to the factory blueprint it would be a much better vehicle than the vehicles he was receiving. It would also be more cost effective, easier to maintain, and command a higher trade-in/resale value. Obviously, a post-production quality-control program like this could not go unnoticed.

Henry Ford II came to Tasca Sr. in 1967 and asked if he'd rebuild a standard Ford for him to drive. When Bob said "Yes," Henry II sent one of his chauffeurs (a man Bob called "Turnpike Smith") with one of Mr. Ford's personal vehicles, a black-on-black 1967 427 Ford convertible to East Providence, Rhode Island, to be debugged. Unfortunately, this first opportunity to show Mr. Ford what he and his agency could do occurred in the dead of winter, which hampered Bob's ability to test the vehicle at speed to ensure a smooth, quiet ride. Undeterred, Tasca brought the vehicle to downtown Providence and utilized the mile-long tunnel that used to run beneath the Providence Railroad Station. When Mr. Ford got his car back he was excited by the improvement.

"Tasca, why don't you start 'de-bugging your cars for your customers?' That's exactly what Henry Ford II called it.

"Bob said, 'You know, Mr. Ford, that's a great idea. I ought to try it!'"

From that point on, de-bugging (which was later renamed the considerably classier-sounding "blueprinting") became a Tasca staple. More than 40 percent of total sales were blueprinted cars.

Longtime Tasca Associate and customer Gene De Graide said, "When you would buy a car from Tasca, Bob would say, 'Let's go for a ride.' Down Route 44 (which is where the dealership was located at the time) we would go. He would be listening to the engine. He would be listening to 'something' and he would have you jot down some of the things that caught his (or your) attention. Sometimes, it would be three, four, five, or six things.

"He said, 'I'll have one of our mechanics check these things out when we get back to the dealership, and your car will be ready by the time you're ready to take it home.'"

Frolics on Tour

Professional jeweler (the late) John Pagano was Team Tasca's logistics guy. However, Pagano often found

---

The Unsung Heroines of Tasca Ford

As told by Dean Gregson

Not only did Bob Tasca Sr. have a great family in Josephine and his children, Bob Jr., Carl, David, and Tricia, he had two aunts who came into the business from the very beginning and made a huge difference.

"Aunty Tess," as they called her, ran the entire office with just two ladies. She handled all the pricing on all the cars we sold. She handled the billing and everything that a dealership would do today, manually, with no computers. Just hand-written ledgers and receipts. It was funny because when we were drag racing, I would go to Aunty Tess and tell her we were leaving for Indianapolis or somewhere else with the crew. I would say, "Aunty Tess, I think I need about $300."

She would say, "Oh, no, Dean. That's definitely not enough. Here, take $500."

When it came to the general managers and sales managers, if they had a big party for the salesman or something like that, they had to get money from Aunty Tess to pay the bills. She would dissect the bill upside down, backward, and forward. Finally the salesmen got smart. They would say, "Dean, would you give this to Aunty Tess. She'll give you what you want. She trusts you." She truly did. She truly became an adopted aunt to all of the employees.

As the Ford dealership closed at the end of August 1971 and the Lincoln-Mercury dealership opened in the following month, September [Dean was appointed Tasca L-M Sales Manager], I went to Aunty Tess and said, "Aunty Tess, I owe you money."

She said, "No you don't, Dean. You've paid [for] everything."

I said, "No, I've got a bill here from H-M for a set of cylinder heads that just arrived."

She said, "No, Dean. You paid everything."

About two months later, she came to me, and said, "You were right, Dean, and I paid the bill."

Aunty Jean Colavecchio was a self-taught Certified Public Accountant (CPA) and like her sister, Tess, she was a well-known and brilliant woman who commanded great respect among both friends and business associates. Jean controlled the bookkeeping end of both Tasca Ford Sales, Inc., and later Tasca Lincoln-Mercury. In fact, Aunty Jean Colavecchio was one of the first female presidents of the Certified Public Accounts (CPA) of America. She was so exacting in her craft that she never lost a case against the IRS and they absolutely hated [yet no doubt "respected"] her.

Chapter Three: "Win on Sunday, Sell on Monday!"

himself on the receiving end of one of Bill Lawton and John Healey's practical jokes. One story goes that the team was racing somewhere on the East Coast, and they had gotten into trouble for cleaning parts in the motel bathtub. John Pagano came to the rescue and cleaned up their mess.

After it was all over Pagano made the offhand remark that a good swim was in order. Of course, John and Bill convinced Pagano that he should go skinny dipping in the motel pool, that it was all in good fun, and that they would join him. However, once John Pagano hit the water, Lawton and Healey ran off with all of John's clothes!

Son of Thunderbolt

In 1966–1967 during the height of the Total Performance Era, Ford's drag racing program attempted to cover all the bases. The sponsorship of funny car racers Gas Ronda, Tommy Grove, and Tasca Ford continued, albeit on a limited basis. However, that was merely for the sake of image. What Ford really wanted to do was get back to selling product that was mainstream, something that could be as easily identifiable by (and purchased by) the masses. The end result was the 1966–1967 427 Ford Fairlane Super Stock cars.

Midway through 1966, Dick Brannan turned over driving duties of his Paul Harvey Ford sponsored stretch-nose 1966 Mustang match racer to Atlanta, Georgia, racer Hubert "Hube Baby" Platt. He then concentrated on developing the 1966–1967 427 Ford Fairlane Super Stock cars. "The 427 medium-riser wedge pushrod V-8 was a great engine for the Fairlanes. It was good on both street and strip," said Brannan.

On March 2, 1966, Ford Stock Vehicles Department V. R. "Vern" Tinsler released an inter-departmental memo titled, "Special Build of Fifty (50) 1966 Model Fairlane with 427 8V Engine," listing Ford's cost per vehicle at $2,730.61. Ford contracted Bill Stroppe & Associates to build the first 57 of these cars. When put in the hands of racers such as (the late) Ed Terry, Bill Ireland, and John Downing, the cars became the holy terror of the NHRA SS/B class. In fact, Downing set a national E.T. record of 11.42 seconds on May 28, 1967, at Raceway Park, Englishtown, New Jersey.

Ten days before (May 18, 1967), Ford Drag Racing Program Coordinator Dick Brannan had submitted a report on the testing of the 1967 version of the 427 Ford Fairlane 500 two-door hardtop prototype. It had been tested and driven by Hubert Platt at Bristol, Tennessee. Platt made 18 runs, which were all in the 11s, with a best of 11.42 seconds, registering a terminal speed of 123.79.

It is interesting to note that Tasca Ford did not actively race one of these cars (the closest association was Healey's involvement in the preparation of John Downing's car), but they sold quite a few 427 R-Code Fairlanes nonetheless. Among those satisfied customers were Enfield, Connecticut's Al and Ellen Hanna, who went on to race a series of Ford Pinto– and Mustang II–bodied AA/Fuel Funny Cars under the "Eastern Raider" banner. They later became involved with jet-engine funny cars and dragsters racing under the Pro Race, Inc./Hanna Motorsports banner. Al's first "real" race car was a Tasca-sold 1967 427 Fairlane, his Robie Ford–sponsored *Hemi Hunter,* which competed in the NHRA SS/B class.

"When we bought the Fairlane, it literally changed our lives forever. I quit my just-acquired after-college-graduation job and went racing. Over the years I have raced in SS/B through nitro funny cars to jet dragsters and jet funny cars. I think I've had close to 50 different cars that I've raced, but it all started with Tasca Ford," Ellen said. She also wrote the following letter to Tasca Ford, in praise of the relationship.

August 5, 1966

Tasca Ford Sales, Inc.
777 Taunton Avenue
East Providence, Rhode Island 02914
Attn: Dean Gregson, High Performance Mgr.

Gentleman:

Just a brief letter to let you know how pleased we are with our new high-performance Fairlane, and what a pleasure it was doing business with Dean Gregson. We were quite anxious to have the deal completed, and Mr. Gregson was helpful and courteous all the while, answering telephone inquiries with amazing patience.

The car is a real beauty and is opening doors for us in more ways than one. We wanted to let Mr. Gregson know that we will forward our guarantee booklet and metal plate on our 1966 Chevrolet to his attention as soon as we receive it from Luby Chevrolet. The plate is presently at the Chevrolet factory, being corrected for an error in the identification number.

If there is an opportunity to refer any business to your office, Mr. Gregson, you can be sure that we will. Thank you again for the excellent customer service.

Sincerely,
Ellen I. Hanna
(Mrs.) Alan T. Hanna

---

98   The Tasca Ford Legacy

Tasca's TGT Fairlane

Although Tasca Ford never actually raced one of the 1966–1967 427 Ford Fairlanes, it didn't stop them from customizing one. In 1966, Tasca and the Alexander Brothers built a mild-custom Kelly Green metalflake 1966 Fairlane GTA, which featured extended front fenders and dual-quad Cibie rectangular headlights (an Alexander Brothers trademark) stacked end-to-end. Other custom treatments included mild dechroming, custom taillight treatment, and side-exit exhaust. The TGT Fairlane rolled on a set of gold-center Hurst 15-inch wheels with special Goodyear tires.

It had a Bill Gilbert–assembled and NASCAR-headed stroked 427 FE (at 447-ci) complete with C8AX (or C/Stock) cam and a 780-cfm Holley 4-barrel carburetor. It was backed up by a Ford C-6 and a 3.91:1 Traction Lok 9-inch live rear axle. As Bill Gilbert put it, "That car could run neck-and-neck with any car out on the open road."

The TGT's interior featured custom black and Kelly Green leather with custom-made round stainless-steel buttons; truly luxurious! The Tasca TGT Fairlane was displayed on Bob Tasca's showroom floor throughout 1966 and 1967 and proved to be a great sales driver. Unfortunately, after the Bopper dropped an intake valve in the engine he disgustedly parked the car outside, leaving it to the mercy of the cold New England weather. Of course, under those conditions the candy green metalflake paint crazed and checked badly, prompting Tasca technicians to brand it "Tasca's Green Tank," a phrase that absolutely infuriated Bob Tasca.

Eventually the metalflake green paint was stripped off and the Tasca TGT Fairlane was painted solid black by local painter Richie Badessa. The car was summarily parked on Tasca's used-car lot and sold to an unknown party. Today, the whereabouts of the Tasca TGT Fairlane is unknown.

Mystery 7 Mustang

Mystery 7 consisted of a Stage II Logghe chassis with a Fiberglas Limited flip-top Mustang fastback body. The car made its grand debut running an 8.32 at the 1967 NHRA Spring nationals in Bristol, Tennessee. Onboard was basically the same fuel-injected, nitro-burning 427 SOHC Ford engine that had powered the now-departed *Mystery 8*. Although originally designed to produce 700 hp on carburetors and gasoline, Tasca's "SOHC motor" was now pumping out 1,400 hp injected (as predicted by Tech Editor Eric Dahlquist in the January 1965 issue of *Hot Rod*), running on strong percentages of nitro methane and alcohol.

"This sort of mutilated the engine and produced all kinds of problems," says John Healey. "But that's what kept me [and crewman Henry "Wimpy" Tameleo] busy."

Of course, *Mystery 7* didn't initially run in the 7s. The injected 427 Cammer won the 2,000-pound class at the 1967 Super Stock Nationals held at Maryland's Cecil County Dragway running in the mid-8s. In one classic York U.S. 30 battle against the late great Dick Harrell, the Tasca *Mystery 7* reeled off runs of 8.40/160.00, 8.62/166.66, and 8.23/176.47 to triumph in a classic Ford-versus-Chevrolet matchup. In October 1967 *Mystery 7* appeared in a Crane Cams advertisement citing its record run of 8.28/173.63 at Atco, New Jersey.

"I remember that we ultimately ran 199.97 injected on fuel," says John. "We were racing and beating all the blown cars. It wasn't until M&H came out with a tire for the blown cars that they were able to catch us."

> "When we bought the Fairlane, it literally changed our lives forever."

Mystery 7's last big win injected on nitro was the King of Kings funny car show at Epping, New Hampshire. Of course, once the blown cars had caught up with (and passed) their injected counterparts, *Mystery 7* stepped up to a supercharger, but Bill Lawton was more than slightly reluctant.

"I didn't like the blower. I saw all the trouble people were getting into and I cherished my life. I said to Mr. Tasca, 'I don't think I want to do this.' This was not my living. I had a business of my own to run. Then after I made that first run, I wanted to dump the can in. The thunderous sound and sheer acceleration: it was truly amazing!"

By mid-summer 1967, the now-supercharged *Mystery 7* was running 7.80s and beating the likes of Malcolm "The D. C. Lip" Durham (7.87/189.06) on their home track, Connecticut Dragway. As the year progressed *Mystery 7* became even quicker and faster, running a career best in the low 7.30s at 201.00. Engine failures and fires, however, had become problematic, and Bob became more and more concerned that someone was going to get hurt.

Lawton continues, "We were at Cecil County and the blower let go right on the starting line. It was like somebody slapped me in the face. Then the sun came out. At first I didn't realize that we had blown the roof right off the car. I think that was the last race Bob Tasca ever went to."

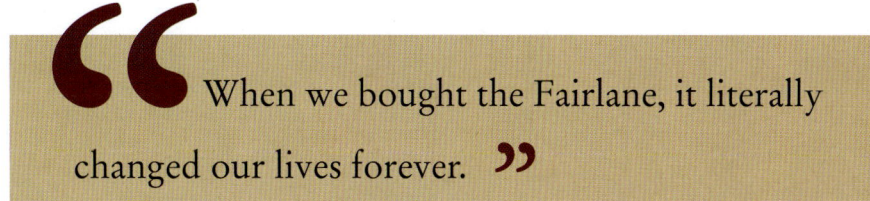

Tasca KR-8, Forerunner to the Cobra Jet

The trend-setting KR-8 began life as a Medium Gold Metallic 1967 Mustang GTA two-door hardtop demonstrator

Chapter Three: "Win on Sunday, Sell on Monday!" 99

model equipped with the top-of-the-line 10.5:1 390 FE big-block engine, and backed by a big-block Ford C6 3-speed automatic. Tasca and company had supertuned the factory-rated 320-hp engine and taken it as far as it would go. Still, Bob felt that the car's performance was lackluster at best so he began making plans to change it. However, you know what they say about the best-laid plans of men and mice . . .

The story goes that Bill "Chicken Fat" Loomis was taking Bob Jr. and Carl out for a test-and-tune run on Taunton Avenue while still sporting its original 390 FE power plant. After accidentally shifting the car into low at speed, the GTA grenaded right in front of Lorber Cadillac. When Bob found out, he was furious. According to Bob Jr., "He ducked underneath the garage door. He didn't even wait for it to fully open. Man, was he upset!"

Fortunately, Bob already had a 428 Police Interceptor short-block through Ford. Tasca's personal mechanic, Bill Gilbert, was in charge of the project and Bill Loomis assisted at the track. Bill Gilbert had tipped Bob off about a very rare set of 1964 date-code 427 medium-riser FE cylinder heads through information provided via Ford's Bob "Jumpy" Snyder.

Those heads differed from their 1965 counterparts in that they did not use a fully machined combustion chamber, and they were better suited for street use. Although no longer in production, Snyder had three of them (NOS), stashed away for safekeeping.

After a series of telephone calls between Providence and Dearborn, Snyder personally delivered the heads to Tasca. Also onboard was a medium-rise, 2x4 aluminum 4V intake with 735-cfm Holleys (which were eventually replaced by Holley 780s). They had a very creative-looking twin-snorkel air cleaner and a special-grind "Poppa Sully" Sullivan/FoMoCo cam. In other words, "Da works!"

Bill Gilbert tuned the suspension on the KR-8. He also performed a few tweaks and twists to the big-block Ford C-6 and Detroit Locker 9-inch rear end. "The KR-8 Mustang was a phenomenal package and it was developed right here at Tasca. If you looked at it from the outside, the car was totally stock in appearance. Well, I like Mustangs, but if you put your foot to it, and once it passes 7,000 rpm, you say 'Whoa, what have we got here?' We took an absolute dud, and made it into an absolute winner."

"KR-8" versus "NO-BRA JET"

In a career that spanned more than 30 years, retired Ford Motor Company engineer Bill Holbrook has worked on some interesting projects, such as 1957's "Blower Bird" and 1964's Ford Thunderbolt program, Conrad "Connie" Kalitta's 427 SOHC Ford engine Top Fuel program (it was Holbrook who designed the blower manifold that all of Ford's nitro racers eventually ended up using). Bill also worked as senior mechanic on the infamous 1967–1968 428GT Mustang pre-production engineering mule, and co-prototyped the infamous nose on Ford's NASCAR Torino Talladegas. He had a pretty cool job, eh?

Tasca's Logghe-chassis *Mystery 7* debuted at the 1967 NHRA Spring nationals in Bristol, Tennessee, running a best of 8.32/170+ mph. Ultimately, *Mystery 7* ran 199.00 supercharged on fuel.

100   The Tasca Ford Legacy

"In 1967 Bob Tasca made a bet with Jacques Passano. At that time, Ford had already been toying with the idea of building the yet-unnamed Cobra Jet Mustang high-performance package as a successor to their phenomenally successful 427 Fairlane program. Other than it being Mustang bodied they weren't all that sure what it would actually be.

"Passano says, 'I bet Tasca a lunch that our car [a candy apple red 1967 Mustang GTA fastback] could beat his car.'

"I said, 'Well, how far am I allowed to go with this project?'

"Passano says, 'You can go as far as you want, but no cheating. It has to be all genuine Ford Parts.'

"I said, 'Well, I'm going to start with a 450-incher. I'll just install a 428 crank into a 427 side-oiler block at 454 ci. It will be backed up by a Ford C6 automatic and then we'll go from there.'

"Jacques said, 'Okay!'

"Bob Hide and I built the package. I had Harvey Crane [Hallandale, Florida's Crane Cams was one of Ford's contract cam grinders throughout its Total Performance Era] grind up

This Crane Cams ad titled "Partners in Time" was featured on the back page of the October 1967 issue of *Super Stock & Drag Illustrated*. It touted Tasca, Lawton, and Healey's record run of 8.28/173.63 at Atco, New Jersey.

This mid-track photo taken by G. K. Callaway shows *Mystery 7* at speed. Ultimately, the car ran a best of 199.97 injected on fuel. Then it was on to a supercharger.

Chapter Three: "Win on Sunday, Sell on Monday!" 101

a number of cams that we tried. Finally, he says 'This one will work best. Run a [timing] gear on there and just retard the damned thing!'

"I was running a set of Firestone Super Sport tires and wound up putting a Hurst Line Loc in the car. What I wanted to do was get the car to where anybody could drive it and run the same numbers without going up in smoke. Then it's done!

"We set the transmission governors to shift at 7,400 rpm. You didn't have to do anything but put it in Drive. When you would come out of the gate, you would think, 'Jesus, is there something wrong with this thing?' Then all of a sudden the car would come to life at the 1-2 shifts and start chirping the tires. It would chirp the tires almost all the way through second gear and it just kept pulling; the thing was absolutely bulletproof!

"Although our race with Tasca was run with closed exhaust, this car had already run 10.90s at 132.00, which was not too shabby for a street tire."

However, Bill Holbrook did admit to just a little chicanery. "The car had a phony-looking hood scoop on it that said '351-C.' I had also installed a batwing air cleaner, which ran back to the cowl so that the engine would get plenty of fresh air. Those were about the only things I cheated with.

"The Bopper Twins [a name given by X-Garage employees to Bill Lawton and John Healey] were running back and forth from the Advanced Engine Garage [where Tasca and "Poppa Sully" Sullivan were testing a number of camshafts] to the X-Garage so I laid out all kinds of lightweight aluminum components on the floor, scattered all around the car. They figured, 'Oh boy, he's really cheating,' and they would run back, and tell Bob.

"So we're all out at the Dearborn Test Track for the big race. They had decided that it was going to be three out of five.

Bob Tasca Jr.'s Indy Story

During U.S. Nationals weekend in the summer of 1967, Team Tasca was staying at the Airport Inn Motel and John Healey was working outside at night in the parking lot. Typically for Indy there was an evening thunderstorm and John needed some light. As these were the days before compact portable generators, etc., Healey rigged up a wire from the hotel transformer to the race rig in an attempt to get much needed electricity out to the parking lot area.

Well, the long and short of it was that it shorted something out. The transformer on the light pole blew up and shut the whole motel down. What happened after that, we don't know!

We didn't have any lights out there so we just decided to race from here to there, and whoever got there first was the winner. I wasn't going to drive Fords; I didn't want to be a party to Tasca's potential embarrassment, so we had the X-Garage's Bob 'Jumpy' Snyder drive instead.

"We had one of our guys stand between the cars with a mechanic's rag in hand. He would point at each car and then he would drop the rag. Every time, the Bopper would leave first but Bob Snyder would pass him at half track, and just about turn him around. Hell, it was like three bus lengths between the two cars.

"Of course, we would walk over and say, 'You guys really got your butts beat!'

"Then Mr. Tasca would say, 'Yeah, but you guys were cheating like hell!'

"Mr. Tasca looked at me and asked, 'What have you got in that thing?'

"I said, 'Well, I've got more cubic inches than yours, Bob, but other than a Crane Cam, it's all production pieces.

"He said, 'Well, what about all those aluminum parts you've got?'

"I said, 'Well, I was just doing that to mess with your boys' heads.'

"Tasca said, 'Those guys kept running back and forth telling me you were

What a difference five years makes. This is the Service Department at Tasca Ford circa 1967 (notice Tasca's TGT Fairlane at the left) with rows of Shelbys and Mustangs in various stages of preparation.

102   The Tasca Ford Legacy

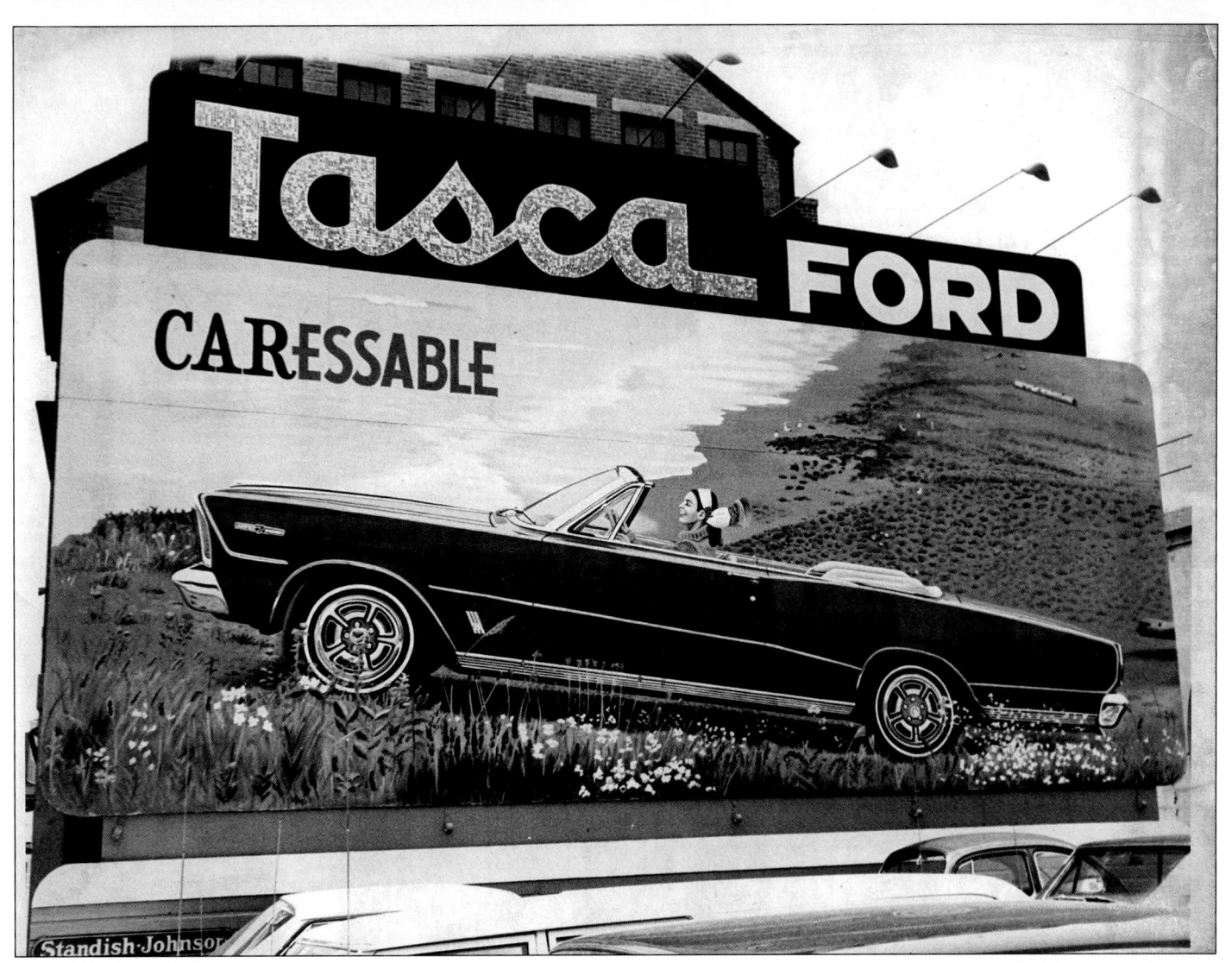

The famous Tasca Ford billboard reflected constant change in Ford Motor Company products as the years rolled by. Note the advertising slogans "Incomparable," "Splurge," and my favorite, "Caressable."

Chapter Three: "Win on Sunday, Sell on Monday!" 103

Tasca Ford's trend-setting KR-8 (for King of the Road) began as a Medium Gold Metallic 390 FE-engine 1967 Mustang GTA hardtop. However, after the original "born with" engine blew up, Bob Tasca, Bill Gilbert, and company put together a killer combination using a 428 Police Interceptor short-block with a set of 1964 date-code 427 medium-riser heads and a 2x4 Ram Air intake. (Photo Courtesy SORC Archives)

To quote Bill Gilbert, "The KR-8 was a phenomenal package. If you looked at it from the outside, you might say, 'Yeah, it's a Mustang.' But when you put your foot to it, and once it passes 7,000 rpm you say, 'Whoa! What have we got here?'" (Photo Courtesy SORC Archives)

Tasca's KR-8 was tested by none other than Eric Dahlquist (former Technical Editor of *Hot Rod* magazine and future Editor of *Motor Trend* magazine). It was featured in the *Hot Rod* November 1967 issue. (Photo Courtesy SORC Archives)

doing this and you were doing that, you were putting on this and you were putting on that!'

"Tasca had gotten whipped three straight, and I knew that really bothered him. But he ultimately won, as his 428 engine combination proved the better way to go. Sure, it had a few weak links that had to be addressed before it was going to become the 428 Cobra Jet production engines [which E&F's Bill Barr and staff did] without risk of breaking. As it was, we had too much of that [going on] with the 427. Until Ford came up with the side oiler they really didn't have anything reliable, but they felt the 427 side oiler was far too expensive of an engine to use from a production standpoint and settled on Tasca's 428 engine package."

Tasca's KR-8: The Unhappy Ending

After the smoke had cleared from the KR-8-versus-Ford battle at the Dearborn Test Track, Tasca's little gold 1967 Mustang GTA coupe remained intact prior to the X-Garage yanking the drivetrain out of it, which Ford kept for R&D. According to Bob Sr., Ford Division General Manager Donald Frey first borrowed the little gold coupe to run up Telegraph Road and engage in a little street racing against the Ramchargers (Bob actually called the famous Dodge-Chrysler team "the Ram-Bums"). Around the Greater Detroit area, these kinds of incidents were common everyday occurrences.

"Ford stripped the car and left us with just a bare shell," Gilbert commented.

"Bob asked. 'Why don't you just buy the car?'

"Ford's answer was, 'We don't need the car. We've got plenty of cars.'

"Bob and I went over to visit Engine & Foundry [E&F]. Over in the corner covered by a tarp was none other than Lloyd Ruby's Le Mans dry-deck tunnel-port 427 engine, which had been salvaged from Ruby's wrecked GT40 car after crashing out on the fourth hour.

"'Oh, you can't have that engine,' the E&F shop foreman said. 'That's special!'

"Tasca replied, 'Wanna bet?'

"Bob got on the phone and reached his old friend Bill Gay who ran E&F, whose comment was, 'If Tasca wants it, then he can have it.' Within a day the little gold Mustang had itself a new power plant."

"Tasca and Gilbert also acquired a salvaged big-block Ford C6, which Bill modified to shift at 7,000 rpm, as well as a 9-inch Traction Lok rear end. Then they drove the car home to Providence. It was a long trip as an oil-starvation problem caused one of the cam lobes to go bad, and the KR-8 barely limped home.

After being fixed, the KR-8 stuck around well into 1968, but it was eventually totaled by Bob Tasca Jr., "The road was slick, and I hit a pole with that son of a gun, and that was the end of the KR-8!"

The Big Announcement

On December 26, 1967, Ford Stock Vehicles Department's newly appointed manager C. R. "Chuck" Foulger sent the following memo to all Regional and District Sales Managers titled "Announcement of 428 Cobra Jet Engine Mustang."

> To All Ford Dealers:
> Effective December 26, 1967, orders will be accepted for a limited number of Mustang 2 plus 2 hardtops equipped with 428-ci Cobra Jet engines. These vehicles will be pre-built to the following specifications (no additions or deletions can be made):
>
> Base Vehicle: Mustang 2 plus 2 Fastback (Model 63A)
> Engine: 428 Cobra Jet
> Displacement: 428 CID
> Carburetion: 4V
> Brake Horsepower: 335 at 5400
> Bore and Stroke: 4.13 x 3.98
> Torque at RPM (Lbs./Ft.) 440 at 3400
> Transmission: Heavy Duty 4-speed Manual
> Axle Ratio: 3.89
> Brakes: Manual Drum
> Tires: F70-14 Wide Oval (WSW) Hood-Ram Air
> Exterior: Wimbledon White (Code M)
> Interior: Black All Vinyl
>
> These vehicles will be built at the Dearborn Plant DSO facility and delivery time will be approximately two weeks from date order is received, depending on proximity to the Dearborn Plant.
> The completely equipped vehicle will be priced at $2,907.67 wholesale delivered excluding Scheduled D delivery charges, and $3,612.69 suggested retail. Warranty will be 12 and 12.

In February 1968 members of Ford's Drag Council received eight H-M/Stroppe–prepared R-Code 428 CJ Mustang drag cars and dominated the 1968 NHRA Winternationals. Tasca Ford was technically represented by Hubert Platt, who drove the Tasca Ford CJ entry in C/Stock Automatic back-to-back at both the AHRA Winter Nationals event at Lions Drag Strip and at Pomona (Bill Lawton was too busy driving the Tasca Ford funny car). Platt also did double duty driving the Paul Harvey SS/E Cobra Jet Mustang where he lost class to eventual Super Stock Eliminator winner Al Joniec.

The True Story of the Mustang Cobra Jet

By Eric Dahlquist, Former Technical Editor, Hot Rod

Looking back now, the birth of the Mustang Cobra Jet was a much bigger deal than it may have seemed at the time. Rereading my stories and notes from the period, 1965–1967, I now understand the progression of events that inexorably led me, like Nick Carraway in *The Great Gatsby*, to Bob Tasca's door that summer of 1967. It had to do with what, at the time, was the Great Ford Performance Anomaly.

You see, despite the fact that Ford Motor Company had gone full-bore into racing in June 1962 as part of its Total Performance Marketing strategy, and eventually dominated professional motorsports in a way no one had done before or since, "total performance" never translated into the kind of hot machinery the average customer could buy at the local Ford dealer.

Oh, yes, there was the pricey Shelby Cobra and the Shelby GT 350 Mustang. You could also get something like a 427 Galaxy or Fairlane sedan but these vehicles were not inside the parameters of the existing intermediate muscle car formula. I tested a 427 Galaxy with four-on-the-floor that went like the hammers but was about as docile in metro traffic as a Mack truck. Meanwhile, Chevrolet, Pontiac, Buick, Oldsmobile, Dodge, Plymouth, and eventually even American Motors, were selling perfectly drivable, attractively priced, stoplight grand prix contenders that even "The Little Old Lady from Pasadena" could take to the Sunday social.

While Jan and Dean, Ronnie and the Daytonas, and The Beach Boys were singing buoyant, chart-busting ditties about Chevys and Pontiacs, the only song for Ford street-performance fans was the blues. As Bob reminded me during my interview, "You know how many high-performance vehicles [with more than 300 hp] were sold in this country in 1966? 634,434! Do you know how much Ford Motor Company had of this market? 7.5 percent. That's shameful for a Total Performance company."

The stimulus to go to Tasca built gradually over a couple of years. When we went to Ford for various briefings or previews, usually the subject of Ford's lack of street muscle came up. Invariably, someone from Ford would respond by saying they had plenty of good pieces; they just weren't packaged in an appropriate car. This "right car," Ford's GTO, or 396 Chevelle if you will, just didn't seem to be in management's approval box, or, in fact, perceived as even being needed. On one such Dearborn drop-by to preview the proposed 427 Fairlane, Bill Holbrook (in the Performance and Economy Section) explained at great length how various pieces from the Ford

Hubert "Hube Baby" Platt drove a Tasca Ford CJ at both the AHRA and NHRA Winternationals competing in C/SA. Of course, Platt did double duty at Pomona also driving the Paul Harvey Ford SS/E Cobra Jet Mustang and was runner-up to eventual Super Stock Eliminator winner Al Joniec in class. (Photo Courtesy Steve Reyes)

parts bin had been combined to create it. Most were available from the dealer. This is what Ford upper management just didn't get. By far, the greatest percentage of potential muscle car buyers were looking to buy, not build, their own cars.

Bill and some of his buddies in Engineering then went on to strongly suggest if I was ever in the neighborhood it might be worthwhile to pay a visit to Tasca Ford in Providence, Rhode Island, to see what one dealer was doing to market and sell high performance the way it should be done. I realized this wasn't an off-handed suggestion on Bill's part but maybe a way to spread the word via *Hot Rod* that Ford had some of the right stuff for the street after all.

So it was I found myself on Route 44 heading toward East Providence, Rhode Island, from Massachusetts after having seen Plymouth Rock. An interesting juxtaposition, now that I think about it. When I arrived, Dean Gregson, Tasca's Performance Manager, was there to greet me and guide me through the Tasca success formula. Dean was a competitive road racer in his own right, a real car guy to the core and the perfect person to make sure a steady stream of hot machinery was available from the dealership for public consumption.

I don't know where Tasca Ford ranks in the pantheon of all-time great Ford dealers but in those days, the mid-1960s, Tasca was the second largest in the country, ironically, from the smallest state. I learned he had started in the automobile business at 16 in a local Ford dealership and by the time he was 27, he had his own store. He was Ford's youngest dealer. He did it on total customer satisfaction. Long before J. D. Power was measuring it, Bob Tasca was inventing it. If the product wasn't right, he made it right and that included performance.

He loved racing; sounds a lot like Roger Penske. And like Penske, Bob Tasca, besides being a great businessman, possessed the ability to hook something exciting, in this case, racing, and performance, to selling automobiles. Certainly, this was not a new concept. Virtually an unknown, Henry Ford himself put his fledgling company on the map by beating Alexander Winton in a match race in 1901. Like western movie hero Johnny Mac Brown, who always had a plan he "thought would work," Tasca had a plan.

I recall when he spoke he painted idea pictures in broad, colorful brush strokes and, like Penske, he populated his plan with dedicated, talented people and turned them loose. Most of the great sports teams and businesses are put together this way. He was living in a motel at the time I was there. When I asked why, he explained it was because he was in the midst of building a new house, which had displaced him, and was consuming a lot of his time. "Well, Eric," he said when this came up in conversation, "you don't build the Palace of Versailles overnight!" Typical Tasca.

Bob Tasca regaled me with the background of the KR-8 Mustang, KR standing for King of the Road and 8 standing for

Where the Name Came From

Who named the Cobra Jet Mustang? Good question. The title for my test story for the March 1968 issue was "The Jet Set" but I don't recall how I came up with it. Recently Bill Bar, another of Ford's great engine engineers and head of the 428 engine program for the car, stated the package was originally called the 428GT but then it was changed to Cobra Jet. He never said why.

Author Note: According to Bob Tasca it was he who gave Lee Iacocca the idea to use the word "Cobra." Ford had just spent a ton of money buying the name "Cobra" from Shelby. Believe it or not, they were considering renaming the De Tomaso Mangusta a "Cobra" and its soon-to-be-released sister car the Pantera a "Shelby!"

Thankfully, sanity prevailed. The term "Cobra Jet" is said to have been uttered by a couple of Ford engineers who said that the KR-8 handled like a cobra and accelerated like a jet. Perhaps we'll never know the entire story.

428. I had driven the car the day before and it was fast, faster than any GTO, Chevelle, or GTX and was totally tractable to boot. Bob laid out how all the KR-8 performance modifications were over-the-parts-counter pieces. It was the same mantra that the Ford engineers had been singing for many years. The KR-8 seemed a no-brainer for the factory to do itself. They just had to push the right button. I intended to see if I could make them push it.

The story I wrote for the November 1967 issue of *Hot Rod*, "Ford's Ultimate Super Cars, Yes/No" was only three pages long, but what made it so impactful was running the title and subtitle as a ballot that the reader could send to Henry Ford II, personally. I talked *HRM* Publisher Ray Brock into doing it because I thought the story needed a dramatic trick to get the reader's as well as Ford's attention. And it worked.

Thousands of ballots turned up at Ford's offices [Henry Ford II's secretary, Jim Cummings, about went crazy]; most, simply torn out of the magazine with the "yes" circled. The impact of the response galvanized Ford into action. The button was pushed! When one of Ford's public relations people called me and said, "Enough already. We're going to build it!" I knew we had done our job. Today, with the perspective of many years in the automotive industry, I realize what a unique, once-in-a-career event it was.

The True Story of the Mustang Cobra Jet CONTINUED

The Cobra Jet Mustang was a win-win from a lot of angles. My reward was scooping the other buff magazines twice, first with the initial Tasca "ballot story" and then with the actual Cobra Jet Mustang in March 1968. For a car writer, it doesn't get any better than that. *Hot Rod* earned some additional readers and a chunk of extra dough from Ford, who bought advertising across the board in all of Robert E. Petersen's car books. The story also reinforced *Hot Rod*'s leadership position in the car book field.

Ford went on to sell over 13,000 Cobra Jets in what remained of the 1968 model year and recaptured some of their street "mojo." Ford enthusiasts finally got the world-beater they were looking for.

Hey, just another day in The Golden Age.

This is the 428 Cobra Jet FE engine that powered Tasca's 1968½ SS/E and later SS/EA Mustang fastback driven by Billy Lawton. He admitted that after driving the 7-second Tasca *Mystery 7*, going 11s in the Tasca Super Stocker felt like he was going backward. (Photo Courtesy Martyn L. Schorr)

Bill Lawton raced Tasca's CJ 017 in both Super Stock "E" and SS/EA. "I kept breaking Toploader 4-speed transmissions, so the Bopper installed a C-6 automatic. I didn't like that too much." (Photo Courtesy Martyn L. Schorr)

108   The Tasca Ford Legacy

These cars all began with the prefix 8F02R1350. Tasca's shipment of ten cars included numbers 16 through 22, 40, 41, and 42. Bob Sr. asked Bill Gilbert that all ten cars be driven and weighed, and the two lightest cars be saved for Tasca's Super Stock and street racing programs. Those cars were 8F02R135017 and 8F02R135019.

In Carl Tasca's words, "The Campanili and Cardi Sand and Gravel Company was located just up the street; they had a truck scale where we weighed all ten cars. I think one weighed 8 pounds less [number 17] than the other ones did, so Bill Gilbert said, 'That's the one we're going to take to H-M to make a race car out of.' [Today, car number 17 is owned by John Koutromanis.]

"Now I'm 15 and Bob Jr.'s 16. So we take off for North Carolina. Billy [Gilbert] and I are in the Cobra Jet and Bobby's with my dad in his purple 460-engine T-Bird. I said, 'Billy, let me drive the car a few miles.' By now we're in Georgia, so Billy pulls over and he lets me drive. Here I am, 15 years old, driving this high-performance Mustang down the highway with nothing but dealer plates on it and no driver's license.

"When we stopped for dinner the old man says, 'Which one of you knuckleheads was driving that car?'

"I said 'I was, Dad.'

"He says, 'Jesus Christ, you don't even have a learner's permit! You're not in Rhode Island anymore, kid; out here they'll lock you up and throw away the key!'"

Between Tasca *Mystery 7* bookings, Bill Lawton drove the Tasca Ford SS/E Cobra Jet Mustang for the remainder of the season.

"I was kind of forced into doing that," says Lawton. "I mean, how the hell do you go from a 7-second car to an 11-second car? At first, I just didn't have my heart in it. Then after awhile, I started to enjoy it. We were able to book both the funny car and the super stock car as a package because by that time a lot of former funny car racers like Sox, Landy, and others were driving these kinds of cars. We would have Heads-Up Super Stock match races!"

Tasca's SS/C Cobra Jet was also raced in SS/CA. "I kept breaking Toploader 4-speeds, so the Bopper put in an [C6] automatic. I didn't like that too much!"

Tasca's other Cobra Jet car (number 19), named *Street Bertha*, was driven by a number of people including Bill Lawton, Bill Gilbert, and on one occasion, none other than Mario Andretti!

Losing Has Its Price

Bob Tasca Jr. owned a pretty fast 1968 428CJ Torino automatic, a car so fast that no one wanted to race him. "I'll never forget this. Most people have their licenses taken away because they've done something bad on the street. I had my license taken away because I lost a race at the track.

"It was a Sunday, my father was out of town, and since nobody would race me with *my* car, I decided to take a yellow 428 Cobra Jet Torino off the lot. Carl, Ray Larson, and I drove it out to Connecticut Dragway. Now the car was 100-percent pure stock, and I had no intentions of racing it but Carl and Ray eventually talked me into entering it. I'll never forget it.

"I went to the final round and got beat by a 442 Oldsmobile. Unbelievable! I didn't think anything of it until that Monday. I got called into my father's office right after school. Now, my father was notorious for asking you a question that he already knew the answer to, so don't lie!

"He says, 'What'd you guys do yesterday?'

"Oh, we went to Connecticut Dragway.

"'How'd you do there?'

"I thought, 'Oh boy, here it comes!' and I said, 'Well, you know, we were watching the races and stuff.'

"'Did you race?'

"Yeah, pop, I raced. I raced a Ford Torino I borrowed off the lot.

"'Oh really,' he says. 'How did you do?'

"Somebody had already told him I got beat.

"He says, 'You took a stock car off the lot that wasn't prepared and you went up there and entered it into a race? After all the time I've spent trying to establish a winning image for the Cobra Jet program and you took a stock Torino to the track and got beat? You damned knucklehead! You're grounded for two weeks!'

"Now, I've wrecked two cars and never had my driver's license taken away from me; he was that angry!"

I Don't Care If You Bring Mario Andretti

Back in the day, (the late) Frank Maratta was a very well known car personality in eastern drag racing circles. As the track owner/promoter/manager at Connecticut Dragway he was always cooking up some type of interesting promotional program that would help shore up the bottom line and pack his stands with spectators. Bob Tasca used to have quite a few hot Mustangs running out at Connecticut Dragway, funny car team included.

One day, Frank Maratta issued a challenge to the Bopper. Frank Maratta's close friend Bob Johnson was the high-performance manager at Greenville, Rhode Island's Scuncio Chevrolet. Scuncio sold a lot of COPO Camaros, Chevelles, and Novas, and had its own race team.

Maratta said, "They're building a Camaro for me, and I'm challenging you and your hot rod Mustang [*Street Bertha*, the same Cobra Jet Mustang that was tested in the June 1968 issue of *Super Stock & Drag Illustrated*] to a race here at the drag strip. You bring your best car. I don't care who drives it. You can bring Mario Andretti for all I care.

"Bob Tasca's response was 'Oh, yeah?' Bob made a telephone call. And who shows up at Cranston, Rhode Island's T. F. Green Airport but Nazareth, Pennsylvania's very own Mario Andretti! This was the year before he had won his first Indianapolis 500. However, Andretti was already a winning race driver on dirt tracks, paved ovals, road courses, and super speedways and one of Ford's contracted racers. Now you're starting to get the picture.

"Team Tasca prepared a hero's welcome complete with a procession of hot Fords led by Tasca's very own Ford GT40. They drove right onto the tarmac at T. F. Green Airport to pick up the famous driver as he stepped off the plane. Anyhow, being that it was early April, Bob Tasca seized the opportunity and threw a huge third birthday party at 777 for the Ford Mustang with Mario as the featured guest. Tasca ordered up a huge, three-tier birthday cake, which said, "Bred First [as in "take that, Camaro"] to Be First. Happy 3rd Birthday, Mustang!"

"Lots of hoopla, autograph signing, and radio interviews followed. But of course the real reason for Mario's visit was for him to participate in the Ford-versus-Chevrolet match race being held that weekend at Connecticut Dragway.

The Case of the Mysterious Cobra Jet

By Mike Perlini

I went to school with a fellow named Mike Chellel. His father had a small body shop in Pawtucket, Rhode Island, called Chellel's Auto Body. In those days (1968) Bob Tasca did not have his own body shop. When Bob got a car in that needed a little bodywork, he had a number of small body shops that he had an agreement with who would do the work. I got a call from Mike one Saturday morning asking me if I knew how to disconnect the speedometer on a Mustang. The answer was "No!" I didn't know but we had a mutual friend who was a bit more mechanically inclined who did.

Mike says, "I've got a Mustang here in my father's shop. When I start it up, it sounds like a real hot rod. If we could disconnect the speedometer, we could take it out for a little ride!" So I call my friend Ralph Pannone and tell him all about the Mustang.

Now Mike's dad also owned a grocery store over in Narragansett, Rhode Island, where he worked on weekends, so nobody else was at the body shop. We walked into the shop and there sits a brand-new 1968 Cobra Jet Mustang GTA, white with a red vinyl interior and red C-stripes on its sides. I immediately recognize the car and know what it is because I had been reading automotive buff books since way back when. I said, "Do you know what this is? It's one of those new 428 Cobra Jet Mustangs." So we disconnected the speedometer and took the car out.

We're driving it around very fast and doing burnouts. Mike was a little nervous at first, but now that's all passed and we think we've got nothing to worry about. The speedometer's disconnected and Mike's father won't be back until Monday. I said, "We might as well go test this thing out against something that's really, really hot." So we decide to take the car around to a few friends we knew with fast cars and try to get a few races.

The first guy that we raced had a 427/425-hp Corvette. We go up on the highway and we hole-shotted the guy as he was just burning his tires. It wasn't until he was halfway through third gear before he passed us. He ended up winning by a couple of car lengths but the Mustang held its own.

From there, we went to a local drive-in called Ratty's Car Hop where there were a lot of local hot rods hanging around. We got a few races and then we decided to drive over to the *big* hangout, Jolly Cholly's in South Attleboro, Massachusetts. On the weekends Jolly Cholly's was always loaded with muscle cars and we beat everyone over there by quite a big margin.

Anyway, we get the Mustang back to the body shop on Sunday afternoon and park it right back in the same spot, or at least where we thought was the same spot, hooked up the speedometer, and figured everything was fine.

Monday after school, Mike calls up, and says, "Boy, am I in trouble! My father chalked the tires and they didn't line up when he came in this morning." So Mike's father didn't know exactly what we had done with the car, but he knew Mike had taken the car out of the shop. Anyway, his father said, "Now you've got to take the car back to Tasca."

Quite a few years later, I'm the Sales Manager at Tasca Lincoln-Mercury. We were sitting around the office on a Saturday afternoon. Business had quieted down and everyone was sitting around exchanging stories. At that point, I felt comfortable enough to tell Bob Sr. the story about the white Cobra Jet with the red C-Stripe.

He said, "You know what I couldn't figure out? I sold about five of those cars and the buyers all told me that they had been beaten by a white Cobra Jet. I was saying to myself, 'How can that be? They just came out, and we haven't sold any of them yet.' Then I remembered we had a couple of cars that had come in with some scratches on the paint so we sent them out to be fixed. You racing that car and you beating those guys so badly made them decide to trade in their cars on Cobra Jets so I'm not mad, but I finally got the answer to the story. I just couldn't figure out how they had been beaten by a Cobra Jet when I hadn't even sold any of them yet!'"

"Now Mario Andretti had never driven a drag racing car before but he was a quick study with Bob Sr. and High Performance Manager Dean Gregson as coaches. Suffice it to say, Maratta and the Scuncio Chevrolet Camaro were no match for Andretti and the Tasca Ford Mustang. Mario blew his doors off three straight running 11.4s to 11.5s in front of thousands of fans. Then Andretti got back on the airplane and flew back home."

The lesson for the day? Be careful what you ask for. You just might get it!

For David Tasca, Mario Andretti's visit was the event of a lifetime. "I came home from school and there he was, Mario Andretti, in *my* house! My mother, who is a terrific cook, fed him classic Italian. I was just absolutely dazzled!"

"We beat over 20 cars with *Street Bertha*," says Bill Gilbert. "We went out on evening trips and ran out on I-95 before it was I-95, in fact. Anthony Pate was kind of like the guru of that area. Many of the kids who had a car that stood any chance of winning a race used to go see Anthony at his father's Sunoco station and get fine-tuned before a race.

"Anyway, he and his father used to take a lot of pride in their work. They used to do a lot of Corvettes and cars like that. Anthony had put together this ratty 1955 Chevy with a healthy small-block in it that he used to race. One night we showed up with *Street Bertha*. They wanted to hear it run, so I pulled right into the service bay. Anthony asks, 'Has that thing got a solid lifter cam in it? No way could a Mustang run like that. I've seen other Cobra Jets around and they're not like this one.'

"Basically, what I did was fine-tune the carburetor and install a set of Jardine Headers. We had also installed a set of Corvair Spyder mufflers on it, which at 2.25 inches in and 2.50 inches out made the engine breathe pretty good. We also re-curved the distributor. Ford used to put their distributors together ass backward [you could turn the cam from around 15 to 10 degrees] and that is what I wanted, and make up the rest of it with initial timing.

"We actually used to have a whole book or pamphlet that we used to give to all the technicians who showed up at our seminars on how to actually set up a Cobra Jet."

Misguided Missiles

By the middle of 1968, Bob Sr. had grown tired of fuel funny car racing. Deep down inside, he was a businessman; his business was running a Ford dealership and selling Ford cars. The transition from racing success on the track to sales success on the showroom floor had become a bit clouded, as he and his team no longer raced the kind of cars Tasca sold. It was becoming increasingly difficult for Tasca to remain upbeat about the subject, much less financially support a program that wasn't even remotely relative. That also went double for primary team members Bill Lawton and John Healey. Both men had full-time jobs and growing families. Precious time spent away from both home and business proved to be problematic, resulting in increased tension all the way around.

The Favorite?

"I would venture to say that for any Mustang enthusiast the icon car of the time would have to be a 1968½ Mustang fastback with 428 Cobra Jet engine, and Tasca Ford dealer plate on the taillight panel!" said Jim King, 40-year automobile industry veteran and retired Ford Motor Company executive.

The following season (1969) proved this point as Bob Sr. severely reduced the budget on his funny car program to where no new car was constructed. Instead, the chassis from *Mystery 7* was sent back to Logghe Stamping Company for updating. The existing roll cage was cut off and a more-laid-back progressive-design roll cage was substituted in its place.

Back again was the same John Healey–tuned and –built nitro-burning supercharged 427 SOHC Ford and C-6 automatic transmission powertrain.

Tasca's "new" funny car was cloaked with a swoopy new Tom Shedlick Mach-1 Mustang flip-top fiberglass body shell complete with Tom Shedlick–applied candle apple red/fade to gold paint job. Named the Tasca Super Boss, which was something of a misnomer as the car was actually powered by a 427 SOHC engine, it may have been the least-popular race car Bob Tasca ever fielded, but it was by far his most beautiful. The Tasca Super Boss was raced on a limited basis and with only minor success. By late summer, Tasca pulled the plug and sold the Super Boss to Division One fuel racers Joe Jacono and "Biddy" Winnard. Unfortunately, the Mach-1 didn't fare all that well with its new owners either; the car was destroyed in a racing-related accident.

As Bill Lawton said, "We pioneered the funny car of today. There's no doubt about it. Not me alone, of course. I'm talking about every guy from that era who got behind the wheel of one of those things and went fast!"

If you're wondering what happened to the old *Mystery 7* 1967–1968 Fiberglas Limited Mustang fastback body, it ended up in the hands of a nameless NHRA Division One racer. It was installed on another chassis and raced for a few more years. The car still exists (you can actually still see some of the original "Tasca" lettering showing through) and *may* possibly be resurrected in some form or another.

Tasca Street Boss

The alter ego to the Tasca Super Boss Mach-1 Mustang funny car was the Tasca

Limbo Lower Now. How Low Can You Go?

By Mike Perlini

I had a friend who owned a 427 COPO Camaro and he was very proud of the car. We were walking through the service area of Tasca's shop, and Bob Sr. had his 428 Cobra Jet Mustang (the car they used to call *Street Bertha*) there. He used to race that car locally, and as he won each race, people would come in and want to buy a new Mustang.

We happened to bump into Mr. Tasca and one of his managers. He says, "Oh, you like that car?"

My friend says, "Yeah, I do, but I have a pretty fast car myself. I have a 427 COPO Camaro."

Mr. Tasca says, "Oh, you have a Camaro? You want to race that car against your Camaro?"

Now my friend was Portuguese and he spoke broken English. He was trying to tell Mr. Tasca that he knew that *Street Bertha* was a highly modified car when Mr. Tasca says, "Wait a minute! I didn't ask you anything about your car. I just wanted to know if you wanted to race *my* car."

My friend says, "You've got the dealership. You've got the money. It's easy for you to say that."

Well, Mr. Tasca had heard all he wanted to hear about the subject and gave us the famous "pointed gesture" toward the door with the comment, "Ou-u-u-t" because he didn't want to hear any more of it. He walks over to the overhead door and opens it up about three feet to where we had to bend over to leave and squeeze our way out the door, and he says, "Get out!"

After he closed the door, we could hear them in there laughing.

Years later I told Mr. Tasca that story and he remembered it!

This famous shot from the roof of 777 Taunton Avenue shows Bob Tasca Sr., Dean Gregson, and Ford's New England Division representatives posing in front of a billboard declaring "Welcome Mario Andretti!" The lineup includes Dean Gregson's aluminum-body Ford Cortina SCCA racer, the Tasca KR-8, a Tasca Shelby GT500, and the Tasca Mustang *Mystery 8*.

112   The Tasca Ford Legacy

Tasca High Performance Manager Dean "Deano" Gregson met Mario at the departure ramp along with Bob Sr. and an unidentified gentleman. Note the highly collectible Shelby jacket, which Dean still has.

Bob Tasca (left) and Ford New England Division Manager R. F. "Bob" Leonard (right) pose with Mario Andretti as he arrives at T. F. Green Airport in Cranston, Rhode Island.

The Tasca/Andretti entourage pulls away from T. F. Green Airport under a full police escort with Tasca's GT40 MK1 leading the procession.

Chapter Three: "Win on Sunday, Sell on Monday!"   113

Parked right in the middle of the Tasca showroom was a three-layer birthday cake proclaiming "Bred to Be First, Happy 3rd Birthday, Mustang!" This is the same GT40 MK1 that Bob Jr. snuck out of the dealership one night. He drove the car at speed only to have it stall out right in the middle of Taunton Avenue.

Street Boss. Bob Sr. was *very* upbeat and positive about that program! "We started out with a Raven Black 1969 Boss 429 (KK-1214) but that wasn't a Boss 429. That car was ultimately powered by an all-aluminum 4.52-inch oil-can-size bore, Boss 494-ci Can Am engine. I told Ford, 'I don't want to call it a 429; why don't we call it Street Boss instead?'

"That was the best car I've ever driven. That was my 'fun' car. However, putting it together was a real challenge. You had 768 hp and more than 700 ft-lbs on a G60x15-inch tire, and that damned thing would take off and never spin a tire. That's how well it was engineered. I spent days working on the suspension making sure of proper weight transfer to make that happen. You could come out of the chute at 3,000 rpm and go, go, go and never break rubber. I don't think anyone's ever built an 11-second street machine with street tires and closed exhaust that went that quick and fast. I think that right now it *might* be a world record."

The Tasca Street Boss was painted by Tom Shedlick in a candy apple red/fade to burnt orange/fade to gold with candy orange "Street Boss" stripes and color-keyed five-spoke aluminum wheels. The car was an absolute stunner!

Bob Jr. commented, "Our father spent three weeks on the Dearborn Test Track working in conjunction with principal engineers Joe Balzzerowick, Joe Eastman, and John Bowers. He and Bill Gilbert must have installed four or five different camshafts before they got one they liked. That car ran 11.00 at 136.00 mph. That was with a G60 bias-ply street tire on it. That's almost hard to believe!"

David Tasca remembered, "That was a great car. My father used to drive it home and nobody passed him; they just followed. When it wasn't on the road he parked it downstairs in the garage and I used to bring all my friends home from school just to see it. I would say, 'Come to my house and see what's in the garage!'"

Bob Jr. added, "Bill Gilbert, who still works here, took me out in the Street Boss after he had tuned it up one day. We were on I-195 heading west. Man, that thing was fast; we had to be doing 140 mph. Then Bill let up. I asked, 'Why did you let up?' and he said an East Providence cop was chasing us. We pulled over and waited.

"The cop said, 'What's your hurry?' Bill told him that we were from Tasca Ford and we had just tuned up the car to take to a race, and he let us go!

"But first, the cop looked at Billy and said, 'That's not a very good example you're setting for that kid.'"

A Really "Super" Stocker

Back in the day, Eastern Publishing Company's *SS&DI* was considered the "bible" for stock-bodied drag cars, exhibition stockers, and Detroit-bred

114   The Tasca Ford Legacy

Bob and Andretti strike a pose for the cameras in front of the third anniversary Mustang birthday cake. The always-promotional-minded Tasca used the Mustang's third birthday as an ulterior motive to "book in" the rising Ford star before his first Indianapolis 500 win (the following year).

Here Andretti is being welcomed by Tasca High Performance Manager Dean Gregson in front of the "Ford Buy Tasca" marquee. The clever play on words proved to be quite popular.

Trackside, High Performance Manager Dean Gregson, along with Bob Sr., gives future Indianapolis 500 winner (1969) Mario Andretti a few pointers. Mario, who had never drag raced before, was a quick study and seemed to adapt to quarter-mile racing rather quickly.

muscle cars. Contained in the October 1969 was a three-page write-up penned by *SS&DI* Editor Jim McCraw on the Tasca Street Boss. Following is a summary of that article.

If you can Beat the Boss with a street car (street tires, closed exhaust system with tail pipes to the rear bumper, and driveline components by the manufacturer) you can get $1,000.00 in cash.

Ford can be Number One on the street or anywhere else if the package is built from carefully chosen pieces. That's why a 3,000-pound automatic transmission car can go 11.10/131 on street tires. That's also why it hasn't yet been defeated; so Mr. Tasca, "The Big Bopper," still has the same one grand in his wallet as when the "Beat the Boss"

Chapter Three: "Win on Sunday, Sell on Monday!" 115

Mario Andretti is seen here warming up the tires in Tasca's *Street Bertha* 1968½ R-Code Mustang street racer. Mario raced Connecticut Dragway's Frank Maratta and his Scuncio Chevrolet-built 427 Camaro running in the 11.4s to 11.5s and beating Maratta three straight!

The GT40 Incident

By Bob Tasca Jr.

Carl and I had been cleaning the GT40 MKI the night before Mario Andretti's visit, and one of the last words I remember my father saying before he and Mario went to dinner was, *"Don't even think about it!"* He knew I really wanted to drive that car!

Well, after they left, Carl talked me into driving it. Our friend Ray Larsen was also there too. I got in the car and started it up. I drove to the top of the Used Car Lot and took off. I headed east. By the time I reached Dick Lorber Cadillac I was doing 120 mph. Now this was 10 or 11 o'clock at night. When I went to turn around and go back to the dealership, the car stalled right in the middle of Taunton Avenue.

I thought to myself, "Oh, my God!" I could just visualize my father coming back with Mario Andretti, and I've got this car I was not supposed to be driving stuck in the middle of Taunton Avenue, and I can't get it started. Carl and I were in complete and total panic. He and Ray were pushing the car down the street while I was inside trying to get the damned thing started; I mean, I tried everything in the world to get that SOB started.

Finally I located a second fuel pump switch under the front seat [evidentially the GT40 had two fuel pumps] and the thing roared to life. I drove the car back to the dealership so fast that I bottomed it out in the driveway. "Bah-Boom!" Man, my heart was pounding.

Fortunately, I didn't do any damage to the car and nothing was ever said.

traveling (road) show started earlier this year.

The chassis is stock, but the suspension carries a lot of thought with it. The left front stabilizer bar bracket is raised 1-inch. The front shocks are 75-25 Autolite heavy-duty units. Rear springs are Ford (Boss 429) but the right has been re-rated by 160 pounds for a total cross weight, left to right, of 237 pounds to compensate for body lift on acceleration. The left rear shock is a 30-70 mounted in stock location behind the rear axle housing, while the right rear ahead of the housing is 70-30.

In addition, at the front of each rear leaf spring is a Koni adjustable shock, pivoted on both ends, which allows the suspension to settle more slowly and evenly upon deceleration. The rear is, get this, a 3.91:1 Detroit Locker.

One Hot Summer Night from a Bygone Era

By Mike Perlini

We returned to the Pink Elephant having just watched our friend "Ecky" and his Plum Mist 1967 Pontiac GTO blow off another unsuspecting victim with a 396 Chevelle. The Chevy guy didn't realize that his pure-stock SS 396 was no match for Ecky's Goat, which turned 12.7s up at Epping, New Hampshire.

Ralph and I were sitting in our friend Dick Macedo's 1955 Chevy. It was a good-looking street machine with a 283, 4-barrel, 3/4 race cam, and 3-speed on the floor with a Hurst Competition Plus shifter. Nothing radical, mind you, but it sure would smoke the tires when you put your foot in it.

As we were ordering cheeseburgers, onion rings, and vanilla Cokes we heard the guys in the next car talking about *Street Bertha* racing a hot Chevelle from Douglas Avenue. So when we finished eating we drove down the road, parked across from 777 Taunton Avenue, and waited to see if there was anything to the rumor. *Street Bertha* was a wolf in sheep's clothing. It was a fairly stock-looking Mustang fastback with the 428 Cobra Jet engine warmed to the point that it was unbeatable on the street.

As I had walked out of the house my father warned, "You be home by eleven!" It was now 10:30. Although I wanted to see *Street Bertha* race I started to worry. "Come on guys; let's go home." Well, the words had just barely left my mouth when the big overhead door of the Tasca Service Department began to open and an assortment of Cobra Jet Mustangs and Torinos came out. You guessed it, *Street Bertha* idled out of the shop into the warm night air.

We took off after them and followed them to a gas station on Douglas Avenue in Providence. About 10 minutes went by and we decided to walk in and see what was going on. In addition to the Tasca entourage there was an assortment of muscle cars parked here and there, in particular a sharp-looking yellow 427 Corvette. Inside a group of guys were standing around bench racing. In the center stood Bob Tasca Sr. talking about his Mustangs and how they were unbeatable.

Up on the lift was the evening's competition, a beautifully detailed, bronze 1966 SS 396 Chevelle. Bob told the car's owner that he knew it was a 427, not a 396, and the guy just smiled a confident smile and said, "Bob, if you're ready, I'm ready." With that, everyone headed out to their cars. By now I had forgotten about the time. The excitement of the moment had taken over.

We all drove to a quiet stretch of highway not far away. The moment of truth was fast approaching. Bill Gilbert, a tall, blond-haired mechanic at Tasca was driving *Bertha* on this particular night. Bob Tasca leaned over and gave Bill some last-minute instructions and then both cars with engines revving pulled up to an imaginary starting line. *One, two, three.* You could hardly hear the count over the sweet sound of screaming engines! Suddenly the smell of tire smoke filled the air, and the Mustang put a car length on the Chevelle but surprisingly seemed to maintain just that margin and no more right to the finish line.

The owner of the yellow Corvette, who had refused to race *Bertha* earlier, now couldn't wait for the white Mustang to return. He was blabbering about how he was going to blow the doors off the Tasca car and finally shut up all his King-of-the-Road talk. It seems that the 'Vette and the Chevelle had raced previously with the 'Vette winning by boxcars. Naturally, he thought since the Mustang just nipped the Chevelle by a car length it would now be easy pickings for the 'Vette.

When the Mustang returned, the challenge was issued. Bob Tasca didn't even flinch; he just said, *"Let's go."*

This was great. What a night. First Ecky's Goat, now *Street Bertha;* not just once, but twice! The yellow Corvette did a burnout then idled up to the waiting Mustang. The whole scene looked surrealistic under the street lights on this quiet stretch of highway as guys were standing around mesmerized by what they were watching.

The RPM started to build. *One, two, three!* Screeching tires and screaming big-blocks was all you could hear. The Mustang put a car length on the 'Vette and once again held it to the very end. The Chevy boys looked bewildered. Bob Sr. just smiled as he chomped on his big cigar. Everyone headed back to their cars and the night grew very quiet again.

By then it was 1:00 a.m. and, boy, was I in trouble!

Street Bertha Lives!

Tasca's *Street Bertha* (8F02R135019) is currently owned by Greenwich, Rhode Island, vintage car collector John Justo, whose specialty is collecting historically significant race cars, well, like this one!

Greenwich, Rhode Island, muscle car collector John Justo is the current owner of Tasca Cobra Jet Mustang 8F02R135019. It's none other than *Street Bertha,* live and in the flesh! This is the same car that was driven by Mario Andretti in that infamous shootout between Tasca Ford and Scuncio Chevrolet.

According to John, "Back in 2007 a couple friends of mine, Richard and Pamela Ellis, who I had some previous car dealings with and knew that I was into rare Corvette and Mustang muscle cars, called me and indicated that they had two Mustangs in their collection that were from the Tasca Ford stables. They wanted to know if I had any interest in acquiring them. They had this particular car (number 19) and another one that was a white 1968½ Cobra Jet with a red interior. It wasn't a lightweight car, but it was a Tasca 1968½ R-Code car with the 428 Cobra Jet High Performance engine.

"Within a couple of months, I flew over for the Mecum Collector Car Auction in Chicago. Since Richard and Pam lived in Idaho, I proceeded to fly over and visit with them and view both cars. Now, these were great cars, with full documentation, and I fell in love with both of them right on the spot. We began a conversation and within a couple hours we came to a mutually agreed-upon dollar figure. I ended up buying both cars and brought them home.

"This car [number 19] needed some paint work so I sent it to Randy Roberts' Muscle Car Restorations in Owasso, Oklahoma. Randy went ahead and repainted the exterior of the car and cleaned up a few odds and ends on it. I also put on new tires. It didn't have the small hubcaps, which are hard to get. At the time, it had some Cragar S/S wheels on the car, which were bigger in the rear and smaller in the front. It had some lettering on the door, which I think Richard Ellis did later on in its life. Randy also straightened out a few things in the engine compartment that weren't correct. He took about four or five months and then the car came home.

"The interior is all original. One of the things I really liked about the car was that it still had its original VIN tag. Then of course, out came the Marti Report that also indicated that it was one of the original Cobra Jet lightweights as delivered to Tasca. With those two pieces, I was pretty certain that it was the genuine, for-real car."

As previously mentioned, the "paper trail" on *Street Bertha* is fairly complete. Although there is no actual bill of sale date from Tasca, a copy of the 1973 State of Rhode Island Registry of Motor Vehicles shows the car belonging to Gennaro Cardella from Richmond, Rhode Island. From there, the CJ was sold in June 1987 to Charles D. Bowers in Mystic, Connecticut. Then Richard and Pam Ellis purchased the car in October 2007.

Of course, the Marti report is very specific about the who, what, when, and where of 8F02R135019, listing its Order Date as 12/04/67, Serialization 12/20/67, Buck Date 12/21/67, Schedule for Build Date 12/30/67, Actual Build Date 12/27/67, and Release Date 1/08/68. The report also lists 8F02R135019 as being a "Marketing Vehicle" as sold to Tasca.

The Tasca Ford Legacy

Street Bertha looks as if it just rolled off the transporter at Tasca, and was officially listed as a Marketing Vehicle by Ford. This is the very same car that Mario Andretti, Bill Lawton, and Bill Gilbert drove.

Justo says, "I've had quite a few offers on the car but I decided not to sell it at the Kissimmee Auction in January, as all bids came in under my reserve. I'm not disappointed that the car came back home. My main interest is in collecting historic race cars. I have a number of other significant cars in my collection, including the Sebring-winning 1960 Corvette big-tank race car owned and driven by George Reed (*Reed's Race Rats*) and the 1963 Gulf 1 Corvette Z06 Corvette racer driven by Dr. Dick Thompson.

"I also have the 1957 number-3 factory production Corvette race car that was raced in 1957 at Sebring and driven by the team of Duncan and Kilborn. I suspect Carroll Shelby also raced it at Cumberland. What's really interesting is that this car [number 19] made it all the way to Idaho, and now it's back here 'living' only two blocks away from Tasca Ford. So for me, having this car in my collection is a home run!"

Chapter Three: "Win on Sunday, Sell on Monday!" 119

Street Bertha Lives! CONTINUED

Powering *Street Bertha* is the original-date-code Holley 4-barrel carbureted Ram Air 428-ci Cobra Jet engine producing 335 hp at 5,400 rpm and 440 ft-lbs of torque at 3,400 rpm.

Street Bertha was technically restored to 100-percent perfect by Richard and Pam Ellis, right down to the F70-14 Wide Oval (WSW) tires, factory 14-inch two-piece wheels, and standard-issue ("cheapo") Mustang hubcaps.

This small-block-letter cast pot-metal emblem went on to become one of the most famously recognized nameplates in automotive history.

Justo's Mustang came with a paper trail about as complete as they come. Shown here are the State of Connecticut original owner registration card, the original VIN door tag, and an original Tasca Ford body tag.

The standard black-vinyl interior inside of Justo's CJ is also original per Tasca right down to the Stewart Warner gauge trio and a set of Simpson Safety lap belts.

Chapter Three: "Win on Sunday, Sell on Monday!" 121

The year 1969 was the last year Bob Sr. funded his AA/Fuel Funny Car program (he famously called them "Misguided Missiles!") The Tasca Super Boss was actually based on the chassis of the former Tasca *Mystery 7*, albeit updated by Logghe Stamping Company with a new roll cage and a swoopy Tom Shedlick 1969 Mach-1 body adorned in candy apple red–fade–to gold, and powered by the same blown 427 Ford Cammer.

Front wheels are American mags, rears are M/T mags 8 inches and 6 inches, respectively, and both have Day-Glo Orange centers. Tires are Goodyear Polyglas front, E60X15 front, and G60X15 rear. Normal tire pressure is 28 to 32 psi depending on the strip. Brakes chosen to haul the Street Boss down are heavy-duty drum units with ceramic linings.

At this writing, it is doubtful that the 494-ci all-aluminum Can-Am engine had yet been installed, as the article refers to the engine as being stock displacement. Nonetheless, with twin 750-cfm Holleys and NASCAR-style cold-air box, a breakerless Autolite Indy four-cam ignition, and a set of Larsen headers, the Tasca Street Boss was driven to 11.40s at 129.00 during an all-day test session at Capitol Raceway.

In conclusion, *SS&DI* said, "The car replete with paint could not be duplicated for about $9,000.00, the price of a ZL1 Corvette that will not beat it, carry as much cargo, and rides a lot rougher. This project will be parked just as soon as it goes 10.60s. In any case, keep watching for a 'Beat the Boss' challenge caravan headed for your local drag strip soon!"

On the Performance Clinic Trail

Bob Tasca had been putting on high-performance clinics for a number of years and they just kept getting better and better. His "Beat the Boss Challenge" campaign was the frosting on the cake. It was an entire road show in itself. A specially equipped Ford tractor-trailer featured fold-down sides that converted into a stage. Parts boards proudly displayed the latest in Ford and Autolite high-performance parts. The hauler also included a modest machine shop, workbench, grinder, welder, air tools, etc.

"One of the things racing taught us is how to fix a car when you're out at the race track and there are no parts available. If something breaks you have to fix it! I told dealers all across the country that I would hold these seminars just as long as we could race on Sunday and sell on Monday!"

The first seminar of the 1969 season was held in Pittsburgh, Pennsylvania, in late May, early June. Why Pittsburgh? Because Bob discovered that through the first three months of that year, not one high-performance Ford car had been sold in that sales region.

This black-and-white photo taken at Aquasco Raceway is actually autographed to Dean Gregson by Edsel Ford II, who studied at Boston's Babson College and accompanied Team Tasca to the drag races whenever he was in town.

"Who the hell would buy a performance car in Pittsburgh when you can't even find a quarter-mile that's flat? That's why Ford was never successful at all drag racing in Pittsburgh, so I decided to take the lousiest district and see what we could do."

Bob Sr. reasoned that if his "Beat the Boss" high-performance traveling road show could turn Pittsburgh dealers on their collective ears, then he (and Ford) could turn anyone on. As things turned out, the promotion proved to be very successful, and the Greater Pittsburgh Ford Dealers sold a lot of product. "We ran seminars in 23 districts across the country, all the way to the West Coast."

Capitol Raceway's Julio Marra remembers the one event Tasca held at their track. "It was the summer of 1969. Tasca set up an All Ford Dealership Drag Race at Capitol Raceway with a huge tent, catered food, the whole deal. He got all the local dealers to come and actually race one another using their own demonstrator cars. I personally set up the clocks for them. When it was over, he gave out a trophy, and some "Cobra Powered by Ford" jackets. It proved to be quite a successful event."

In Kansas City, Kansas, Tasca lined up 120 428 Torinos on one side of a field and 116 Twister Mustangs on the other side. (Note: Bob Tasca also alluded to creating the "Twister" Mustang concept.)

"When they picked me up at the airport, Ford's District Manager Chuck Tuston and Assistant District Manager Earl "The Pearl" Watson said, 'What are we going to do with all those cars? Who's going to buy them?' I said, 'Don't worry. Before the day is over, they'll either be owned by the dealers in your area or I'll buy them.'"

That day, Tasca's dog-and-pony show consisted of a series of drag races pitting dealer against dealer and car (Mustang) against car (Torino).

"I got the oldest guy there; I think he was a 66-year-old dealer from West Topeka, Kansas. I think he was selling 6 to 12 cars a year; he was a very small dealer. He could have cared less about high performance. I put him behind the wheel of a hot Torino and said to him, 'Now you're going to race.'

"He said, 'I don't know anything about racing!'

"I said, 'It's very simple. When the light turns green you put your foot on the accelerator pedal and you hold it there until you see the light turn white at the end. Then take your foot off the gas and brake.'

"He said, 'Well, what do you mean?'

"I said, 'Exactly that.'

"We get up to the starting line and I tell the guy to let out the clutch a little bit and give it some gas. Soon as the light goes green, "GO!" The old man got beat out of the chute but that was all right because he won the race. In fact, he won the trophy for the day.

"He said, 'I want this car! I want to take this car home and show it to my grandson!' Before that day was over he had called his son and grandson back at the dealership and they bought 14 hot cars. That was more than what he sold in one year. He got turned on to performance at that race and that was in Topeka, Kansas."

Later Bob admitted to finagling just a little, as he had put the old man in the fastest car at the event. Regardless, it had proved his point: You can sell high performance even in Topeka, Kansas, to a 66-year-old grandfather!

By day's end Tasca sold every car there. "I gave them [dealers] two order blanks. One for how to order a Mustang and one for how to order a Torino, properly, in all the right colors and all the right equipment. They filled in the blanks, and I collected them at the end of the day. There were 133 dealers there. On average, that was 1½ cars per dealer. And they sold them all!"

Smile When You Say That, Pardner!

Bob ran a clinic in Houston, Texas, that was so popular that it started at 7:20 p.m. and ended at 1:40 in the morning. He still couldn't get the kids out of the dealership.

"I didn't know that day who they were. It turns out that they were a group of so-called bad boys who came from various questionable neighborhoods in the Houston area. Some of them had been behind bars, or shall we say 'off the highway.' Unbeknownst to me, the Mayor's son was [also] in the crowd.

Chapter Three: "Win on Sunday, Sell on Monday!"

Bob Sr. may have been down on fuel floppers but he was totally upbeat when it came to the Tasca Street Boss, a 494-ci, Can-Am aluminum-engine Boss 429 (KK-1214), which ran 11.00 at 136.00 on a G60XD15-inch Goodyear Polyglas street tire! In the October 1969 issue of *Super Stock & Drag Illustrated* magazine ("Top This, If You Think You Can!") Editor Jim McCraw wrote, "If you can beat the Boss with a street car (street tires, closed exhaust system with tailpipes to the rear bumper, and driveline components by the manufacturer) you can get $1,000 in cash!"

124   The Tasca Ford Legacy

"The next morning I was at Houston Dragway, running a clinic, when Ford Public Relations got a call from the mayor's office saying, 'We would like to see Mr. Tasca at the mayor's office around 11:30 a.m.' I went downtown where Mayor Louie Welch [a Republican] gave me the keys to the city live on TV and presented me with a large 10-gallon [Texas] hat. I remember like it was yesterday. I put it on and said, 'Gee, Mr. Mayor, thank you very much. I appreciate your generosity. Now I feel like LBJ [a Democrat]!'

"The mayor slams his hand down on the podium and says (on live TV), *'Don't ever mention that name in Texas.'*

"Man, I felt like two cents. I wanted to crawl under the table. I'm talking about the President of the United States and they disliked him! I had no idea. That was Houston!"

Street Boss, Street Boss, Who's Got the Street Boss?

Toward the end of 1969, Bill Gilbert and company converted the Street Boss to the Strip Boss by bolting up a set of M&H drag slicks and open headers. Bill said, "That car ran high 9s with Billy Lawton driving, but the Bopper had no interest in it. He said, 'You just ruined a million-dollar car.'"

It's kind of a shame that Bob Sr. didn't become involved with the Heads-Up Super Stock movement (and specifically the United States Drag Racing Team extant from 1968 to 1969), as they were the forerunners of NHRA and AHRA Pro Stock class, which was instituted in early 1970. When you stop and think about it, the Tasca Street Boss–turned–Strip Boss would have made a great Heads-Up Super Stock car. It was basically running the same speeds and ETs as the USDRT cars once equipped with drag slicks and open headers.

It would have been the perfect transition car for John Healey and Bill Lawton in lieu of them going their separate ways. Who knows? Tasca might have gone on to dominate early Pro Stock (or at least be a key player) just as they had done with their Super Stock and A/FX cars.

With regard to the Tasca Street Boss' ultimate fate, Bob stated in the October 1992 issue of *Mustang Illustrated* that it had been sold to a Brooklyn, New York, street racer and was extensively street raced. Furthermore, as Bob, Bill Gilbert, and a couple other Tasca employees have previously stated, the Tasca Street Boss was destroyed by fire resulting from a fuel leak while in the trailer. Or was it?

A Tasca Street Boss 429 Mustang is currently owned by a well-known Ford hobbyist, but (depending on who you're talking to) its authenticity is in dispute. At this writing, that's a can of worms that's best left unopened.

Thunderbird, 1. Corvette, 0!

In 1969 Bob Tasca built a custom purple Thunderbird with a white top (the *Purple Cow*) and powered by a Ford 460. The car also had a Cobra Jet shaker hood scoop, which kind of looked out of place, almost silly looking, but the car ran like gangbusters.

"Bob got the idea that the Thunderbird [which shared the same platform as the Lincoln MK IV at the time and was built on the same Wixom, Michigan, assembly line] needed more power," says Bill Gilbert. "All those luxury items weighed the car down. It was never meant to be performance oriented. Bob pitched the idea to Ford and they didn't think that they needed a 460-powered Thunderbird. Whether it helped or not (I am not a salesperson), Bob had faith in it and wanted it. So we built one. We also installed a better exhaust system and a Holley carburetor with a spacer and Cobra Jet hood scoop on it."

The story goes that while John Healey and Bill Gilbert were driving to Michigan to meet the Bopper, they encountered a guy in a Corvette. Gilbert continued, "You could hear the guy before you could see him. Well, this guy pulls up alongside and he's laugh-

> " *I used to bring all my friends home from school just to see it. I would say, 'Come to my house and see what's in the garage!'* "

ing at our car. Healey was driving at that point.

"I said, 'John, did you see that? You just got insulted. The guy's laughing at our car!' Healey just looks over at the guy and makes a forward motion like this [repeatedly pointing forward]. The guy shifted up to third gear just as John mashed the throttle. The guy got the jump on us because of the weight of our car, and being that it was an automatic, but we went by him at about 130 mph with that thing.

"Thinking that it was a fluke, he pulls alongside us again and gives *us* the forward motion and a look like 'I really wasn't in it.' So we take off again. He daylights us a car, then we blow by him again.

"As we're slowing down I said, 'Well, that's the end of this guy. We'll never see him again.' But sure enough here he comes again up on our left side and I see him shift into third gear. I say, 'John, hit it now!'

Bob Tasca Sr.'s Total Performance seminars (which also incorporated his "Beat the Boss Challenge") were popular with Ford dealers across the country. Bob and his staff showed up in a fully equipped Ford van complete with machine shop. They unfolded a stage out of the van and then ran a dealer drag race.

Of course, at the end of the race there was an overall winner. Tasca and Ford won even bigger by selling more cars.

126   The Tasca Ford Legacy

"Well, he was right on our back bumper. We made the guy look foolish. How do you go 130 mph in a Corvette and say to your buddy, 'I just got beat by a Ford Thunderbird!'"

The conclusion of that story was when Healey and Gilbert pulled in for coffee up the road, the Corvette owner comes roaring up and says, "What the hell have you got under the hood of that thing?"

Once the guys told him that it was Bob Tasca Sr.'s car the guy in the Corvette says, "Holy Christ! I should have known better!"

Tallying Talladegas

At its zenith, Tasca Ford's 777 Taunton Avenue showroom always had several high-performance Fords on display. When Ford brought out the Torino-Talladega model for 1969, Ford had to build a certain number of street cars and make them available for sale to the general public before the car was eligible to compete in NASCAR (called "homologation") and most specifically its season opener, the Daytona 500. Ford furnished NASCAR with a list of dealers that sold these Talladegas, and you can bet that someone from Chrysler sent someone around to see that they were really there.

Of course, Ford was checking Chrysler-Dodge dealers to ascertain the availability of the Dodge Daytona cars as well, says SAAC's Howard Pardee, "The Talladega I saw in Tasca's showroom had a 'Sold' sign on the window. It was hard to understand that the car [only] had a 428-ci engine and a C6 automatic. I didn't know at the time that Ford had to qualify only the body style, and not the drivetrain."

By the Numbers

Performance car sales at Tasca Ford were brisk at the height of the muscle car era. The truth of the matter was that from 1961 to 1971, Tasca Ford Sales sold more high-performance Mustangs, Fairlanes, Torinos, Cobras, Shelby GT350s, and Shelby GT500 Mustangs than any other car dealer in America.

As Dean Gregson put it, "What fun it was back then just being out in the country with all those high-performance cars at our disposal. No radar, no cell phones. I remember having sold seven Boss 302 demos in one week. Every time we got one ready I would take someone out for a [demonstration] ride down Taunton Avenue, turn right onto Fall River Avenue, down the hill at the old grist mill as the road went right again, with a half-mile power slide down the road. You couldn't get away with that kind of stuff today. Then I would take a right onto Waterman Avenue and stop and ask them if they would like to drive (the Boss) back to Tasca Ford. They would (usually) say, 'No. But we'll take it!' Mind you, I'm not complaining; it was a good problem to have!"

The following figures were provided by SAAC, The Boss 302 (Mustang) Registry, the Boss 429 (Mustang) Registry, and former Tasca High Performance Manager Dean Gregson, based on ownership information and dealer sales invoices, which are considered to be fairly accurate although not all inclusive. Some of the figures may be even greater as they do not include those of other Tasca salespeople.

- 289 Cobra Sales: 7
- 427 Cobra Sales: 6
- 1965 Shelby GT350 Sales: 17 (plus 29 more on consignment sold to dealers from Maine to Long Island, New York)
- 1966 Shelby GT350 Sales: 11
- 1967 Shelby GT350 and GT500 combined sales: 69
- 1968 Shelby GT350 and GT500/GT500 KR combined sales: 40
- 1969 Shelby GT350 and GT500 combined sales: 18
- 1970 Shelby GT350 and GT500 combined sales: 3
- 1969–1970 Boss 302 Sales: 14
- 1969–1970 Boss 429 Sales: 9 (including Tasca's 1969 Street Boss and Carl Tasca's Grabber Blue 1970 Boss 429)
- 1971 Boss 351 Sales: 6 (including one custom-built car for Edsel Ford II)
- 1971 Mustang 429 SCJ: 7

Sales figures for Falcon, Fairlane, Galaxie, Torino, Torino-Talladega, and LTD totals are unavailable, but as you can imagine, the amount sold no doubt eclipses total Mustangs sales and then some.

> "Who the hell would buy a performance car in Pittsburgh when you can't even find a quarter-mile that's flat? That's why Ford was never successful at all drag racing in Pittsburgh."

Carl said, "Richard Petty had driven for Ford the previous year, and I ended up with the Boss 429 from his Daytona car, which we installed in my second car, a Grabber Blue 1970 Boss 429 Mustang (KK2124). I'll never forget it. We went to pick up the motor at the Railway Express station in Lincoln, Rhode Island. When we got back to the dealership Bill Gilbert and John Healey pulled the heads off.

"My father said, 'See that carbon on those pistons? That's Daytona carbon!' That Boss 429 was totally set up. I took Edsel Ford II for a ride one afternoon on the back roads. When I hit second gear the seat track broke and Edsel ended up in the back seat, but I just kept on going."

Boss 302 versus Track Boss 302

In the summer of 1969, *Autodriver* magazine's Bill Oursler contacted Tasca Ford High Performance Sales Department Manager Dean Gregson to arrange for a track test between one of Tasca Ford's 1969 Boss 302 demonstrator cars (a yellow one) and Gregson's red-and-black Boss 302 1969 Trans-Am Mustang racer on Thompson Speedway in Connecticut.

In reality, the article (published in the February 1970 issue) proved to be more of an apples-to-oranges comparison as Deano's Trans-Am Mustang racer was obviously superior in every respect. However, according to Gregson, it gave him much-needed track time on Thompson's new surface, as the configuration of the track had been recently changed, so that was a plus.

In closing, the author of the article was sufficiently impressed with the Tasca Boss 302 street demonstrator, comparing it to being "the closest thing to a race car that they had ever come across."

"It was a good article and it sold a lot of cars for Tasca," commented Gregson.

Handwriting on the Wall

By early 1971, word was out that Ford Motor Company was pulling the plug on high-performance racing and would shift its corporate focus to federally mandated motor vehicle emissions testing instead. It was the end of an era, and Bob Tasca knew it.

"I had a lot of fun building cars that I could drive. Once it got to the point where we didn't have anything to race I wanted to get the hell out of it. There was nothing there to get involved with. You couldn't build anything hot. You couldn't modify a car for the street because of the emissions laws. That would be illegal. All there was were sleds. You couldn't go fast downhill even with a sail!"

Almost as if his prayers were answered, Bob received a telephone call from Ford Chairman Lee Iacocca asking him to take on a new project. The Lincoln-Mercury Division had built a brand-new dealership in nearby Seekonk, Massachusetts (the popular line "Seekonk where?" was commonly used), and needed an experienced management team to run it.

"At the time, Lincoln-Mercury held .8 percent of the market and Iacocca

> " *It's kind of a shame that Bob Sr. didn't become involved with the Heads-Up Super Stock movement as they were the forerunners of NHRA and AHRA Pro Stock class.* "

asked me if I would take it. I said that I would just as long as he [Ford Motor Company] bought out the Ford dealer. I didn't want to run two dealerships. He accommodated me by buying out Tasca

An Involuntary Hood Ornament

As told by Mike Perlini

We're up at Connecticut Dragway in East Haddam, Connecticut, on a Sunday with a couple of friends. It happened to be a day that some of the Tascas were there. Mr. Tasca had the Tasca Street Boss. They had the Super Boss funny car. There was another guy, Bob "Yeager" Andreozzi, with a Cobra Jet Mustang. Carl Tasca had his Grabber Blue 1970 Boss 429 Mustang.

Now Carl's Boss 429 was a really fast car. As I remember, it ran high-10-second elapsed times; I think the car might have even run a few low-10s. At any rate, this was during time trials, and the fellow that was coordinating the lanes sending the cars out to race called Carl's lane out. At the time Carl was outside the car talking to somebody. I was crossing in front of those lanes of cars walking toward the timing stand to another set of bleachers on the other side of the track where you could get a different perspective of the cars.

So anyway, Carl was not in his car. The guy kept calling up Carl's car and was waving frantically as Carl was simultaneously running back to his car.

To make a long story short, the track official got a little aggravated and he started making motions for us to cross. I start crossing but by then Carl had jumped into his car and came flying up the lane. I jumped out of the way. It was only a matter of inches or I would have become a hood ornament.

Of course the official at Connecticut Dragway became really upset and walked over to Carl's door and began yelling.

128   The Tasca Ford Legacy

In the summer of 1969, *Autodriver* magazine asked Tasca High Performance Manager Dean Gregson if he would be interested in doing a comparison test between a stock 1969 Boss 302 and his 1969 Boss 302 engine Trans-Am Mustang out at the newly reconfigured Thompson Speedway track.

Ford [which became Crocker Ford Sales, Inc., named after then–Tasca sales manager Bob Crocker] so I could start selling Lincoln-Mercury products from scratch. I knew damned good and well that I couldn't do anything but go straight up!"

Of course, it wasn't quite that simple. Things never are. In fact, the deal almost didn't happen. When Bob Sr. went down to the Industrial Bank in Providence, he took Bob Jr., who was 20 years old and had become hands-on in car sales, and Carl, who was 18 years old and had become involved in the financial side of the business. He also took his Aunty Jean Colavecchio, who by then had become one of the top CPAs in Rhode Island.

"We all sat around in a big conference room for a while, just talking. Then the Ford manager suggested that we get down to business. He said, 'Get those kids out of here.'

"Bob Sr. slowly got up from the table, snapped his briefcase closed, and started to walk out of the room. The Ford rep excitedly asked, 'Where are you going? We've got to get this thing over with!'

"'The deal's off,' Bob said. 'If my kids aren't here then I'm not here. Let's go!' The Bopper always included us in everything he did; otherwise 'How are you going to learn?' he would say. 'Sit there, keep your ears open, and your mouth shut, and you just might learn something.'

"As you can no doubt imagine, the Ford rep practically went into cardiac arrest. 'Stop, Wait! It's okay if the kids stay. We can't lose this deal now.'

"To which Tasca replied, 'Okay, we go ahead [with the sale].'

"So in September 1971, Bob Tasca sold Tasca Ford Sales, the small one-stall gas station dealership that he had founded some 18 years previously, which had now become the second-largest Ford dealership in the world, for $1,771,000. That was major bucks back in the day.

"To everyone's astonishment, as Bob Tasca departed from the room, he turned and handed the $1.7-million cashier's check to 18-year-old son Carl and said, 'Here, take this check and invest it.'"

Obviously, Gregson was up for it. "Seat time is seat time," he would say. The article was actually more of an apples-to-oranges comparison and most of the photos featured Dean's race car. "It was a good article and sold a lot of cars for Tasca."

Chapter Three: "Win on Sunday, Sell on Monday!" 129

Tasca Lincoln-Mercury: the End of One Era; the Beginning of Another

In September 1971 Bob Tasca sold the second-largest Ford dealership in the world for $1,771,000. For his sons, the stark realization that there would be no more Tasca Ford (although Bob Sr. retained ownership of the property) was like putting a padlock on the front gate at Disneyland. It was just unthinkable, as Carl Tasca later commented.

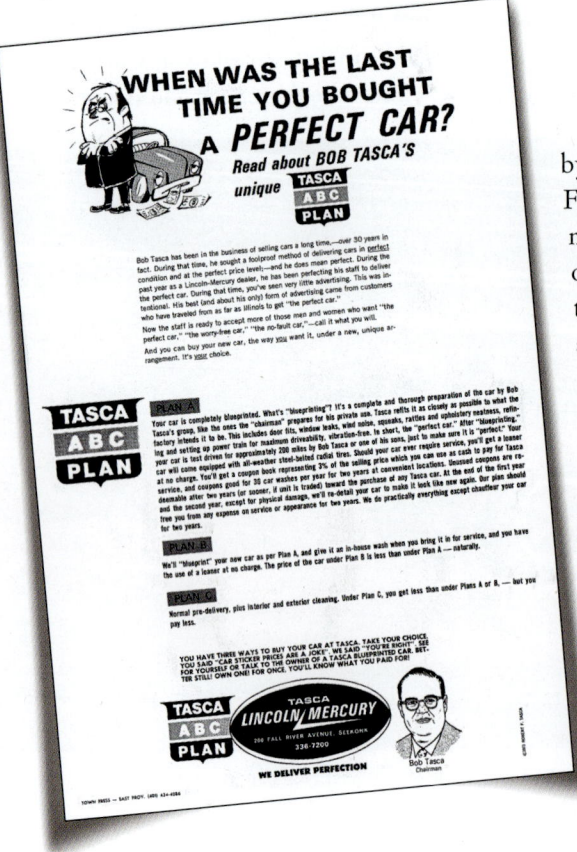

"Our father was asked by Lee Iacocca to sell Tasca Ford. Now here's Bobby and me, two young kids right out of school, and we're going to inherit [along with David and Tricia] the second-largest Ford dealership in the world. We're going to be in good shape, right? Then the old man goes and sells the joint. We're thinking, 'What? Is the old man going crazy?'

"He says, 'Let me tell you one thing. If I gave you the place and you were successful they would have said that the old man gave it to you. If I *did* give it to you and you weren't successful you would feel like dirt, so I'm going to buy this little Lincoln-Mercury dealership up the street in Seekonk, Massachusetts.'

"At the time L-M was at the bottom of the sales market in the Greater Boston area; they virtually had nothing. He would say, 'You guys are going to build it. We're going to build it. We're going to make it or break it.'"

Obviously, Bob Sr.'s "empty box theory" was based on love, devotion, and an unwavering faith and confidence in his offspring. Bob and Josephine had taught

This "Tasca A B C Plan" advertisement touts Tasca L-M's vehicle "blueprinting" program. It's a prime example of the creative marketing strategy that was put into play at the agency.

The Tasca Ford Legacy

CHAPTER Four

their sons and daughter well. They were all capable of standing on their own two feet while moving forward in a positive direction.

"I was 18 years old and the Bopper handed me a check for $1.7 million," says Carl. "He said, 'You're the treasurer. Your brother's a good salesman, so you don't have to worry about selling cars. You just worry about the money.' I went to the bank to invest it and he never once asked me what I did with the money."

And so began the next chapter in the Tasca legacy. Tasca Lincoln-Mercury opened its doors October 1, 1971. Ford had capitalized the venture to the tune of $177,400. From its inception, Tasca L-M was designed to handle just 390 units per year. Of course Tasca ultimately moved ten times that much product annually. When Ford asked Bob what kind of salary he wanted, he elected to take a small salary in lieu of allowing his profits to accrue, thereby being able to buy out Ford's share of the business at a much quicker rate.

"Quick" indeed! To Ford's astonishment, Tasca L-M made money the very first month it was open for business, write-offs and start-up expenses included. In fact, Tasca L-M never had a red month. In July 1972, Bob Tasca bought out Ford. He later said that he "didn't buy the dealership, he earned it," and in less than one year. All along it had been Bob's plan to keep the business fairly small until his sons could join him in the budding enterprise.

> " To Ford's astonishment, Tasca L-M made money the very first month it was open for business, write-offs and start-up expenses included. "

According to Bob Sr., "Bob Jr. [who became the Sales Manager at Tasca Lincoln-Mercury in the late 1970s] came into the business straight out of college. That was in 1975. Carl entered the business shortly thereafter and David entered the business in early 1979.

"We were the team at Tasca Lincoln-Mercury. Bob is president of Tasca Lincoln-Mercury. He is in charge of marketing, merchandising, and customer relations. He goes to all the weddings and funerals. Carl is CEO. He's the treasurer. He runs the dealership.

This is the "house" that Lee Iacocca and the Lincoln-Mercury Division built. It's the house that Bob Tasca Sr. and his three sons turned into a "home." Tasca Lincoln-Mercury opened its doors October 1, 1971, and never had a red month. Originally designed to handle 390 unit sales per year, Tasca ultimately sold ten times that many and established Tasca Lincoln-Mercury as the number-one volume dealer in the country. They sold 3,664, earning them the Ford Motor Company Chairman's Award.

Chapter Four: Tasca Lincoln-Mercury

This is the Tasca Lincoln-Mercury "Our Commitment to You" plaque, which still hangs in the lobby at Tasca East, site of the former Tasca L-M dealership. It pretty much says it all.

It's a proud moment for Robert F. Tasca as Ford Chairman Harold "Red" Poling congratulates him and the entire Tasca L-M organization for becoming the country's number-one volume dealer in the country.

He knows the financial end of it. Bob worries about selling cars, Carl worries about making money.

"David runs a very unique system we have here called 'Pre-Trade,' which means we'll put you in a new car every two years. We started that program in July 1982 and we've got 7,600 customers on the two-year plan. Out of that number, 4,200 are active. So even in this [1992] recession, we've been flourishing with a repeat-customer factor of 97.3 percent."

Pantera. Funny, but not so Funny

Bob Tasca actively sold the Lincoln-Mercury–marketed De Tomaso Pantera but he felt that they weren't really good cars. In actuality, the Pantera was sort of a tail-end project (or leftover) from Ford's Total Performance Era, a program that had already been in place when Ford decided to pull the plug on high performance. What made the Pantera program even more unusual was that the cars were marketed through the stodgy Lincoln-Mercury Division and not Ford.

"They were kind of like trying to fit a square peg into a round hole," as Bob Tasca Sr. sarcastically stated. "I really didn't enjoy selling them. You see, I can't sell something if I really don't like it. They [De Tomaso] used to build those things using parts they stole from Fiat the night before! You never knew what you were going to get. You could get a 171-inch speedometer cable on one day and a 103-inch speedometer cable on another. You would get one spindle bigger on the right side than the left one. The Pantera was a joke!"

"Joke or not, it was quite easy to make the 351 Cleveland engine in the Pantera come alive," said Bob Tasca Jr. "I had just souped up the engine in my Pantera. It was about 1:00 am. Frank Barba and I are on I-195. He drove the car west and I drove it east. Now I'm flying, a buck thirty, a buck forty. I see blue lights in my rearview mirror. I never ran from a police officer, never! I said to myself, 'Well, I'm going to go to jail.'

"If I had run, he never would have caught me but I pulled over. I had to wait for him to catch up with me. I mean, *for a while!* It was a Massachusetts State Trooper. I said to myself, 'Man, I'm in serious trouble.'

"'Get out of the car,' he says. Frank starts to get out of the car too. The trooper says, 'No, just the driver. I want to talk to you.'

"I sat in his cruiser and told him who I was, bop, bop, and bah-bop! He said, 'How would your father like to get a phone call right now? I've got a good mind to take you back to the barracks.'

"I said, 'Don't call my father; just put me in jail. Please don't do it!' On his seat between us was this clipboard with two Providence College basketball tickets. I was in Providence College at the time so I said to him, 'You like PC basketball? I go to PC.'

"He said, 'Well, did they teach you how to drive that way at PC?' Then the officer says, 'You know what, kid? I'm going to give you a break. I'm going to let you go but if I ever catch you doing

132 The Tasca Ford Legacy

that again on this road, I'm going to put you in jail. And I don't give a s*#t who your father is!'"

Tasca L-M TSE Cars

Like the family-owned Ford agency before it, Tasca Lincoln-Mercury built a number of specialty cars, or "TSEs." They differed from mainstream product offerings such as the Tasca LM 250 based on a 1975–1980 Mercury Monarch. Another was the Tasca Mini-Mark Montego Phaeton based on a 1976 Cougar XR7. Regarding the former, Bob Tasca Jr. tells a funny story about how that car came to be, and the unanticipated commotion and consequences it almost caused.

"The Ford Granada-Lincoln-Mercury Monarch cars [produced from 1975 to 1980] were supposed to be a car or "cars" that somewhat resembled the Mercedes-Benz; a far reach to be sure but Ford and L-M were both banking on the fact that a large percentage of their customers would buy into the concept. However, there was no excitement there. The cars were, in Dad's words, 'American' in appearance. The resemblance didn't go very far."

Bob Sr. and sons decided to wake up the Mercury Monarch and created the Mercury-Benz.

"We thought we saw an opportunity there. What if we added some Mercedes-Benz styling cues and partly paid for them by deleting some American options such as whitewall tires, which saved us $35 per car? Then we'd have a unique product offering: a Mercedes-Benz look-alike at one-third the price of the real thing. We decided to bet on the come and do it."

Tasca's Mercury-Benz featured Mercedes-Benz–type hubcaps and "250 LM" lettering on the trunk lid. It also featured a Mercedes-Benz–type hood ornament. The radio antenna was relocated to the passenger-side rear fender just like the real McCoy. The trunk lock cover on the deck lid was also changed to a Lincoln cover. They also pinstriped the bottom of the car.

Where did Tasca get the hubcaps, MB250 nameplate, and hood ornament?

"I went over to the local Mercedes-Benz dealership and bought them at the parts window. The Mercedes-Benz hubcaps fit the Monarch 14-inch rims perfectly. The LM part of the signature was meant to stand for Lincoln-Mercury and came right out of the L-M parts bin!"

In no time at all, Bob Jr. had succeeded in putting together the prototype Mercury-Benz, which sold almost immediately. "We menu-priced them at a level that gave us a fair profit and started selling Mercury-Benz cars by the gross, 35 to 40 a month. Needless to say, I became a pretty regular customer at the Mercedes-Benz parts window. That is until we got a very official letter from Daimler-Benz telling us to 'cease and desist' or they would sue us.

"I panicked and ran to Dad, who told me that I'd gotten us into the mess and I would have to figure a way out.

> **"** That's one of the wonderful things Dad did for us. When he gave us responsibility, he gave us total responsibility. **"**

"That's one of the wonderful things Dad did for us. When he gave us responsibility, he gave us total responsibility. If we got into the soup we'd have to find our way out. It was his way of telling us he trusted us."

Bob Jr. was faced with a real dilemma. Tasca L-M was doing very well and didn't want to lose that revenue. But he knew that his visits to the local Mercedes-Benz parts window were over. In fact, it didn't take their regional management long to figure things out and Tasca L-M was shut off.

Bob Sr. and Bob Jr. were able to locate a hubcap manufacturer in New York and together they designed a Mercedes-Benz-looking hubcap that bore a stylized "T" (for Tasca) in the center. With John Pagano's help they located a jeweler in Providence, Chris Catanzaro at Catamore Jewelry, who cast a hood ornament. It looked like the Mercedes-Benz ornament but with a circled "T." Catamore Jewelry also manufactured new "250 LM" lettering plates for the rear deck lid.

It appeared Tasca L-M had dodged a legal bullet, and they were back in the Mercury-Benz business within a matter of weeks. That program lasted until Lincoln-Mercury Division discontinued the Mercury Monarch in late 1979.

Getting "Bugged" about De-Bugging

Bob Tasca's de-bugging program began back in his Ford era with the encouragement of Henry Ford II after Tasca and his team of technicians de-bugged one of Ford's own personal cars. That program continued through the Lincoln-Mercury era, which brings up an important story. To drive home the message that buying a new car from Tasca L-M meant that the customer was buying a superior product, the terminology "de-bugging" was frequently used in Tasca L-M advertising. "Buy Your Debugged Car from Tasca," for example. Because of it two things happened.

Tasca built his Lincoln-Mercury organization on two unshakable concepts, customer service and quality. When he noticed that the quality was slipping, he borrowed a page from his Tasca Ford playbook and began blueprinting cars. The hammer above and a depth gauge are testimony to Bob Sr.'s devotion to quality.

One, customer interest level increased almost immediately, which was reflected in increased sales. And two, Tasca L-M got a visit from Ford District Manager Tom Riddell, who threatened to cancel Bob's franchise because Tasca was indicating that Ford Motor Company products had "bugs" in them.

Bob told Mr. Riddell that he would become famous for being the one who threatened to cancel Bob Tasca's L-M franchise agreement with Ford. But also Bob told him not to worry because if Ford agreed with him and told Bob he could no longer improve the quality of the vehicles he sold then he would resign the franchise himself!

"I said to him, 'Well, is that a secret? You mean [to tell me] that Ford Motor Company products are perfect?'

"He said, 'Well, you can't use the word 'de-bug' then!'"

"I said, 'It was the Chairman of the Board's suggestion that I use the term de-bug. But if you want to change it that's fine. I'll call it something else!'"

That was when the more politically correct and technically sophisticated term "blueprinting" came into vogue. Of course, Tasca continued to blueprint cars and tout it in Tasca L-M advertising campaigns. "Drive a Car Like the Chairman's," but of course they didn't say who the "Chairman" was. If asked, they were told either Henry Ford II or Bob Tasca.

It represented a certain degree of exclusivity, according to Bob Jr. "The fit and finish of our blueprinted Tasca Lincoln-Mercury cars was second to none. When you think about his vision, I mean, we had something no one else had to offer. We had an edge that was second to none. You could go and buy a car and drive it onto our lot and my father would say, 'You didn't buy that Lincoln from Tasca.' 'You didn't buy that Mercury from Tasca.'

"They would always ask, 'Why?'

"And he would say, 'Because I can just tell.'

"He knew that it was something in the overall fit and finish of the car. And people were willing to pay more money for a car from Tasca. Imagine telling someone back in those days, 'I'm going to charge you 5 percent more for one of our cars but I'm going to blueprint it. You're going to get a car wash every time you drive in for service, we're going to guarantee it against squeaks, rattles, or leaks for as long as you own the car, and if you opt for the 'A Plan,' we're going to offer free pickup and delivery service and we'll give you 3 percent of the selling price back on the car that you can use in service coupons not only on that car but on the next new [Tasca] car that you buy. Plus, every blueprinted car is driven for 200 miles by a Tasca.'

"Just think of it. I buy a new car, I buy a new Lincoln. I've got to pay more to get it right. I'm going to let someone in the Tasca family drive it for 200 miles and I've got to pay 5 percent more for it? Only Bob Tasca can get away this, but our more astute buyers saw the real value in that."

Going to the Dogs

In the summer of 1978, Bob Sr. embarked on a whole new hobby, which, in the true Tasca tradition of family excellence, he transformed into a refined art. While attending the 1978 Frankfurt Auto Show, he was introduced to a breeder of German Shepherd dogs, which kindled a new-found interest in the breed. Bob returned home with a male German Shepherd dog named Olaf, a beautiful specimen with a huge head and neck.

134 The Tasca Ford Legacy

The first car Bob Sr. ever worked on at age four was a Model A Ford. For his 65th birthday, the Tasca children got together and bought this 1930 Model A Cabriolet, which had been restored by former Georgia Tech alumni and retired Ford Atlanta Assembly Plant Manager Pete George. Of course, the Bopper proceeded to practically rebuild the entire car. This photo, taken in the early 1990s, shows Bob with some of his grandkids and three of his prized German Shepherds.

Bob began to breed his own dogs from the superior German Segar bloodlines. One of his earliest successes was a female named Gabriella, who won several national events. Several of Gabriella's sons went on to become national champions and established the name Tasca as a force to be reckoned with in national dog show competition. In fact, Bob Sr. became so accomplished at breeding these prized dogs (which became known as Tasca Shepherds) that when one of Tasca's buses pulled into an event, the competition packed up and went home!

Timber Lane's Jakarta won the prestigious American Kennel Club (AKC) Best in Futurity for 1993 and Maturity Victor for 1994. Even more significant was the fact that he was one of only three dogs to win consecutive AKC titles since 1913. Another Tasca Shepherd, *Timber Lane's Derringer,* won his class at the AKC's Annual Madison Square Garden Dog Show in 1993. Of course with show-winning credentials such as these, Bob was *very* selective about who he sold or gave his dogs to.

"As a dog breeder and retailer, I'd need to know each potential buyer, know his own or his family's needs. I'd need to know the personalities. Maybe a show-quality German Shepherd isn't for them or maybe a puppy isn't for them. Maybe a puppy would be too much change in their family's routine and they would be better off with a more mature house-broken dog. In that case, I'd show them another 'model.'

"In the dog business there are no bad dogs but there *are* dog owners with problems. Dogs are a family commitment. How loyal are you prepared to be to your dog? That's how loyal your dog will be to you!"

Bob Sr. was so devoted to his animals that he helped develop a patented formula in conjunction with the Ukanuba dog food company. For the Tasca kids and grandkids, however, the definition of "loyalty" took on an entirely different meaning, as David Sr. related.

"Almost everyone in the family did 'kennel duty.' I used to clean up after the dogs. I would give them baths. I would lock them up at night. They had automatic door locks [on their kennels] so that when they came in they would stay in and wouldn't bark. Yeah, I did all of that."

Although Josephine Tasca was extremely supportive of everything her husband did, the dogs became a somewhat exasperating experience for her, especially on Sunday afternoons.

"He [Bob Sr.] used to drive my mother crazy. On Sundays, she would make dinner then have it ruined because she had to wait for the Bopper because he was outside in the kennels

Chapter Four: Tasca Lincoln-Mercury

showing off a dog to a prospective buyer!" Carl says laughingly, "Everybody that bought a dog bought a new Ford or Lincoln-Mercury as well, so we really made out on that deal!"

As I mentioned, Bob Sr. was very selective as to whom he either sold or gave his dogs to. That list included New England Patriots second-string quarterback Matt Cavanaugh, former John Force Racing Crew Chief Austin Coil, and Mustang and Thunderbolt restoration specialist Randy Delisio. Bob continued raising German Shepherds until his health began to fail him. His last AKC National was in 1996.

The Tasca motorhome chauffer was veteran Tasca employee and distant relative Louis "Lou" Tullie (Bob Sr.'s grandfather and Louis' grandfather were brothers on the Colavecchio side). He had started with Tasca in 1957 working in the Parts Department.

"Bob knew that I maintained a commercial driver's license. One day, he put a picture of a bus in front of me and asked, 'Can you drive one of these?'

"I said, 'Yes, if I can fit behind the wheel.' From that day on, I drove Bob and Josephine everywhere. I drove two MCI motor homes and, later, the Prevost. I can't begin to tell you how many times we drove back and forth across the country. It was great to see the United States through the front window of that coach.

"In the summer of 1996, we attended the AKC National in Louisville, Kentucky. As you've probably been told by other people, the standard [colors] for German Shepherds are black, red, and tan. But they put an all-black Shepherd up. They would never put an all-white one up but they put an all-black one up for whatever reason. And it was awarded Grand Victor.

"Bob said to trainer Tommy Castriana, 'I'll never show another damned dog again!'"

Kicking the Rattles out of Detroit Iron

Bob Sr. may have liked German Shepherd dogs but he had a tremendous dislike for cars that were "dogs." On March 13, 1984, the Sunday edition of the *Boston Globe* ran a feature article by A. S. Plotkin in the Business Section called, "Kicking the Rattles Out of Detroit. Dealer from Seekonk Tells Ford: Build Cars Right, or Else!" Following are some paraphrased highlights of that article.

Bob Tasca sells automobiles in Massachusetts. But one day two weeks ago he was in an assembly plant near Detroit telling Ford Motor Company that he had a better idea about how to make better cars.

He holds strong views on what car buyers want and has so impressed the number-two carmaker that he regularly joins corporate brass on plant inspection trips.

For Robert F. Tasca, quality is like a personal Holy Grail.

Other dealers are occasionally invited to visit the plants. But Tasca, say Ford officials, is the only dealer who is a regular on official inspection parties at the assembly plant. In fact, he is an unofficial plant consultant and trouble-shooter.

Tasca, who stands at an impressive 6'1" and weighs 260 pounds, happens to be a good, if unorthodox, businessman, a crackerjack mechanic, and no shrinking violet.

Tasca's first visits, starting 2½ years ago, generated some apprehension, even suspicion. But now he is welcomed by both management and workers.

Some of Tasca's Lincoln-Mercury competitors in southeastern Massachusetts say he has a big ego and that satisfying that ego with the trips is compensation of sort. And they gripe that Ford favors him with a large share of hot-selling cars and protects his area from competing dealerships. But none derides his technical expertise or his intense striving for product quality.

They [Detroit] built lousy cars, big and frilly. We fooled the public. In their selfishness to earn money, they neglected what the market wanted.

Today he says he is convinced that US-built Ford cars are now as good as, or better than, the imports.

Tasca's own standard for maximum body gaps is 5 mm [less than .02 inch]. But he would actually prefer it to be 3.5 mm.

> "One unusual marketing aspect of Tasca's program that drew corporate attention was his offer to deliver a "blueprint," or perfect car."

One unusual marketing aspect of Tasca's program that drew corporate attention was his offer to deliver a "blueprint," or perfect car. He blueprints about a third of the new cars he sells. "We take the assembly line error out of the car."

In the customer reception room in Seekonk the walls hold framed documents, pictures, citations, and letters. Among them is one dated March 25, 1982. It is from P. C. George, plant manager from Ford's assembly plant in Georgia. It reads, "Not only did you tell us what must be done, but you showed us how it could be done."

Plant Tours

Bob Tasca was one of the key figures outside Ford Motor Company

Blueprinting Cars—Not Quite as Easy as It Sounds

As told by Carl A. Tasca

The 11th Commandment, according to Bob Tasca Sr., was, "You build a car for the 'taker' not the 'maker.' Don't cheat where you can see it, feel it, or hear it!"

The old man had a maximum tolerance gap of 5 mm. Any of the seams in the car's hood or doors couldn't be any wider than that. So we're watching him do this for a couple of months.

Anyhow, the Bopper went away on a Ford trip somewhere one weekend, and we said, "Let's see if we can blueprint a car." I'll never forget it. There was Bobby, myself, and Bobby "Yeager" Andreozzi, blueprinting this 1972 Lincoln, or at least trying to.

I mean, we took a brand-new Mark off the lot and started re-fit it. We were absolutely lost!

The Bopper comes in Monday and knock, knock, knock. "Dad, we're in trouble."

He says, "Jesus Christ!" It took him and his technicians a day and a half to re-fit the car.

We thought we could do it without him, but we couldn't!

who helped make "Quality Job 1," says Bob Jr. "When I used to go with him on some of the assembly plant visits, I was amazed at how everybody responded to him. My father used to have a great relationship with the UAW workers at the Ford assembly plants. They [managers] would tell him about problems they had and they weren't always right. My father would say to them, 'Now, if I get such and such, you're going to build a better car,' and they would. These running changes were made for the good of the company and for the good of the customer!

"On one of his plant visits to the Edison, New Jersey, Ford Assembly Plant, which was a tough environment where management and the unions weren't getting along, Dad notices that the quality [control] wasn't all that good. He's watching this UAW worker gruffly fitting the door onto a Mercury Cougar. But he wasn't fitting it properly.

Dad walked up to him and said something like, "You know, you're not fitting the door right."

The guy says, "Mr. Tasca, I've been fitting doors like that for the last 30 years."

To which Dad replied, "Well then sir, if you've been fitting doors like that for the last 30 years, you've been fitting them wrong for the last 30 years! I'll tell you what I'm going to do. I'm going to show you how to fit them properly and I'm going to make your job easier."

Dad rolled up his sleeves and showed the guy how to do the job the right way, and the guy really appreciated it. That's the kind of rapport he had with Ford's workforce. He had their respect. He had no problem telling someone he was doing the job wrong and he was always able to show the person how to do it right.

"My father used to have his own parking space for his [Prevo] motorhome at the Ford assembly plants that said 'Reserved for Mr. Tasca.' Sometimes, we thought that he believed that he was Henry Ford, that he owned Ford Motor Company. Every once in a while, we had to pull him back to reality and remind him that he wasn't Henry Ford; he was Bob Tasca."

Let's Do Lunch!

Another incident that clearly underscores the incredible connection Bob Sr. had with Ford and Ford/UAW workers was the time he visited the Wixom, Michigan, Ford Assembly Plant and spoke with the UAW workforce.

Water Test? What Water Test?

By Louis Tullie

This happened in the mid-1970s at the Wixom, Michigan, Assembly Plant. At the time the Lincoln had a cowl leak that was really causing a lot of warranty problems. The guys on the assembly line were supposed to shoot some dum-dum material up into the seams of the cowl beneath the dash where the firewall sections came together, but it was a difficult area to get to. A lot of the time they just didn't do it.

Mr. Tasca got wind of this, so we drove around to the back of the plant where the new Lincolns were coming off the line. These cars would be driven through a 50- to 75-foot water trough that had an uneven surface, so it would rock the cars back and forth. The idea was that they would become thoroughly inundated with water so that any leaks could be detected.

When we got out back, Bob asked the plant manager, "What do you see?"

The plant manager replied, "I see a lot of beautiful Lincolns."

Mr. Tasca said, "No, what do you really see? They're all dry! Why aren't they wet?"

The workers knew that there was a problem and they were driving the cars *around* the water trough, not through it.

Now Bob was a strong advocate of workers' rights, no question about it. Apparently, the workers were going to strike and they were being given a real hard time by management. Bob had lunch with them and their demands actually weren't that unreasonable. They wanted some picnic tables outside. They wanted a few small things done inside. The managers weren't listening to half of the things they were asking for, which weren't even money related.

Bob said to Ford management, "You damned fools! You're going to have a strike over a few damned picnic tables! You better listen to these guys."

> "Bob said to Ford management, "You damned fools! You're going to have a strike over a few damned picnic tables! You better listen to these guys.""

Within a week or two, one of the UAW representatives called Bob and said, "All the things we asked for we now have. Thank you, Mr. Tasca!" Paying attention to the little details usually makes a big difference.

The next time Bob came back to visit the plant, the manager suggested that they have lunch in the company cafeteria. Bob replied, "Where do the workers eat?"

The manager quite frankly didn't know. Bob replied, "Well, today you're going to find out!"

Having a Pre-Christmas Christmas

By Tricia Tasca-De Cristofaro

The Sunday after Thanksgiving, we would all pile into my dad's motor coach and drive up to F.A.O. Schwartz in Boston. That was *his* Christmas present to the kids. He would take them shopping.

In the early days we would go when the store was open. But as the family grew larger the manager said to my dad, "Mr. Tasca, you just spent $10,000 at F.A.O. Schwartz. Next year, you come an hour early and we'll open up the store just for you."

I mean it was absolutely incredible. Imagine being a kid in such a place. It reminds me of the movie *Toy Story*. We had the whole store to ourselves for an entire hour. We played with whatever we wanted to play with, and whatever we wanted, we got.

After visiting F.A.O. Schwartz, Dad would take us over to Copley's and he would buy us new clothes. Anything you wanted. Then we would have dinner at Regal Sea Food. The experience was unbelievable. For my father and mother, that was the happiest day of the year.

That was one of the best memories we all have of our father; memories that will last forever!

This photo was taken outside Boston's F.A.O. Schwartz store where Bob, Josephine, and all the Tasca kids and grandkids would spend an entire hour picking out whatever they wanted for Christmas. Imagine being a kid and having the entire toy store to yourself for an entire hour.

The Twin Cities Ford Assembly Plant Team and the Ford Kansas City Team presented these plaques to Robert F. Tasca Sr. in their appreciation of Bob's unending quest for quality. "He liked them and they liked him," commented distant relative and veteran Tasca chauffer Louis Tullie.

The Cougartown Follies

One day Bob Tasca Sr. came back from the Ford Lorain, Ohio, Assembly Plant where they built the Mercury Cougars. He was clearly aggravated. He had had an argument with one of the engineers about one of the machines they used to install the doors on the 1985–1986 Mercury Cougars.

If you recall, those particular cars featured an airplane-door design that closed into the car just like the Ford Thunderbird's did. He said to the engineer, "The way you've got the machine calibrated the doors will leak air and water." To him, that was the make-or-break scenario to building a well-made car. Tasca wanted to do a blueprint car so that he could re-do the door fit the proper way. That's one of the reasons why we blueprint a car. The blueprint is perfect. Mass production is where things get screwed up.

Anyway, Bob was concerned that the gap of the door was going to start off narrow and get too "thick" toward

> "He said to the engineer, "The way you've got the machine calibrated the doors will leak air and water." To him, that was the make-or-break scenario to building a well-made car."

the back of the car. He had an argument with one of the engineers who was setting up these robots. He said to the guy, "I'll tell you what. You set it up the way you say and I'll work with your team setting up the other door on the other side and we'll see which side comes out better." That was how the argument ended.

"Bob tells us this story in a sales meeting," said Mike Perlini. "It was 1985 and I had just started working at Tasca L-M.

"He said to us, 'I want you to keep your eyes on the Cougars that are coming in. Here's what you're going to see. On the left-hand side of the car you're going to see a big gap at the bottom of the door. If that happens you're going to have water leaks, and . . .'

"Anyhow, a customer comes in and he's interested in buying a new Cougar

Chapter Four: Tasca Lincoln-Mercury

This pin was given out by Bob Tasca Sr. to Ford assembly plant workers and management to show his appreciation for the quality work that they were doing. Heck, Bob even had an assigned parking spot for his motorhome at most assembly plants!

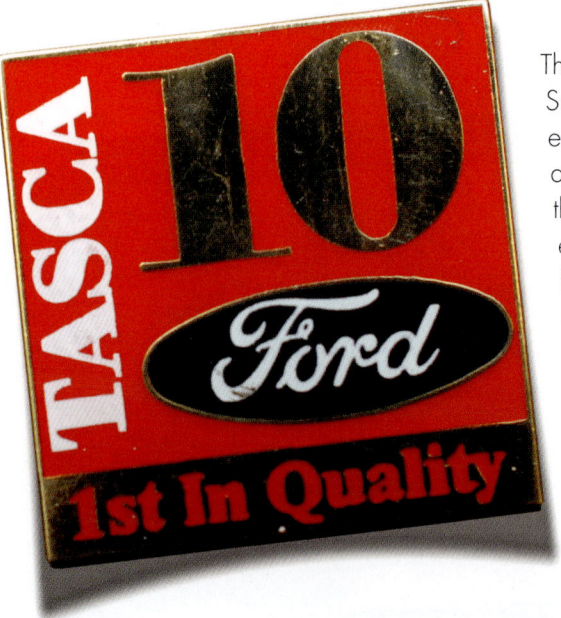

but he says, 'They just started building these cars, right?'

"I say, 'Right!'

"'Well, I noticed that there's one out there, and there may even be more of them out there, that are not right.'

"Since we had just heard the same story from Mr. Tasca I inquired, 'Why aren't they right?'

"The guy says, 'I think they're going to leak water.' So I asked him to show me what he was talking about. Damned if we don't go out to the car and on the left-hand side, the gap of the door is way too big, just like Mr. Tasca had said, but the other side (the side he and Ford's UAW workers had worked on at the factory) was okay.

"I said, 'You know something? Mr. Tasca was just telling us something about this. I want you to go inside with me and talk to Bob Tasca Sr. and tell him about your findings.'

"We go inside and I introduce Mr. Tasca to the customer saying, 'This gentleman wants to buy a new Cougar but I think he's got something to tell you that I know you're going to be interested in.'

"He [Tasca] said, 'Didn't I tell you that?' He says to the guy, 'Have a seat; I'm going to call up Lorrain [Ohio]. I'm going to call the assembly plant where they build the Cougars and tell them what you said.'

"Bob got the plant manager on the phone. Based on that call, they [Ford] stopped the assembly line. I mean, if there was any doubt in my mind that the man had that much power at Ford, from that moment on, I no longer had any doubt.

"At 6:00 am the following morning I drove Bob to T. F. Green Airport where Ford had a Gulfstream jet waiting on the tarmac. Bob flew to Lorrain, Ohio, where he met with Ford engineers. They re-calibrated the door and there were no more gaps."

At the height of the Ford assembly plant visits, Bob Sr. awarded a pin to managers and key Ford/UAW workers that said: "Tasca (Top) 10. Ford First In

The Best Place to Buy a Bad Car Story

As told by Mike Perlini

When I was Sales Manager over at Tasca Lincoln-Mercury, a fellow with whom I had grown up came in with his wife. They were interested in buying a Mercury Topaz, which was a nice little car. It wasn't a great car but it was a nice little car for transportation, especially when the window sticker was only about $10,000.

At any rate, I'm talking to him about the Topaz and it looks as if he was pretty close to making the commitment to buy one. As I'm beginning to finalize the details of the sale, Bob Sr. walks by.

I say, "Mr. Tasca, do you have a moment?" He pokes his head into my rather small office and introduces himself to my friend Greg and his wife.

He says, "So you're buying a car? What are you getting?"

Greg says, "It's a Topaz."

The Bopper says, "You need to know that this is the best place to buy a bad car," and he walks away.

My friend Greg says, "What does he mean by that?"

Then his wife asks, "Are we doing the right thing here buying this car? Why would Mr. Tasca say it's such a bad car?"

I really didn't think Mr. Tasca meant that, but to tell you the truth, I really didn't know what the hell he meant.

Mr. Tasca comes walking back within a matter of minutes and sticks his head through the door and says, "I guess you're wondering what I meant by that?"

I say, "Well, I am, Mr. Tasca."

My friend Greg says, "I can't help but start wondering, is the Mercury Topaz a bad car?"

Mr. Tasca says, "Oh, no! Topaz is a nice car. But you know, have you ever heard of a Friday car? That's the kind of car they build at the end of the day on Friday when the workers are not up to speed. Anybody can build a bad car. If you ever buy one from Tasca, I'll fix it, I'll replace it, or I'll buy it back from you and burn it; you bring the matches!"

What he was saying was that Tasca stood behind its products. "If you get a car from us that wasn't built right, we'll replace it for you."

---

140   The Tasca Ford Legacy

This marquee coincided with Tasca L-M being named number-one L-M volume dealer in the country. The building is located at the south end of New York City's Times Square, the same one from which the ball is lowered on New Year's Eve.

Quality." Today, these pins are highly sought and are highly collectible as keepsakes from the Bopper's dedication to making quality Job 1.

Customer Satisfaction Practiced Here

Tasca greeter and longtime friend "Uncle Gene" De Graide tells the story of a dissatisfied customer who approached Bob Sr. about a billing problem, which Bob addressed in typical Tasca fashion, turning the negative into the positive and, in the long run, making everybody happy.

"One day this customer came in and said to me, 'Gene, I am very upset with my repair bill.'

"I said, 'Would you like to talk to Bob Tasca Sr.?'

"He said 'Yes,' so I took him into Mr. Tasca's office.

"The customer said, 'Mr. Tasca, I'm very upset with this bill. [I think it was $200.] I had my car serviced, etc., etc. I think it's exorbitant, etc., etc.'

"And Bob says, 'Wait just a minute.' He picked up the telephone, called his top mechanic, and inquired about the charges.

"The mechanic said, 'Yes, Mr. Tasca, that bill is correct. We didn't overcharge him.

"'I see,' he says, hanging up the telephone. He said to the customer, 'Would you accept $100 and I pick up the other half?'

"The man didn't expect that. With a surprised look on his face, he went and paid his bill and was gone. Two weeks later that same customer came in and bought a new car!"

A Sable for Mabel? Well, Mable Not

In 1986, Ford Division created the Gen I Ford Taurus and Lincoln-Mercury created the Gen I Mercury Sable. Of course, other than headlight, taillight, grille and wheel treatments, the cars were virtually identical.

Bob Sr. and one of his sources at Lincoln-Mercury Division thought that it would be a great promotional idea to hold a "Sable for a Sable" contest in which every so many Mercury Sable buyers would win a genuine sable fur.

Quite typically, Bob conducted a thorough research and educational program about sable furs. He paid a visit to a top-name furrier in New York City whose specialty was sable fur. He spent quite a few days with this gentleman learning everything there was to learn about the subject. Ultimately, Bob purchased a sable fur coat for his wife, Josephine, as well as a couple of sable fur hats.

When he returned to Seekonk, Bob more or less gave a full dissertation on the subject at one of the Tasca L-M sales meetings, citing what made that fur different from mink, sable farms versus wild sable, domestic versus Russian sable—the whole ball of wax. Just like the car, it seemed as though Bob had

Chapter Four: Tasca Lincoln-Mercury

A Lifetime of Community Service

Bob Sr. presents the keys to a pair of Lincoln Town Cars that he donated to Providence College. Accepting for PC are Father John Petersen and Father Thomas Petersen. Over the years, the Tascas have actively participated in several car-oriented charitable events to benefit both church and the college.

Bob, Josephine, and the entire Tasca family are devoutly Roman Catholic and have always been supportive of the church. One day, seven-year-old grandson Carl Jr. came home from school with tears in his eyes and said, "Popi, they're going to close my school. Popi, please give them some money! I love my school!"

Bob said, "It won't close."

He went to the parish and said, "If I can make the school an asset, rather than a liability, to the parish, will you keep it open?"

Of course the answer was "Yes!"

The Blue Ribbon Award

By Father Alfred Almonte ("Father Al") of Our Lady of Grace Parish

I came to St. Rocco's in 1988 and that is when I got to know Bob and the entire Tasca family. At the time, St. Rocco's School was going through some tough times. They were having serious financial problems. Enrollment began to fall. Money was not coming in and I appointed Bob a member of the Finance Council for the parish.

When we got together, he said, "Let's try and call in a group of financial experts from Providence College," as Bob was also on the Board of Directors at PC. "We'll have them come in and give you an evaluation based on what's happening."

At that time, we also had a very, very excellent principal in [the late] Sister Mary Carol Gentile. I was just in the

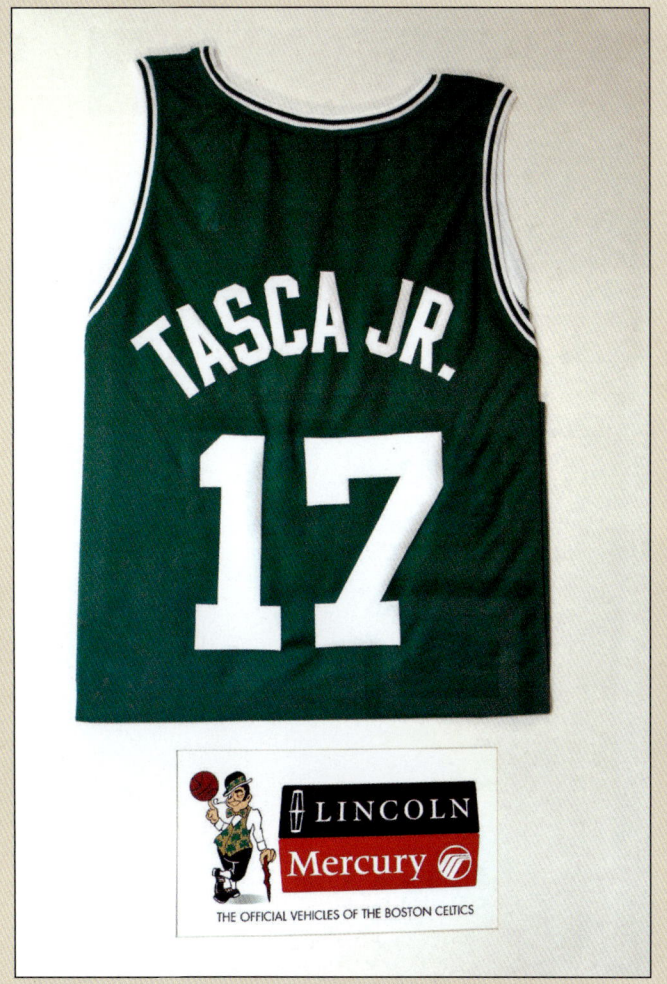

This Boston Celtics basketball jersey hangs right outside Bob Jr.'s doorway in the executive offices at the Tasca Automotive Group's Cranston, Rhode Island, facility. It was a gift from the Lincoln-Mercury Dealers Association in appreciation for his service as president. At the time, Lincoln-Mercury was also the official vehicle sponsor of the Boston Celtics.

Bob Sr. proudly stands alongside a plaque dated December 12, 1985, in recognition of the efforts of the entire Tasca family and Ford Motor Company that went into the building of a hall at Providence College.

background; it was she who spearheaded the project. At Bob's suggestion Marty Goldfarb Associates came in and with the sister's help prepared an evaluation.

Whatever recommendations they made we followed. We increased our enrollment so that when I left in 2001, it was up to 505 children, so at the time when Bob became involved, enrollment had doubled. The end result of all that work was that St. Rocco's was chosen out of nine schools in the nation to receive the National Blue Ribbon Award, which was presented to Sister Mary Gentile by President Bill Clinton in Washington, DC. As far as Catholic schools are concerned, that really put us on the map.

St. Rocco's became the largest parish school in the diocese. That was in December 1995.

Is It a Raffle, or Is It a *Raffle*?

Bob Tasca knew how to get things done. In the late 1980s the church wanted to build a new gymnasium. Bob made the suggestion, "You know, you ought to hold a car raffle [to be held in conjunction with the annual Feast of St. Rocco]," and he left it at that. The church went out and bought a stick-shift base-level Ford Escort because that's what they could afford.

However, they said to Bob that the whole idea of a car raffle wasn't working out. They weren't making that much money.

Tasca replied, "You bought a car that nobody wants. Get a Lincoln Town Car or something like that."

Father Alfred Almonte said, "We can't afford a Lincoln Town Car, Bob."

Bob replied, "You're going to find out that people want the Town Car. I'll give you the Town Car up front and you can pay me after you raffle it off. You're going to get a lot more money raised with a raffle on a car that people want instead of a car that they don't want."

Saint Rocco's ended up raising three times the value of the Town Car, and suddenly the church began buying Lincolns from Tasca for other fund raisers because they realized that that strategy was a much better strategy than their initial plan.

Chapter Four: Tasca Lincoln-Mercury

A Lifetime of Community Service CONTINUED

Robert F. Tasca Sr. speaks to the graduating class of 1985 in the hall named in his honor. The strong sense of giving back to both church and community has been a deeply rooted Tasca family tradition from day one.

Angels to the Rescue

By Bob Tasca Jr.

My father has always been good to Providence College and they've always been good to us. In fact there's a scholarship there named after him. Father John Petersen was the treasurer and (the late) Father Thomas Petersen [Father John's brother] was the president. In the late 1960s, or early 1970s, my father donated a Dark Blue Metallic Lincoln Town Car to PC. Father Tom went to New Jersey to visit his mother, I believe, and his car was vandalized. The hood was all caved in as if somebody had jumped in the middle of it, which they most likely did.

Father Tom had a big meeting to go to later that day and called my father because he didn't know what to do. He said, "Let me call you back, Father; I may have a plan." My father took the hood off a brand-new Lincoln that he had on his lot. He put it in the back of a service truck and had two of his technicians drive down to New Jersey. I think he told Father Tom to leave his keys somewhere.

When Father Tom got out of whatever meeting he was in, he walked up to his car and the hood wasn't dented anymore. He called my father and said, "I guess the 'angels' came down and repaired my car." That's a true story. That's the kind of stuff my father would do. It wasn't about the money. It was all about making someone happy, which was his personal business philosophy all of his life."

learned everything there was to know about its namesake.

However, one of the most important things he learned was that a top-quality sable was cost-prohibitive, so much so that a promotional giveaway program was totally out of the question. Furthermore, it was also suggested that such a promotion might be ethically, as well as politically, incorrect with the Animal Rights Movement protests beginning to gain national attention.

Ultimately the "Sable for a Sable" idea was scrapped.

The Tasca Challenge

Since its earliest beginnings, Tasca L-M has been consistently ranked among the top 10 in dealer sales. Then in 1986, Tasca L-M was rated number one in dealer sales with 3,664 cars sold. Tasca L-M also received the Ford Motor Company Chairman's Award for being the number-one satisfaction dealer in their market segment as voted by the customer nine times! Then Tasca L-M Sales Manager Mike Perlini tells of the day Tasca L-M's sales force received the good news for the first time.

"We're all sitting around the table in the conference room congratulating ourselves. I remember it as clearly as if it were yesterday. Saying 'None Bigger, None Better' always meant a lot to Bob Sr., so after a torrid December where the race between us and San Antonio, Texas, North Park Lincoln-Mercury was very close and always in doubt it was a great relief that we found out that we actually won.

"So there we were in the morning's sales meeting. Bob Jr. had just received congratulations from upper-level Lincoln-Mercury officials in his father's office with Bob Sr., Carl, and David. He came into the sales meeting with the good news.

"I don't know if 'smug' is the right word but we were certainly pumped up and proud to have finally accomplished the long-standing Tasca goal of achieving the right to say 'None Bigger, None Better.' Ford was in the process of checking CSI [Customer Satisfaction Index] scores worldwide to see if our CSI score

> " Since its earliest beginnings, Tasca L-M has been consistently ranked among the top 10 in dealer sales. Then in 1986, Tasca L-M was rated number one in dealer sales with 3,664 cars sold. "

was the best in the entire Ford world but we knew we had the highest CSI score for Lincoln-Mercury dealers.

"As we congratulated ourselves for the accomplishment Bob Sr. walked in with an intense look on his face and the room grew quiet, waiting on what he was going to say. He circled the long conference table that we were sitting around making stern eye contact with everyone, including his three sons.

"As he returned to his starting point near the door he stopped and finally spoke. 'I suppose you are pretty full of yourselves right now,' and then his booming voice rising in volume accompanied by his big fist slamming down on the table in unison with that last word he explained, 'A true champion repeats!'

"With that he walked out of the meeting room. Bob Jr. looked around with a semi-amazed look on his face and said, 'We can't even enjoy this for five minutes. You heard my old man; now let's get back to work.'

"Not only did we receive word from Ford Motor Company that we had indeed earned the highest CSI score in the world for any Ford or Lincoln-Mercury dealer, we did in fact repeat as Volume and CSI Champions in 1987. True champions, just like the way we were."

The Sam Walton Story

"Uncle Gene" De Graide was probably one of Bob Tasca's best friends. They met quite a few years ago (1963) when Gene purchased a new Fairlane from Tasca Ford. Then, in the early 1970s, Bob Sr. and Tasca Lincoln-Mercury were advertising locally on station WJAR. De Graide and Bov did a weekly radio show called the "Tasca Times," which was quite popular in the Greater Boston area. With Bob being first a mechanic as well as a salesman he offered advice and came up with viable solutions that would help his listeners.

When Gene De Graide decided to retire, Bob posed the question, "Well, Gene, what are you going to do now that you've retired?" Gene really didn't have an answer to that question, so Bob quickly followed up with yet another question, "Gene, why don't you come to work for me?"

Of course, Uncle Gene retorted, "I don't know anything about selling cars!"

Tasca replied, "No! You're too personable to be selling cars. I would like you to become my greeter. When people come in, you greet them, they tell you what they want, and then you direct them to a salesperson or a manager or send them to whatever department they need."

For more than 30 years, Gene De Graide served as greeter at Tasca L-M and, later, Tasca Ford's official greeter. People liked him and he was a great conversationalist. One day a man walked into Tasca L-M, and Gene asked if he could help him. The man immediately figured that Gene was trying to sell him a new car. "Oh no, no, no! I'm not here to buy a car."

Uncle Gene says, "Well, I'm not trying to sell you a car, I'm just a greeter."

The man says, "A greeter? That sounds very interesting. What is it you do?"

De Graide replied, "Well, I meet people when they walk in like I did with you. I try to find out what they're looking for and then I move them along to wherever it is they want to go."

The man says, "You know, that's great. Is Bob Tasca Sr. here? I would like to meet with him."

De Grade inquired, "Can I tell him who's asking for him?"

The man said, "Tell him it's Sam Walton!"

At first, De Graide took a step backward and said "Sam Walton?" By then Uncle Gene had recognized him because Sam Walton was relatively short. He was a pretty casual guy. He wore a baseball cap and a pair of jeans. Walton was taking a look at a piece of property in Seekonk where he intended to build a Sam's Club, which was a relatively new deal at the time. Seekonk already had a Wal-Mart. The gentleman who owned the property was a man named Fred Darling; the two were going to meet to talk about Walton's company leasing the property for 99 years.

When Walton was talking to some of his automotive friends in Detroit, they said, "You know, one of our best Lincoln-Mercury dealers is there in Seekonk, Massachusetts. Why don't you look him up?"

They knew Sam liked to visit with businesspeople and anybody in the community who was doing a good job. Sam Walton was always looking for ideas and he wanted to meet with them, according to then Tasca L-M Sales Manager Mike Perlini.

"Long story short, Sam Walton met with Bob. I remember when Uncle Gene walked him in he whispered, 'That's Sam Walton,' to which I said, 'Oh my goodness! *The* Sam Walton from Wal-Mart?' and he said, 'Yes!'

"Sam Walton and Bob Sr. spent about 40 minutes together talking about this and that. After he left, Mr. Tasca was kind of shaking his head and said, 'You know what he asked me? He thought it would be a great idea to have a greeter in his stores and wanted to know if I would mind if he adopted the concept and used it in his stores.'"

Sam Walton's idea to use greeters in Wal-Mart stores worldwide was from an idea given him by Bob Tasca Sr. A few years ago, Mike Perlini had a Wal-Mart manager turn in a lease vehicle, and Mike told him the story. The guy said, "Oh, that's interesting."

"You could tell that he really didn't believe me. Then he says, 'That's about the time [early 1990s] when the greeters went in. He actually got that from Bob Tasca?'

"I said, 'Yes!'"

"About a month later he was at a big Wal-Mart manager's meeting and he called me up and said that he talked to a number of people from Wal-Mart and they all said that [all] they remembered was that Sam had met with a car dealer [they didn't mention Mr. Tasca's name specifically] and said that he got the idea from a car dealer!"

Witnessing the Business Model that was Tasca L-M

In 1996, Bob Tasca Sr. and co-author Peter Collins wrote a book titled "U WILL B SATISFIED" (Harper Books, a division of HarperCollins Publishers). It covered Bob Sr.'s philosophy about sell-

Balls Over the Walls

Tasca Lincoln-Mercury was, and Tasca Useful Cars (or "Tasca East" as it is officially known) is still located at 200 Fall River Avenue, which just so happens to be located right next door to Seekonk, Massachusetts's Firefly Golf Course. Errant golf balls were always something of a problem ever since the grand opening of the dealership, even though the tee on the driving range was pointing in the opposite direction.

Nonetheless, errant golf balls seemed to find their way onto the lot, and there were quite a few close calls as well as damage done to cars. Fortunately, no Tasca customer or employee ever got beaned with one.

Eventually, the management at Tasca L-M started to draw "smiley faces" on the golf balls and throw them back.

ing cars, service, and customer satisfaction, citing numerous real-life instances that occurred throughout the Bopper's storied career. The book became a top seller (with proceeds donated to St. Rocco's School, Johnston, Rhode Island) and became a veritable "bible" for anyone who was serious about pursuing a career in automotive sales.

The book became so popular that a dealer and management team from the island of Reunion (in the Indian Ocean) paid a visit to Tasca L-M in Seekonk just to see "the house that Tasca built" firsthand. In fact Ford dealers from Germany and Spain also sent representatives to the little L-M dealership in Seekonk to learn those principles that had made Tasca so successful.

On one such visit, a group of German Ford dealers walked in and took a look around. One of them declared, "Impossible! This can't be the real store!

You can't possibly do this much business out of this tiny little space. Where's the real store?" Upon visiting the Service Department, the reaction was pretty much the same.

One delegate commented, "You can't possibly service 3,000 new car sales out of only nine service bays. In Germany, we need 54 bays to do that much work!"

In essence, Tasca L-M was six times more efficient than the German operation! Pretty incredible business model, eh?

The Centennial Wreck

Georgia Institute of Technology's *Ramblin' Wreck* is a 1930 Model A Ford Cabriolet that has been the official mascot of the student body since the early 1960s. It has been present at all the major sporting events and student body functions. In actuality, there have been a number of *Ramblin' Wrecks* beginning as far back as 1916. However, the most famous of them all is the 1930 Model A Ford Cabriolet, which is mechanically and financially maintained on campus by students from the Ramblin' Reck Club.

The phrase "often imitated, never duplicated" comes to mind when speaking of this particular 1930 Model A Ford Cabriolet. It is currently owned, maintained, and displayed in the lobby at the Tasca Automotive Group's Cranston, Rhode Island, dealership. Officially, this car is known as the *Centennial Wreck* as it was built and used by Georgia Tech to celebrate its 100th Anniversary. It actually accompanied the original *Ramblin' Wreck* 1930 Model A Ford Cabriolet onto the tarmac at Bobby Dodd Stadium at historic Grant Field throughout the Yellow Jackets' 1985 football season.

Tuscaloosa, Alabama's Larry Fanning purchased Model A 372740 out of a junkyard in 1973 and drove the car for a number of years before performing a minor restoration job at his home garage. In February 1984 the A-Bone was sold to a group of Georgia Tech Alumni. Ford Atlanta (Hapeville, Georgia), Assembly Plant Manager Pete George had dedicated his life to Ford Motor Company, his family, and Georgia Tech and planned to donate the Model A to the school. Mustang restorer Tom Gattis was charged with assembling a team of five Atlanta Assembly Plant co-workers to orchestrate the restoration led by team leader R. T. McDaniel.

The car was completely disassembled; NOS Ford parts were ordered from outside vendors. Its body was completely stripped down to the bare metal and sent through the plant's Bond Rite E-Coat prime, paint, and clear-coat process. The interior trim was replaced with reproduction Model A trim using original factory patterns. Ford's X-Garage mechanic Ed Stone coordinated chassis restoration and final (re)assembly. After being inspected by project consultant R. T. McDaniel and certified to be a 100-percent technically correct restoration, the Model A was delivered to the Alexander Tharpe Fund Corporation at Georgia Tech on August 23, 1984.

In 1985 they entered the recently christened *Centennial Wreck* into the 18th Annual World of Wheels exhibition at the Georgia World Congress Center where it was declared the first-place winner in class.

In 1986 Georgia Tech raised more than $250,000 in raffle ticket sales with *Centennial Wreck,* and alumni Jeffery L. Parker was declared the winner. The Model A was kept in a garage until 1987, when Pete George repurchased the car and sent it back to the Ford Atlanta Assembly Plant (where the Mercury Sables were built). The car was cosmetically reconditioned and sat on display in the lobby for a number of years. When Pete George retired as plant manager in 1991, he decided to sell his prized Model A.

During one of his many visits, Bob Tasca Sr. saw the car and expressed a bit of nostalgia about old Fords and how he would like to have one. Just before Bob's 65th birthday (October 1, 1991) the Tasca family approached George about buying the car. When he found out that the car was going to be for Bob Tasca Sr. he felt honored. Bob Jr. was quoted as saying, "Dad said that the car looked pretty good, but that it ran like crap. He rebuilt the engine, the transmission, and rear axle. In fact, he rebuilt everything on the car except the windshield-wiper motor."

Bob Sr. may be gone but his prized Model A sits proudly on display in the lobby of the Tasca Automotive Group's Cranston, Rhode Island, dealership. It is a lasting tribute to the young boy from Rhode Island who fixed his first Ford (a Model A) at age six.

In Summary

On June 2, 2010, Ford Motor Company announced the cessation of the Mercury brand after a run of 71 years. When you consider that Tasca Lincoln-Mercury was in business for some 39 years, it stands as the oldest institution in the Tasca family, eclipsing the original Tasca Ford Sales by some 21 years. It still exceeds the combined (old and new) Tasca Ford businesses by (at this writing) a full two years.

Although the original Tasca Ford was widely recognized first and foremost as the "king" of high-performance Ford muscle car sales, Tasca L-M became the flagship dealer of Lincoln-Mercury Division worldwide. It re-established Lincoln and the upscale Mercury as "status cars" among the American motoring public. While the Tasca Automotive Group's Cranston super dealer continues to sell Lincolns, the former Tasca L-M dealership in Seekonk, Massachusetts, continues as a full-service facility (Ford, Mazda, and "Tasca Useful Used Cars") under the Tasca East banner.

TASCA

The Rebirth of Tasca Ford

The fall 1994 re-opening of 777 Taunton Avenue occurred for several reasons. When Bob Sr. was asked by Lee Iacocca to assume the reins of what became Tasca Lincoln-Mercury, it was with the proviso that Ford Division purchase Tasca Ford Sales, Inc. The actual sale of the dealership occurred in September 1971, and former Tasca Used Car Sales Manager–turned–current Tasca Ford Sales Manager Bob Crocker became its new leaseholder.

The fall 1994 grand re-opening of the remodeled Tasca Ford store back at the old 777 Taunton Avenue address was (to Rhode Island residents) like seeing an old friend for the first time in more than 20 years, which is exactly how long it had been since the name Tasca (note the updated sign) had been on the building. That's the last production 1965 Shelby GT350 (SFM 5S409) parked in front of the east door. (Photo Courtesy Howard Pardee & June Veader, SAAC)

148   The Tasca Ford Legacy

CHAPTER Five

The agency was renamed Crocker Ford, Inc., and it continued to operate at the now-famous 777 Taunton Avenue address. However, Crocker Ford eventually pulled up stakes and moved down the street to 500 Taunton Avenue. Sometime later, Bob Crocker passed away after an illness. Then a local automotive family by the name of Fournier, who owned and operated the local American Motors dealership, purchased Crocker Ford and moved it back to 777.

The enterprise that became known as Fournier Ford was unsuccessful, and the dealership was forced to close. It is company policy for Ford Motor Company to step into business situations like this to protect its market-share holdings, and 777 became a company "store" known as East Ford. Although nothing has been finalized as of this writing, there are other changes in various stages of negotiation. One of them is the acquisition of Berlin, Connecticut's Morande Ford, a medium-size Ford dealership located several miles south of Hartford. How big the Tasca Automotive Group will become is anybody's guess but two things are certain: Tasca will always work tirelessly to ensure their customers' complete satisfaction, and they will always strive toward the ultimate goal of the Tasca family, which is to be able to say, "None Bigger, None Better!"

It is generally agreed that this was about when Ford began talking to Bob Sr. about re-acquisition. Bob could see that his ever-growing family, which now included five grandsons (Bobby III, Carl II, David II, Michael, and Nicholas) and four granddaughters (Jaime, Carrie, Nicole, and Rebecca), couldn't possibly all work together at Tasca Lincoln-Mercury, so he warmed up to the idea of reopening 777. Of course, Bob's ruffled pride and disappointment in seeing his "baby" go from the second-most-successful Ford dealership in the nation to last in customer satisfaction ratings and the lowest in sales volume among the seven Providence Area Ford dealers could not go without comment.

> **"Tasca will always work tirelessly to ensure their customers' complete satisfaction, and they will always strive toward the ultimate goal of the Tasca family, which is to be able to say, "None Bigger, None Better!""**

"While my little Lincoln-Mercury dealership just down the road in Seekonk went from nothing to number one under my business agenda, 777 went from number one to bankruptcy under the traditional businesspeople's agenda. What made this turn of events even stranger is that my business practices have never been a secret. I've regularly run seminars for Ford Motor Company dealers since the late 1950s. What I've done has been an open book. Hence the operators at 777 could have easily followed my formula. They chose not to, and the results speak for themselves. I've agreed to take back the Ford store so that the next generation of Tascas have room to grow in the business."

Although the entire Tasca family became involved with both stores, which was the root of Tasca's hands-on business philosophy, Bob Sr., Carl Sr., and Bob III worked on the "777 Project" while Bob Jr. and David Sr. remained at the Lincoln-Mercury store. In addition to the Tasca family members, holdovers from the Fournier Ford era included Dave Laliberty, who was hired to continue his role as Sales

With Tasca's acquisition of Ford-owned Volvo in 2001, the 777 Taunton Avenue and 200 Fall River Avenue (Seekonk) stores were both basically one-brand dealerships. The need arose for expansion and, ultimately, an all-new mega-dealership was located at 1300 Pontiac Avenue (yes "Pontiac"), Cranston, Rhode Island. Shown here at the August 2001 ground-breaking ceremony are (left to right): David Tasca Sr., Carl Tasca Sr., Bob Tasca Jr., Bob Tasca III, Bob Tasca Sr., Rhode Island Governor Lincoln Almond, former Rhode Island governor Bruce Sundlund, and Cranston Mayor Michael A. Traficante.

Chapter Five: The Rebirth of Tasca Ford

TASCA

Two full years were required to complete this multi-million-dollar project. This beautiful night shot of the Tasca Automotive Group's 165,000-square-foot facility certainly does the place justice. Styled by former Ford Land Architectural Design and Development chief Sadd Chehab, the design is modular so that it can continuously be added upon.

Manager. Bob "Yeager" Andreozzi (a previous employee and longtime friend of Bob Jr.'s) came back to serve as Carl's right-hand man. Many other East Ford employees, some holdovers from the Fournier Ford days, were retained along with current and past Tasca Ford/Tasca L-M employees, who were all blended into one happy "family."

The Evolution of "777"

Over the years, the 777 Taunton Avenue property has undergone a number of changes and revisions. The 1961 expansion program was the first. Then, in the late 1970s, Bob sold off a corner of the property to McDonald's Corporation (which still operates a store at that location) that *may* have had something to do with the Crocker Ford move. Bob Sr. later commented, "We reopened the re-modeled store in October 1994. Eight months later (June 1995) we'd built the Ford store up to where it ranked number one in customer satisfaction, and number two in sales volume."

Tasca Ford's growth cycle continued throughout the remainder of the decade. The company's multibrand acquisition process initially began with Volvo in 2001, according to Mike Perlini. "Bob Sr. could see the direction Ford Motor Company was headed. For him, if it was a Ford Motor Company brand, then he was all for it. The interesting thing about the Volvo acquisition was that the people who owned the 'Auto Show' Volvo franchise walked into our showroom at 200 Fall River Avenue in Seekonk. They wanted to sell their dealership and came see if Tasca was interested.

"As an ex-Volvo salesman I knew who those people were. I went over to Bob Jr. and asked him what it was all about. He told me that the father was sick, the son didn't want to run the business, and that the family wanted to sell it. I asked him if he was interested. Bob Jr. said, 'No, my father would kill me. Volvo? That hasn't got anything to do with Ford.'

"I said, 'Thank you for considering us but we're not interested.'

"It was about a year or so later that Ford bought Volvo. I went into Bob Jr.'s office with a copy of *Automotive News* and said, 'Ford bought Volvo.'

"He said, 'Yeah, I know. I've already called up the Leonard family and told them if they haven't sold the dealership we would be interested in talking to them again.'

"It wasn't too long after that that we acquired the Volvo franchise. Prior to that, Bob Sr. would not have approved of us buying a franchise that was not within the Ford family. He always felt like he had a long-term marriage with Ford and he didn't want to cheat on them!"

However, the addition of Volvo posed something of a logistical problem as both the Seekonk store and "777" were essentially "one-horse," or single-brand, operations. With the completion of Tasca's new Cranston, Rhode Island, mega-dealership located at 1300 Pontiac Avenue, that problem was solved.

Tasca's New Super Dealership

Bob Tasca III said, "I think the decision to build the dealership in Cranston, to expand to that level, was really a testament to how much my grandfather, my father, and my uncles believed in the third generation of Tascas. In most businesses, it's very rare to see a first and second generation continue successfully, although it happens. It's almost impossible to see a second and third generation be half as successful, or even successful at all, to be quite frank.

"When it came to the Tasca family [at the time] everything was paid for. They had no mortgages. It was a testament to the confidence they had in us because the last thing they needed was to take on a $15 million mortgage. To move a successful business to a different location and basically start from scratch from rebuilding cash and growing what they already had. As the oldest of the third generation, I had great belief in my brother, my sister, and my cousins. I knew the only way we were going to continue to grow as a family was to reposition the operation and give us more opportunity for growth.

"That is what really drove the whole decision. It was a lot of responsibility. I mean, at the time I had pretty much just gotten out of college and here we're moving a huge, huge operation to a new facility. It was a massive undertaking. That really is what started the 'run,' I would call it, of the Tasca Family Automotive Growth.

"At the present, the Tasca Automotive Group facility covers just under 17 acres. The architect who designed this building was Sadd Chehab. Sadd is currently the president of Chrysler-Lancia, which is the brand's name in Europe, but at that time he was the head of Ford Land Architectural Design and Development. Working so closely with him on this project, I realized how dynamic he was. He had a great, great relationship with my father and my grandfather. My grandfather really loved talented young people. He gravitated to them. He knew that they were the wave of the future.

"It was really a lot of fun. We called him 'Blank Check Chehab.' If you walk through the building, you'll see that no cost has been spared. It was like a Niagara Falls with thousand-dollar bills going over it. For example, the building is a very intelligent design. It's modular so that we could add on 'pods.' In fact, we're just about to add a brand-new Lincoln showroom to one end of it."

At the inception of the Cranston facility, Ford was moving in the direction of the Premium Auto Group concept. They had Lincoln, Aston-Martin, Jaguar, Volvo, and Mazda, all considered premium-brand marques. The conventional wisdom behind the building of these large facilities was to feature interior appointments, or "styling cues," which would reflect the character of each of these Ford brands. Bobby III worked hand-in-hand with key people at Ford Design to come up with a place that had that brand-indicative "feeling."

For example, on the Ford side, in the showroom [which features highly polished dark texture floor tile and is painted in traditional "Ford Blue" colors], you find a lot of lifestyle posters, an American flag, and a huge "Mustang" running horse on the walls. On the [current] Lincoln side, which is meant to be the luxury side, you have light-colored tile on the floors, high ceilings, and very luxurious interior appointments. The transition between the showrooms is marked by well-appointed hallways, which are decorated with numerous awards and framed copies of magazine articles on the Tasca family, their dealerships, and their past and present racing programs.

Then of course, there's Bob Sr.'s beloved 1930 Model A Cabriolet, which is parked across from Bobby III's NHRA National record-holding Top Alcohol funny car. The waiting room in the service area is done up in highly polished black tile; the furniture is as nice as you'll find in some hotel lobbies, and quite comfortable. If you're hungry you don't have to go far, as the deli-style Tas-Cafe on the upper level features some of the finest food and pastries you'll find anywhere.

Yup, you read it right! This is the plaque placed near that beautiful fountain, known as Lake Force, in honor of the World's Greatest Drag Racer, John Force.

Just completed and ready for move-in day, Tasca Cranston represents the Tasca family's belief in the third-generation Tascas: Bobby III, Carl Jr., David Jr., Mike, Jaime, and all their children.

This picture of the patriarchs of the Tasca family, Robert F. Tasca Sr. and his wife, Josephine, was taken shortly after the grand opening of Cranston. What a legacy the "Bopper" and Mrs. Tasca have forged.

Even the executive offices feature this concept. Mr. Tasca's office (which is now Bob Jr.'s office) emulates the Aston-Martin theme. Its door has the metallic look of titanium. The desk is a highly engineered and polished mechanical framework with a glass top. The walls are a rich saddle color with a black floor covering. All of these things are brand elements of Aston-Martin.

The next office down the hall is David Sr.'s and it is obviously Ford themed, using various elements of Ford blue.

Bobby III's office is Volvo themed, using a different shade of blue and light-colored wood. All brand elements of the Volvo franchise.

Carl Sr.'s office incorporates the Jaguar theme. It uses medium-tone woods and Jaguar Green carpet.

Carl Jr.'s office uses red Mazda colors and is meant to emulate the Mazda brand.

Hitting on All Eight Cylinders

Bobby III said, "Those acquisitions and the accompanying growth factor have really put the third generation of Tascas in a position to win. As an owner of a growing company I really have to put our team in a position to win. I take a lot of responsibility in making that commitment. Cranston was a big part of the commitment they [family] have made in us when they opened up their checkbook and made a big investment in our future.

"To make one of these kinds of operations run, you just can't be good in one area, you have to be [to use the drag racing vernacular] hitting on all eight cylinders. Clearly, we've worked very, very hard to make Cranston a success and continue to grow the family business. We have talented people. I'm blessed to have had an amazing supporting cast around me: my grandfather, my father, my uncles, and my cousins.

"I take a special role in the third generation, being the oldest one, having spent the most amount of time [in the business] with my grandfather, father, and uncles. Now my cousins, brothers, and sisters are getting involved and I'm really proud how they have performed in the family business. I spend a lot time with them and I don't take for granted all the time my grandfather, my father, and my uncles spent with me. I've spent that same time with them,

The Tasca Ford Legacy

This is an inside view of the "Ford side" of the Tasca Automotive Group showroom in 2013. It was taken through the conference room window on the executive level; the same room where Tasca's Mike Perlini instructs would-be salespeople at Tasca University.

Tasca Cranston is an automotive shopping mall carrying many brands including Ford, Ford Trucks, Lincoln, Volvo, Mazda, Jaguar, and Aston-Martin vehicles plus Ford Motorcraft, Tasca Parts, and Tasca Mobile Service. The list just goes on and on.

Chapter Five: The Rebirth of Tasca Ford

The "Big Day" in More Ways Than One!

By Bob Tasca III

The day before my son Robert F. Tasca IV was born [August 9] I went to work that morning and said to my wife, "Whatever you do, don't have the baby this weekend" because we were opening the dealership the following Monday, August 12.

I'm up on a lift installing the last phone antenna for our wireless telephone system and my wife calls and says, "I'm going into labor."

I said, "Well, I'm literally in the middle of opening the dealership."

She said, "Don't worry; it'll be awhile. I'll keep you posted."

I finished working that day and rushed to the hospital. They thought I was the doctor when I literally ran through the door. That's how close I cut it but I was able to see my son born. When he came home from the hospital we brought him by the dealership. I'll never forget it. There was my grandfather, my father, and me all together for the first time. I remember my grandfather appointed him "Chairman of the Board, 2033!" It was amazing how much happened in that period of time!

However, for Bobby III there were also a lot of sleepless nights, as a lot of things didn't go right during the build.

We missed our opening date a number of times as delays in the construction kept pushing it back. It was a lot of work and very, very stressful. The construction of Cranston was a grueling two-year project to get completed. Then we had to make the move and go from an operation that was a stand-alone Ford store to suddenly selling Fords [cars and trucks], Mazdas, Lincolns, Mercurys, Volvos, and pre-owns all under the same roof.

We call it the "campus concept." We took every process that we had and threw it out the window. From how we run Fixed Operations, to how we run an office, how we run sales, having multiple sales managers all in the same building. It was a major, major undertaking.

Around that time, I [also] started to go racing. I started to put together an NHRA Top Alcohol funny car team. Subsequently, the racing is what got me into the Ford Motorcraft parts business and we bought the building behind us. That was an interesting conversation with my Uncle Carl, who is treasurer.

We had just got finished building one of the largest Ford dealerships in all of New England and spent the most money that my family's ever spent in 50 years on this new facility. Less than two years later I went to him and said, "We need to buy the building behind us because I ran out of room in our parts department in the new building."

Obviously, he believed in the vision that I wanted to sell more [Ford Motorcraft] parts and he knew I needed more room, so we acquired the building directly behind us. That was in 2004. About six years later we outgrew that building and bought a 55,000-square-foot building about five miles up the road.

teaching them what I know, and they've certainly taught me an awful lot along the way. It's been pretty cool for me to see my brother, Michael, my sister, Jaime, my cousins Carl Jr. and David Jr. really thrive in the Tasca culture.

"I use this line, and I don't use it lightly, when I sign all of my e-mails, 'The best is yet to come!'"

A Mazda for the Bopper

Bob Sr. was involved with the Mazda-derived Lincoln Mercury CX9 crossover SUV project from the very beginning. He really loved that kind of vehicle. When Mazda was about to come out with the CX9 seven-passenger Crossover SUV, a number of the company's top engineers came to the dealership and asked him for advice. Bob Sr. thoroughly dissected the prep-production "mule" they brought with them. He showed them a number of different things that he would improve upon and made suggestions.

As such, he felt that he had taken a hands-on role in the final engineering phase of that vehicle. As Bob always appreciated a fine vehicle, he was eager to drive the production version. He felt the car was very smooth. It had a very responsive suspension. It had very responsive braking, and its 273-hp V-6 engine definitely drew from Mazda's extensive racing heritage.

So, Bob Sr.'s last daily driver became a Mazda CX9. He was once asked, "Why are you driving a Mazda?" His answer was, "Because the G.D. thing is better engineered than anything we make over at Ford!" He loved his Mazda CX9. It's all he drove until the very end!

Becoming Fast Friends

Although Henry Ford II and Bob Tasca Sr. were longtime friends and business associates, Bob Jr. and brothers Carl and David didn't get to know Henry's son Edsel II until sometime in 1970. Sure, they had met Edsel II a couple of times as kids while accompanying their father to Dearborn, but it wasn't until they became teenagers that they really forged a lasting friendship.

Bob Jr.: The first time I met you was at [the original] Tasca Ford. You were driving a candy apple red 1970 Boss 302 with black interior, and I don't know what the heck we were doing to it. I just said to Bob [McClurg] we were all a lot younger, and our hair was a lot longer!

Edsel II: You know [laughing], that's true! I was just thinking about that this morning. That was quite a long time ago. I think it was around 1970. I was at Babson College. I remember coming to the store at 777 Taunton Avenue. My car needed to have some work done to it and I had called someone at Ford. They said, "Call Bob Tasca Jr. He's about your age and he will take good care of you." I think that's how we met.

Bob Jr.: I remember that. My father was so involved with Ford Motor Company that every once in a while he thought he was a Ford. We used to say, "Dad, your last name's Tasca." As I have a great relationship with you, my father used to have a great relationship with your father, Henry II. It's been generation after generation, a long, long time.

Edsel II: I can remember meeting and talking with your father. He would tell me that he had been to some assembly plant somewhere in the Ford world and had sat down with the plant manager and had given him some pointers. I know your dad loved going out to the plants and I know the company loved having him visit. I think it was a feeling of mutual respect. Your father did a lot for our manufacturing system for Ford in the early days, and yes, he was a good pal of my father's!

Bob II: I remember the time right before you left Boston and went to work for Ford of Australia. You arranged a meeting at your father's office. I remember there was Carl, David, my father, you, and me. We met with your dad in his office. I'll never forget how cordial he was.

We were talking, he made coffee, and my brother David said, "Mr. Ford, do you have tea?"

Your father's answer was classic. "You want tea? Okay, I can press a button and have someone get it, but I'll make the tea for you myself."

Mr. Ford got up and actually made tea for my brother David.

I said kind of frustrated, "Why the hell can't you just drink coffee?"

Edsel II: Your father always had a unique way of doing things. I thought the blueprint concept was really a terrific idea!

Bob Jr.: He took that concept to the assembly plants. He was very well respected and I can honestly say that he really helped the Ford Motor Company appreciate fit and finish.

Edsel II: There's no doubt about it. I know that all our plant managers, the ones I knew pretty well like Pete George at the Atlanta, Georgia, plant, really appreciated working with him.

Bob Jr.: Pete George is the one who sold us the Model A. We gave it to our father when he turned 65. That's the car Ford Motor Company rebuilt on the assembly line. That car actually went down the assembly line. It even went through E-Coat!

You know, the Ford family is a very special family in our lives. My father's lifetime ambition was to become a Ford dealer and he became a damned good one.

My father was a character just like your father was and they got along famously!

Edsel II: I remember we went to a few drag races together at New England Dragway. There was also a lot of interaction with the crew, (the late) Bill Lawton, John Healey, Dean Gregson, and the rest of the guys. In fact, I just got a very nice e-mail from Dean Gregson, just checking in to say "Hello."

I knew the Tascas at so many different points in my life and career, from when I was a college student at Babson, when I came back to become the Assistant Managing Director at the Boston Regional Office. When I had my official Ford Motor Company hat on, I used to call on the Tascas, so there were a lot of interesting times when I interfaced with Bob Jr. and the entire family. We've been friends for 40 years, and it's always been an interesting relationship.

The Up-and-Coming Generation: Tasca Grandkids

Carl A. Tasca Sr. once humorously commented, "There are only so many dogs that can eat off the same bone. Ultimately, you need less dogs, or a bigger bone!"

A new era in Tasca Automotive history began when Bob III (son of Bob

---

Cranston Stats

- Original square footage of the dealership, first and second levels: 165,000 sq. ft.
- New Lincoln showroom addition: 5,859 sq. ft.
- Square footage of back building: 55,000 sq. ft. Tasca Truck Center, Body Shop, Dyno Shop, and Museum
- Square footage of off-site parts building: 58,000 sq. ft.

Here's how the ratio worked out: 60 percent was taken up by Service Inc. and Fixed Ops; 40 percent was taken up by new- and used-car sales.

With the opening of the Cranston facility, 777 Taunton Avenue sat vacant for a number of years before being sold to Scott Volkswagen. The building has been extensively remodeled and bears little resemblance to the original Tasca Ford Sales agency of old.

Tasca University

Tasca University Dean of Instruction Mike Perlini teaches the "Tasca Way" to properly deal with people while succeeding in the profession of selling cars. Tasca U's six-week classes in groups of three to four per year cover virtually every facet of selling automobiles. And I mean every subject under the sun.

When Ford Motor Company gave a party (1993) at the Henry Ford Museum in Dearborn, Michigan, to celebrate Bob Sr.'s fiftieth anniversary as a dealer with the Ford Motor Company, Chairman Harold "Red" Poling cited the fact that over those five decades, "Tasca University" had trained 165,000 people for Ford.

Of course, this is not to imply that Tasca University (a term first used by Bob Sr. in the late 1960s) has its own campus with ivy-covered walls and a championship-winning collegiate football team, although they do have a couple of strong drag racing programs. Red Polling's reference was based on the much broader concept and was referring to the sum total of sales training programs and high-performance seminars Bob Sr. had instituted, conducted, and participated in on behalf of Ford-Lincoln Mercury, for the benefit of Ford companywide.

Tasca University holds three or four classes per year with a curriculum covering the correct way, or Tasca Way, of selling automobiles. The classes take place at Tasca Automotive Group's Cranston, Rhode Island, facility. Tasca's Dean of Instruction is Mike Perlini, who was also the informational liaison for me during the writing and production of this book.

"I had the opportunity to meet Bob Sr. in 1985. Having grown up in this area, I had gone down to the [Ford] dealership many times just to look at the race cars and the muscle cars on the lot. So, for me to be interviewed for a job by Bob Sr. for three hours? Well, let's just say I came out of that interview walking three feet off the ground because when it came to the automotive business, Bob Tasca was a legendary figure. That was 28 years ago."

Regarding Tasca University, the realization was that a lot of salespeople never really received proper training when they started off in the business. Many of them learned "it" from other salespeople who had the time to teach them, and they were typically the least productive salespeople. What they learned was how to sell the minimum number of vehicles and complain a lot.

"When you hire new sales consultants you can hire either inexperienced people or people with experience. Inexperienced people you can train. Some of the experienced people you hire have baggage. Experience is okay but baggage is not good. Baggage is the accumulation of bad habits that they develop over the years, and baggage is what gives the automotive sales industry such a bad name. We developed a more focused approach to training that, depending on the individual, can take from two to three months to complete."

Program Beginnings

"Our current training program came from a meeting our ownership and management team had with representatives from BZ Results. That company started as a website-development company called BZ Productions whose principals were Adam De Graide, Sean Wolfington, and Bob Tasca III. They showed their website templates at the NADA [National Automobile Dealers Association] convention, and quite a few dealers asked them to come into their stores and show them more. What the dealers realized is that effective websites could supercharge their showroom traffic counts. However, as one dealer told them, 'The additional traffic sounds great but what worries me is that we do not do a good job of handling the traffic we have now. What are we going to do with the additional traffic that our website is going to generate?'

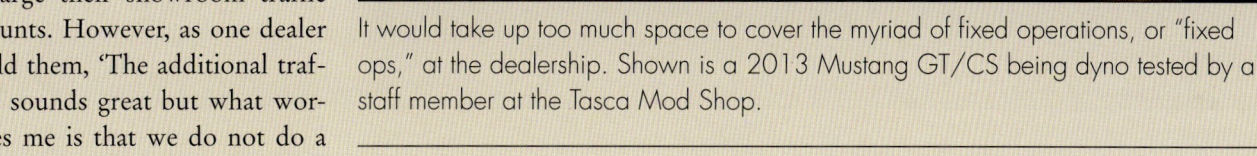

It would take up too much space to cover the myriad of fixed operations, or "fixed ops," at the dealership. Shown is a 2013 Mustang GT/CS being dyno tested by a staff member at the Tasca Mod Shop.

"Sales training has been around for quite some time but most of it has an essential flaw. The trainer comes in to install his program and while he or she is there it's Rah! Rah! and there is lots of excitement for a short time. Then, after they leave, the situation usually reverts back to the way it was before. This is due in part to the fact that in most dealerships most managers have relatively strong, well-developed egos. They believe that they already know the right way to do things and that the trainer's way of doing things was, after all, his way, not 'our' way.

"Bob Tasca III and his partners at Tasca Automotive Group realized this so they decided to go about things differently. Our owners and managers were off-site for three days with facilitators from BZ Results. BZ training reps had a general outline and they facilitated conversations among us. They threw out questions such as:

- What do you consider the most important aspects of your training program?
- What principles do you strongly believe should make up the underpinning of your program?
- Do you think a mission statement that clearly communicates your beliefs and business agenda is important?
- How do you want to state it?
- What process do you deem essential in the way you handle every customer who comes into your store?

"Those were not all the questions they posed but I think you get the idea. What we ended up with was a program we created ourselves, signed off on by all the owners and all the managers. It included fixed-operations managers as well as sales, finance, and office managers. We had the blueprint going forward and it was our program, specifically designed by and for us."

Training Elements

"Our hiring process is rooted in inspiration, not desperation; it is continuous as is the training. We process three or four training groups per year so that we can supply our showrooms with trained eager consultants who can fill the demand from our sales managers regardless of whether that demand arises due to retirement, resignation, or replacement. Coverage is important in any sales environment and our continuous training program ensures adequate coverage for all our locations."

Company History and Business Philosophy

"We begin training with Tasca Culture, in which we take all trainees through our company's history and indoctrinate them into Bob Tasca's business philosophy, which

Tasca University CONTINUED

Shown is the 58,000-square-foot Tasca Parts warehouse located five miles away from the Tasca Automotive Group. This building addition became an absolute necessity with the explosive growth of the Tasca Parts and Ford Motorcraft Parts operations.

was, as he stated so many times: 'I've never planned the bottom line, I only planned the top lines, which are how do I sell and service more vehicles [volume] and how do I satisfy my customers once I have them. I figured if I could do that, the bottom line would take care of itself.'

"This may sound strange but we really don't teach people how to sell a car to customers. Rather, we teach them how to help our customers buy a car from us. I know that Bob Tasca always strived to do things *for* his customers and he never would do things *to* his customers. I also remember Bob teaching us to focus on all things leading up to the sale and not the sale itself. As noted sales trainer Joe Verde once put it, 'The sale is the end result and you don't just focus on the end result, you first must focus on all the things that produce that end result.'"

Professionalism

"We spend a lot of time in our training teaching professionalism, the 10-step selling process, and product certification as well as effective prospecting techniques, things that should be mastered if you expect to become a productive and consistent sales consultant. During every facet of our training we make sure trainees understand the whats, the whys, and the hows. *What* we want you to do, *why* we want you to do it, and *how* to do it. So in addition to traditional classroom work we incorporate role-playing and video role-playing as well."

Finance Terms

"Another point of emphasis is our Pre Trade, or short-term cycle, plan. While our industry has turned to longer finance terms as a way to keep customers' payments within their budgets on the constantly escalating prices of the vehicles that we sell, we believe that shorter finance terms on new vehicles benefit everyone. Our customers drive more cars, more often, for less, and in most cases under the protective umbrella of the factory bumper-to-bumper warranty.

"Our dealership has renewal opportunities with our customers after two to three years. Manufacturers can build more cars over the same time than if each customer had to keep their vehicles for longer periods due to five- or six-year finance terms. Here at Tasca we believe that the lowest cost of driving is our Pre Trade program.

"Because of the novelty of offering affordable payments to our customers for shorter, not longer, terms [24 to 39 months] our sales consultants must be very knowledgeable on this subject. It really is not something new, as Bob

Tasca piloted this program for Ford Motor Company in the early 1980s with the concept's creator Eustace Wolfington. Consumer questions remain and our consultants must be trained to answer those questions and satisfy any concerns our customers may have."

Department Interaction

"The final piece of the training puzzle is experiential. I think in order to get our sales consultants to work cooperatively with all the other people in the dealership it is helpful if they 'walk a mile in their shoes,' so they spend some time working with service advisors, parts counter people, and prep department people, all areas where they will have to interact once they become sales consultants. Gaining insight into those job functions and getting to know the people who perform those functions is a big part of creating and maintaining that necessary chemistry among people and departments."

Mystery Shop

"The other component that Tasca U students experience during training is the Mystery Shop, where they visit local dealerships posing as a buyer so that they can feel what a consumer feels as they shop for a vehicle. They invariably come back with either horror stories about their experiences or praise for a professional experience. In either case as we discuss all their experiences it becomes apparent to them which behaviors they should emulate and which they should avoid."

Tasca on Profit

Bob Sr. used to say a lot of things. One of the things he used to say in relation to the training program was, "If you want to sell a lot of bread, make your profit a slice at a time. If you try and make it a loaf at a time, you won't sell as much bread."

Sales Confidence

"We tell our people, 'Look, it's going to take two years before you look in a mirror and really begin to feel as though you're getting good at this.' Two years because this is not an overnight business. This is not instant pudding!' Of course, some people begin selling well before they complete their first two years, but learning the nuances of negotiation and going through the various different experiences they have to go through on the journey to professionalism takes some time.

"Considering the money they can make in the automotive sales business [good salespeople easily make well over $50,000 per year], the two-year investment of time and effort to become a true professional is well worth it.

"I believe you cannot be competent in sales unless you are confident. And our training program was designed to instill that confidence in our sales consultant's ability to serve our customers with their transportation needs. It fits perfectly with Bob Sr.'s business philosophy on volume and customer satisfaction. And it creates a strong foundation for our trainees as they begin their careers. More important, it reinforces our founder's credo that when you buy from Tasca, 'You Will Be Satisfied!'"

Parked in the entranceway between the Ford and Lincoln showrooms is Bob Sr.'s beloved 1930 Model A Ford Cabriolet on one side and Bobby Tasca III's 5-second Top Alcohol funny car on the other.

Tasca, the third generation, from left to right: David J. Tasca Jr., Jaime Tasca-Frateschi, Michael J. Tasca, Carl A. Tasca Jr., and Bobby Tasca III. They continue to guide and shape the destiny of this huge enterprise.

Jr.), the oldest of the third generation of Tascas entered the business. Although Bob III was first, he was followed by his sister Jaime, his cousin Carl Jr., Bobby's brother Michael, and cousin David Jr.

You could call the entry of the Gen III Tasca offspring part of the "expansion." In 2001 the Volvo brand was added to the Tasca family fold. Then with the opening of the new Cranston store, Mazda joined in, followed by Jaguar and Aston Martin. The Tasca Automotive Group's product roster currently features Ford cars and trucks, Lincoln, Volvo, Mazda, Dodge-Chrysler, RAM, Jeep, and Nissan.

Michael Tasca is the principal dealer at Tasca Chrysler, Dodge, Jeep, RAM in Westerly, Rhode Island. Just like his older brother Bobby III, sister Jaime, and cousins Carl Jr. and David II, Mike was born into the automotive business and spent his summers doing hands-on training with his grandfather Bob Sr. and father Bob Jr. at the dealership. This Tasca worked his way through virtually every department prior to assuming the helm of the Tasca Automotive Group's first "non-Ford" automotive enterprise.

Tasca's latest acquisition is Tasca Nissan located at 845 Taunton Avenue, East Providence, Rhode Island, which is housed in what was the former home to "ex-next door neighbor" Dick Lorber Cadillac. This most recent acquisition occurred in June 2013. At the present, the entire Tasca organization is engaged in the restructuring of this new enterprise, with Carl Jr. and David Jr. acting as point men.

Tasca's Outdoor Ford Shows

In September 1998, Tasca Ford held its first outdoor Mustang & Live Music Event at 777 Taunton Avenue with John "Brute" Force as the featured guest. The autograph line extended completely around the dealership. In fact, John has appeared at 15 of the last 16 events, prompting many to call it "The John Force Car Show."

Over the years, other featured guests have included Bobby III, who annually "cackles" his 8,000-hp, Quick Lane Tire and Auto Center/Ford Motorcraft Parts Shelby GT500 Mustang for the fans, (the late) Bill Lawton, John Healey, Ralph Poirier, Billy Gilbert, and Dean Gregson.

Past event highlights have included the grand re-debut of the 1964 Tasca Ford Thunderbolt and 1968½ Tasca Ford Cobra Jet Mustang as well as corporate displays from Ford Racing, Ford Motorcraft, etc. The 2013 event unfolded September 7 and featured NHRA Fuel Funny Car celebrities John Force, Bobby III, and Tim Wilkerson. Also present were Carl Sr. and his 2010 Cobra Jet Mustang, the quickest and fastest CJ in the country. Admission was two canned goods to benefit the Rhode Island Food Bank.

Every September, usually the week after the U.S. Nationals at Indianapolis, the Tasca Automotive Group holds the Mustang & Live Music Event, a one-day outdoor car show featuring celebrities such as John Force, Bobby Tasca III, Tim Wilkerson, and other great names from Ford Racing history. Proceeds go to the Rhode Island Food Bank.

You like cool Fords? Tasca's got cool Fords! On the left is Carl's 7-second 2010 Cobra Jet Mustang and a passel of Cobras and Cobra replicas.

This is David Sr.'s 1966 Shelby GT350 (SFM 6S0050) that he has owned for more than 27 years. What a beautiful car.

Chapter Five: The Rebirth of Tasca Ford

2012 Boss 302 RFT Edition

To surprise Bob Jr. for his 60th birthday, Ford Motor Company and Ford Custom Accessories built this special one-off 2012 RFT Edition Boss 302 Mustang. It's a rocket!

To this day, Bob Jr. fondly remembers the Calypso Coral 1969 Boss 302 Mustang he drove some 44 years ago. To surprise him for his 60th birthday, Bob's friends at Ford Motor Company and Ford Custom Accessories built a special one-off 2012 Boss 302 Mustang especially for him and christened it the "RFT Edition."

Straight off the showroom floor, Ford's new second-generation Boss 302 Mustang is a very special car. Under the hood lies an 11.0:1-compression aluminum-block 5.0L four-valve Ti-VCT modular V-8 that features stainless-steel headers and boasting 444 hp and 380 ft-lbs. Backing it up is a 6-speed transmission and 3.73:1-geared limited-slip live rear axle. Big Burly Brembo disc brakes provide ample stopping power. A specially tuned race-bred suspension with adjustable front struts and rear shock absorbers ensures quick and nimble handling on street and track. This 2012 Boss 302 features Ford's special TracKey feature, which is a special key that really unleashes the power in the beast.

TracKey automatically tells the powertrain control module that the driver wants a competition-ready track experience. The TracKey engages software Ford calls TracMode. It alters more than 200 engine-management parameters, most noticeably an increase in low-end torque. It's like having a race mechanic in the key capable of taking a powerful street machine and tweaking it for the track.

As great as the new Boss 302 is in stock form, the RFT Edition is a one-of-a-kind version. From the moment it left Ford's Flat Rock, Michigan, Assembly Plant and rolled into the Ford Custom Accessory building, it signified the transformation into custom beauty. The Competition Orange paintwork is accented with Silver Pearlescent mirror caps and rear fascia appliqué.

A big boy and his toy. Bob Jr. proudly stands alongside his super fast Boss, which pumps out 444 hp and 380 ft-lbs of torque.

Custom side scoops, custom two-tone rear spoiler, and a special billet-aluminum grille add pizzazz. The black rear-window louvers (an original Boss 302 and Mach-1 styling cue) were added to provide a retro touch. The RFT Edition gets its ground-hugging appearance from the orange-accented black ground-effects kit. The crowning touch to the exterior comes from the fat 19-inch soft-compound Pirelli P-Zero sticky tires mounted on unique color-keyed wheels.

The folks at Ford Custom Accessories didn't just work their magic on the exterior. The interior is also pretty racy looking as well. The centerpiece is a pair of eye-popping white Recaro seats featuring competition orange stitching and embroidered "RFT" initials. The rest of the interior is black with white leather inserts in the doors. The dash and console feature white titanium trim. All of the gauges, including the special Laguna Seca Edition gauge pack, are accented with competition orange trim. Even the steering wheel is wrapped in white leather, another unique feature on the RFT Edition.

This is not the 1969 Boss 302 Bob Jr. drove so many years ago; this version might be even better. One thing is for sure, this one-of-a-kind Boss 302 made one heck of a birthday present!

Powering Tasca's Mustang is a 5.0L four-valve 11.0:1-compression Ti-VCT modular V-8 featuring factory Boss 302 intake, stainless-steel factory tubular headers, Tremec TKO 5-speed transmission, and 3.73:1 limited-slip live rear axle with TracKey feature.

The Boss rear taillight panel is titanium trimmed and features a distinctive Boss 302 deck spoiler. This is a bold look even for a low-production specialty car like the Boss 302 and is more than reminiscent of the tail-panel treatment on the original cars.

The specially appointed interior includes white leather Recaro seats with competition orange stitching and "RFT" initials. The rest of the interior is black leather with white inserts on the doors, titanium trim dash and console, leather-wrapped steering wheel, and special Laguna Seca Gauge Pack.

Bill Lawton Remembered

The 1995 *Super Stock* Magazine Drag Racing Hall Of Fame inductee and Tasca Ford super shoe, Bill Lawton, may no longer be with us (he passed away from the effects of cancer of the kidneys June 24, 1998) but his memory definitely lives on in the hearts of those who knew him best. William Perseverance Lawton Jr. was born August 9, 1940, to parents Christina Muri-Lawton and William P. Lawton Sr.

This autographed picture of Bill Lawton kneeling in front of his most famous ride, the Tasca Mystery Mustang, is particularly significant because it was originally signed by Bill back in the day (upper left). Later, in 2009, John Healey, Bob Sr., Bob Jr., Carl Sr., Bobby III, Dean Gregson, and well-known drag racing components manufacturer Sid Waterman signed it.

According to longtime friend and Tasca Racing Team Chief Mechanic John Healey, "Billy was a straight shooter and possessed a terrific sense of humor. He was a fun-loving guy who enjoyed pulling pranks on his friends. But when it came time to race, he could be as serious a competitor as there ever was!"

Throughout this book I have spoken much about family and sense of family, so it is only fitting that we hear from members of Bill Lawton's family to get their take on things. Recently I had the opportunity to sit down with Bill's wife of 36 years, Maddeline Di Biasio-Lawton, sons Todd and Christopher, and grandsons Christopher Jr. and William IV to record their thoughts.

Author: Maddeline, when did you and Bill first meet?

Maddeline Lawton: We met at Mount Pleasant High School. I invited Bill to my Sweet Sixteen party and we dated all the way through our senior year.

164   The Tasca Ford Legacy

CHAPTER Six

Author: So basically, you were high school sweethearts?
Maddeline Lawton: Yes!

Author: Was Bill your typical car-crazy kid back in those days?
Maddeline Lawton: Well, he had a 1950 Studebaker that had originally belonged to his grandfather. There was something wrong with the starter, so when he would pick me up from school he had to keep the engine running. He would honk, I would jump in, and away we would go!

Author: Jeez! That must have not set well with your parents?
Maddeline Lawton: No; they really liked Bill. My father really loved him. In fact toward the end of my father's life, he wouldn't ride with anyone else but Bill.

Author: Billy was in the National Guard wasn't he?
Maddeline Lawton: Yes. He worked as a clerk typist. Actually, he typed far better than I did!

> "Our youngest son Todd was born while Bill was out in California. I think he was at the NHRA Winternationals!"

Author: So after the Studebaker, did Bill have a series of hot rods?
Maddeline Lawton: Well, no, not like the traditional hot rod you would see driving around town. He had a 1957 Chevy, a 1958 Impala with a 348 engine. He had a 1960 Impala also with a 348 engine. He had a 1961 Corvette, and then he had a 1962 Impala convertible with the 409 engine. Those were *his kind* of hot rods.

Author: What did Bill say when Mr. Tasca gave him the ultimatum to go racing with him?

Maddeline Lawton: Oh, he was really excited. He came home and told me all about what all had happened. That was the beginning of it.

Author: Did the kids go to the races with him?
Maddeline Lawton: No, not at first. They were too young and I was too busy being "Mom" to go along with Bill. When Bill was racing for Tasca he traveled quite a bit. In fact, our youngest son Todd was born while Bill was out in California. I think he was at the NHRA Winternationals.
Todd Lawton: My father said if I was born a girl he was coming right back home. But if I was born a boy, he would wait because he already had two boys.

Author: Maddeline, how nervous were you about Bill getting hurt as these cars kept going faster and faster?
Maddeline Lawton: Very! I didn't want to go to the races with him because it was so dangerous.

Author: Was that while he was still racing with Tasca?
Christopher Lawton Sr.: My father wasn't ashamed to say it: The first time he drove *Mystery 9* it really scared the hell out of him. The car was so loud. He said it was like little bombs were going off inside his head. But once he got to the starting line, he lost all fear. It just went away.

Here's Billy all spruced up and ready for the high school prom of May 1957. Pretty snazzy, eh? Bill and his high school sweetheart Maddeline Di Biasio-Lawton tied the knot on January 27, 1962. They had three boys (William, Christopher, and Todd) and were married for 36 years. (Photos Courtesy Lawton Family)

Chapter Six: Bill Lawton Remembered

Author: Out of all of Tasca's cars, which one was your favorite?

Christopher Lawton Sr.: Of course *Mystery 9* is the car you hear the most about. But the Cobra Jet Mustang Super Stock car was my favorite. Maybe it's just because you could see those cars on the street and you could relate more to them.

Dad drove the Cobra Jet home one time. There was no passenger seat in it but we kept begging him to give us a ride. Finally he said, "Okay; you want a ride? Get in the car; I'll give you a ride!"

When he fired the thing up it blew out the neighbor's window because of the open headers. He pulled a small wheelie out in front of the house and we all rolled into the back of the trunk. We practically crapped our pants. We never asked him for another ride again.

Author: Maddeline, with three boys, I bet you must have had mixed emotions when Bill quit racing?

Maddeline Lawton: I felt sad for Bill because he loved racing so much but I was happy that he was back home again with the kids. They were about eight to ten years old when he quit, which was a very ideal time to have their father be home with them.

Author: I take it Lawton Moving and Storage is a family-run multi-generation business?

Maddeline Lawton: Yes. My father-in-law started the business, then Bill took over, and now my kids have it.

Christopher Lawton Sr.: Lawton Moving & Storage is located at 100 Crescent Avenue in Cranston. The warehouse is at 25 Frost Avenue in Warwick, Rhode Island, and our website is lawtonmoving.com.

Author: How many children do you have?

Maddeline Lawton: There's William, Christopher, and Todd. I also have four grandsons, William IV, Christopher II, Nicholas, and Conner.

Author: So was that the reason your father named his funny car *The Mover*?

Christopher Lawton Sr.: Actually, my father ran two different cars under that name. He had bought a car from Charlie Allen out in California, installed a Mustang on it, and named it *The Mover*. Then he had Rollie Lindblad (Lindblad Chassis) build him a brand-new car, a Ford Pinto with a Keith Black Racing Engines Chrysler in it. He had a bad fire with that car at Englishtown, New Jersey. After he got out of the car, he said to one of his crewman, 'I can't believe I still want to do this.' After he sold the Pinto to Al Hanna and Joe Mundet from the Revell Eastern Raider racing team, he said that he could never go back to another race again. It really bothered him; he just couldn't watch from the stands.

Author: Yes, but there was a financial aspect to that as well. In the tape that your father made before his passing, I remember him saying that if you didn't have a sponsor, you weren't going anywhere!

Todd Lawton: My father also said, 'When you're a winner and all of a sudden you become a loser it takes the heart right out of it!"

Author: Yes, Butch "California Flash" Leal, who raced Thunderbolts with your father on the Ford Drag Council, once commented, "Bill really hated getting beat." Speaking of Ford Thunderbolts, there's a story about the resurrection of your father's T-Bolt in Chapter Three of this book. Given the chance, if you found one of your father's old race cars, would you like to have it back in the family?

Christopher Lawton Sr.: Yeah, sure! The Grand Opening Car Show at 777 Taunton Avenue in 1994 was the first time I had seen that car. That thing was beautiful but the coolest thing about it was the fact that the guy who restored it still had the original ignition key, which was still on the original Tasca Ford key chain. The current owner of that car is a good guy. He invited us all down to his place to have lunch and sign the car. You just wouldn't believe the cars that he has in his collection!

Author: Actually, your father's Winternationals–winning 1965 427 SOHC Mustang A/FX car was found about 15 years ago, and it will be restored to the original "as raced" Tasca configuration.

Christopher Lawton Sr.: By the time they get the Mustang back together there probably won't be much left of the original car.

Author: No! Actually, that car is in amazingly good condition. In closing, how would you say having a famous father affected you when you were growing up?

Christopher Lawton Sr.: These guys [pointing to Bill and Maddeline's grandsons] can't appreciate it. But my whole life growing up I walked around with a Lawton Movers shirt on. I can't tell you how many times I've had people come up to me and start telling me stories about watching him race. It happens all the time.

Christopher Lawton Jr.: I was playing basketball and there was an old guy walking his dog and he noticed my sweatshirt. He asked me, "Oh, are you related to Bill Lawton?" Then he started telling me about how good of a driver my grandfather was; how he could shift gears without even slowing down!

Christopher Lawton Sr.: I was just in the bank last Friday and I had a Lawton Movers shirt on and a guy came up to me and asked, "Are you part of the same Lawton family whose father used to drag race?" I said, "Yeah." Then he started telling me the story about the time my father drove Frank Federicci's *Shark* Corvette funny car because Frank had some kind of family function to go

This is Bill and Maddeline hanging out with the family on Christmas Day. To their left is Bill's mother Christina Lawton. (Photo Courtesy Lawton Family)

to. "Your father ran the best time the car ever ran. He called Frank and said, 'See Frank? It's not the car; it's you!'"

Author: What is your favorite Bill Lawton story?
Christopher Lawton Sr.: It's probably a stupid one. He used to tell me about some crazy things he used to do back in the day. He had a bus that was converted into a race car hauler. They pulled up to a red light one day and this bum came up to the bus and started banging on the door. He wanted in so Dad opened up the door and let him in.
Maddeline Lawton: What about the time he and John Healey had been driving all night and they fell asleep and drove off the road? When they woke up they found themselves in a ditch and had no idea how they got there. Fortunately, no one got hurt and there wasn't much damage done to the race rig.

Author: I'm glad that all you folks are here at Tasca today. When I came up in 1969 to photograph the last funny car, the Tasca Super Boss, Bill would do his cricket imitations in the restaurant and Healey would join in with bird whistles. It was driving all the customers crazy. I'm just sitting between these two and trying not to burst out laughing.

Christopher Lawton Sr.: I remember when Bobby II would come over to the house. They would get out the old car magazines and talk about the good old days. They would point to pictures and say, "Remember when we beat that guy? I remember when we beat that guy." They knew all the places, times, and speeds!

I'll never forget how close the Tascas were to my father. When he first went into the hospital he had to have an operation at 6:00 am. He had to be there by 4:00 am to get prepped. Bobby and Carly were right there with him. They were always with him.

Making *Shark* Meat out of the Track Record

Dickie Williams was another Northeastern racer acquaintance of the Tasca and Lawton families who tells the story about Billy Lawton driving Frank Federicci's Chrysler-powered *Shark* Corvette fuel roadster in the summer of 1969. This was shortly after Tasca had suspended its funny car racing program.

"Billy and I lived two houses from each other and he was my daughter's godfather. Frank [Federicci] had some kind of family obligation to go to so he asked Billy if he would like to drive the car for him. Billy came to me and told me what Frank had said. Then he asked me if I would like to wrench on the car. To me that was really a compliment. I was finally getting the chance to work on a fuel car all by myself. I had been hanging around with John [Healey] and was going to the races with those guys forever it seemed. I learned an awful lot, so I thought that was pretty neat.

"We went to a funny car race at Long Island Dragway and ran pretty well. All the heavy hitters were there, Don 'Snake' Prudhomme, the 'Mongoose,' the 'Ramchargers,' 'Jungle Jim,' the Hill Brothers, King & Marshall. At that time, the best the car had run was a 7.60. That night, Billy ran a 7.02 and that was with the old steel-block 392 Chrysler. That was pretty neat, especially due to the fact that the Ramchargers ran the first 6-second run ever that night. It was a very rewarding experience.

"We actually got bumped out by one thousandth of a second to come back for the second round. Then one of the guys who was in the show broke a motor, so that put us back in again. I remember what a frantic effort it was to get everything put back together again. The Hill Brothers pitched in and so did Jimmy King. We lost to Clare Sanders in the number-two Jungle Jim car on the final. We really thought we were going to beat him as the *Shark* Corvette ran exceptionally well that night.

"That was the only time Billy ever drove Frank's car and, of course, Frank took a ribbing afterward. There was such a huge rivalry between those two! Later on, Billy got his own car.

"I went to California to pick up Charlie Allen's old car and brought it back. We replaced the Mopar body with a Mustang body and he renamed it the *Mover*. That first car really didn't do much for Billy and me. Then he built the *Mover* Pinto, which ran pretty good but he had to give it up because without a sponsor, he just couldn't afford to run that much."

John Healey Weighs In

John Healey (left) and Bill Lawton (right) raced together under the Tasca Ford banner for eight years. They campaigned everything from 406 big-block Galaxie lightweights to their last car (pictured), the blown fuel-burning *Tasca Super Boss Mach-1 Mustang*. The Team of Tasca, Lawton, and Healey was inducted into the 2009 Super Stock Magazine Drag Racing Hall of Fame during the Muscle Car Madness event held annually in York, Pennsylvania.

I knew Billy Lawton way back before he became involved with the Tascas. We used to go to this place in Seekonk, Massachusetts, called the Pink Elephant. Billy was always there with his 348s, 409s, and what not. I was working nights at Tasca's and I had my own family car, which I also street raced.

At first, Billy and Bob Sr. had, let's call them "personal clashes." The next thing I heard was that Billy was going to try out for the job of driving the [1962] Tasca Ford Super Stocker. Once he joined the team we started spending a lot of time together, getting to know each other on a more personal level.

We also socialized together with our spouses. It all started blooming from there. The higher up the ladder we went the more famous we became, or as I've always said, "The higher up the pole you go, the more people you have shooting at your ass!" I don't want to call it "stardom." We just became *very* competitive.

As the years went on we grew together as an organization and as a team. We won together. We lost together. We never gave up. We always kept the pace going and got better at what we did. The more we raced, the more we learned, and the more we learned, the faster we went.

Billy and I spent a lot of time together on the road. We shared the same motel rooms. If there weren't two beds in the room we had to share the same bed. We always used to have a series of wisecracks that we would make to each other but it was all in fun.

By early 1969 we knew the end was coming. Billy and I talked about if we could make a living match racing. My input was we could but we would have to make some major changes. I felt that without sponsorship it just wasn't going to happen. I told him that it's just not going to work because I've got family to think about, you've got family to think about.

I got an offer to go to work for the Ford Drag team and head up the West Coast operations as engine builder for Ed Terry and Dick Wood. I would be building all the 427 'cammers, the Clevelands, and 429 Shotgun motors, which was a great opportunity. So Billy went his way and I went my way but we always stayed in touch.

[Around 1972, Lawton had his Pinto-bodied AA/Fuel Funny Car and John was co-owner of the Besch & Healey Pro Stock Ford Pinto.]

A number of people came to me and asked who was going to drive the Pinto. There were other people from the area who wanted to drive the car. I said, "If anybody's going to drive the car, and we can get together between schedules, my choice is Billy Lawton. He's my number-one pick." Steven Besch agreed with me.

After that, I didn't see Billy that much or talk to him. When I learned that he wasn't feeling so good I talked to him about it. He said, "I'm fine." Then I would hear from Bobby or Carly that Billy wasn't doing all that good.

Bobby would say, "Why don't we go and see Billy?" We would all sit down and talk.

One day he said to me, "Why don't you come back? Pick a day, and you and I will just sit and reminisce about things." It was a lot of fun to go back and talk about how we started in 1962 and so forth.

As time went on, I learned of the exact nature of Billy's illness. The operation was coming up and we both knew where he was headed. We would start to talk about it then I would say, "Let's change the subject and talk about

> "We won together. We lost together. We never gave up. We always kept the pace going and got better at what we did. The more we raced, the more we learned, and the more we learned, the faster we went."

the good old times." He would just look at me and smile and we would talk. Those thoughts he shared with me will always stay with me.

When I was told the news, I was really taken aback. I just said to myself, "I just lost another friend!" It's hard to weigh out in life what a friend really is. I have a saying, "I can actually put [all my] real close friends in the palm of one hand." And Billy Lawton was one of them. Yeah, we would have our disagreements. But so what? That was normal; Billy was Billy. If he had something to say, you never heard it from someone else.

Of course, anyone who knows me will tell you that my nature is just a couple of steps higher than grumpy, and that would be putting it mildly. He would say to me sometimes, "You know, Healey? You're a miserable bastard."

And I would look back at him and say, "You know, Billy, you're right!"

Bill Lawton was one of those people you can never forget. It is unfortunate that a lot of guys [Lawton, John Pagano, and Larry Metivier] who made Tasca Racing what it was are no longer with us.

TASCA

Bob Tasca III, Mover and Shaker

The name Tasca instantly evokes images of hard-charging, wheels-up Mustangs, thundering down the quarter-mile off to yet another stellar victory.

Although Tasca Ford's original 1965 427 SOHC A/FX Mustang driven by (the late) Bill Lawton, and Bobby Tasca III's high-3-second Quick Lane Tire & Auto Center/Ford Motorcraft Shelby GT500 Mustang are worlds apart, both vehicles proudly carried the Tasca and Ford brands into battle. Recently, I visited with Bob Tasca III.

Robert F. "Bobby" Tasca III is a busy, busy man. He is one of the heirs apparent to the multi-brand Tasca Automotive Group, a legacy begun by his grandfather, Robert F. Tasca Sr., and guided to greatness by his father, Robert F. Tasca Jr., and his uncles Carl A. Tasca Sr. and David J. Tasca. Bobby III is (as of this writing) the pilot of the world's quickest and fastest Ford Mustang–bodied AA/Fuel Funny Car, his Quick Lane Tire and Auto Center/Ford Motorcraft Shelby GT500 Mustang, at 3.988/316.97. Busy hands are happy hands!

170   The Tasca Ford Legacy

CHAPTER Seven

Author: When did you first become aware of your "world," as far as automotive influences were concerned?

Bob III: That's a great question. Truthfully, I don't remember a world without it. As a young child, I remember the car dealership. I remember coming to work with my dad, Bob Jr. I remember seeing my uncles Carl and David and my grandfather, Bob Sr. I remember washing cars when I was just a kid, and wanting to drive them. I started driving a go-kart when I was just five years old. I just had a natural passion for the automobile business. I was simply infatuated with the "World of Ford" as far back as I can remember!

Author: Your grandfather, Bob Sr., and your father, Bob Jr., were obviously the most supportive influences that you had in your formative years. Was there any word of advice that your grandfather gave you that has stuck with you throughout your life?

Bob III: For as long as I can remember, I don't know that there's a day, or significant decision, that goes by in my life that my grandfather's teaching and experience hasn't [directly] influenced. There was so much that he's taught me over the years.

One of his most famous phrases, his "Secret to Success," was to ask the right people the right questions and remember the answers. I remember him laughing and joking with me, saying, "That can be dangerous because if you ask the right question to the wrong people and remember the answer you didn't do yourself any good. If you ask a lousy question to the right people you're not going to get much out of it." I think that advice has been something that I really took to heart; ask the right people the right question and remember the answers.

Now when it comes to the racing business, I've modified that somewhat. In the racing world you ask multiple people the same question and try to decipher the answer because everyone [fellow competitors] is always trying to hold something back that would give them a competitive edge.

Being around my grandfather, he exuded confidence. He was always confident that the direction he was going

> **"** *I started driving a go-kart when I was just five years old. I just had a natural passion for the automobile business.* **"**

was the *right* direction. And if it wasn't the right direction, he was going to figure out how to make it work, one way or another. When my grandfather made a decision, it wasn't a quick decision but you always believed that it was the right decision! I really learned so much from him. Family was first and then came everything else. Every decision he made was really grounded with his family and with the best interests of his family.

Those are just two of so many of life's lessons he taught me over the years.

Author: People say that generation after generation of show-business people are taught the business at the dinner table and it's passed on to each generation. Has that same principle been applied to the Tasca family through the car business?

Bob III: Absolutely! My grandfather and I have had many, many dinners together. When I was younger my grandfather took me to every state in the union except Hawaii. When it came to Hawaii, he said, 'You're on your own. It's up to you to get there by yourself.'

Just being with him, going on a lot of the Ford Assembly Plant Tours, being around him when in the company of many top-ranked Ford executives, I mean, I've been so blessed in my life to have been around so many extraordinary people. I'm just a byproduct of the great people that surrounded me. My grandfather was most certainly at the top of that list. To be able to have spent the years I've spent with him.

I'll never forget one idea I had. It was called the "Tasca Time Capsule," which was about my grandfather. I asked all of his friends the question, "If you had to ask Bob Tasca Sr. one question, what would it be?"

Someone asked him, "Is there anything you have left to do in your life?" He said, "Nope. There's nothing left for me to do but watch my children, grandchildren, and great-grandchildren carry on and continue [and develop] what I've started."

At more than 80 years old, what a peaceful place to be in your life. To have such confidence, love, and admiration for a family that he and my grandmother started. The man lived an awesome life!

Author: Bobby, you and I did our first magazine article way back in 1992; a 5.0L Mustang LX was your first car. Being that was quite some time ago, I may not be aware of all the cars that you've driven in since then and your current Mustang-bodied AA/Fuel Funny Car. Perhaps you could walk

Chapter Seven: Bob Tasca III, Mover and Shaker   171

Bobby III mashes down hard on the loud pedal while competing at the NHRA Gatornationals, Gainesville, Florida. (Photo Courtesy Steve Reyes)

My father and grandfather were actually involved in street racing, but like I said, none of them drove professionally.

I just wanted to be a race car driver for as long as I can remember. When I turned 16 I started driving my 1992 5.0L Mustang LX, which ran 12.6s in the quarter-mile. That's where it all started. Like any serious drag racer I just wanted to go faster and faster.

I have had a tremendous relationship with Roy [Hill] over the years, and I have attended the Roy Hill Drag Racing School. I've driven door cars, Super Comp dragsters, dragsters, Pro Stock cars, nitrous cars; I've driven a Pro Street nitrous Mercury Capri belonging to my father. That car ran in the 7s. Then

me through the list of race cars you've driven.

Bob III: Believe me, I couldn't turn 16 fast enough, coming up in this family and being around high-performance cars. My passion for racing started with stories as a kid listening to what my grandfather did on the race track, "Win on Sunday, Sell on Monday!" Bill Lawton, John Healey, Ralph Porier, Bill Gilbert, and Dean Gregson were the icons in my life. However, no one in the family drove professionally until now. My grandfather always owned and tuned the cars.

It takes a lot of heavy hardware to chase the points on the Full Throttle/NHRA Drag Racing Series national event trail. In fact, 13 18-wheelers and a motorhome are required to haul everything from crew to race car, tow vehicle, spare engines, sometimes two cars or car bodies, and all the necessary parts and shop equipment. One race rig is strictly for hauling souvenirs.

172   The Tasca Ford Legacy

The Shelby GT500 body shell on Bobby's current ride is made of Carbon-Kevlar by championship-winning B-Bottom Offshore boat builder Mike Feorie from Outer Limits Boats fame. It's one of the strongest and lightest bodies in the sport. (Photo Courtesy Tim Marshall)

I decided to take the step up to blown alcohol funny cars. That was my first foray of competing in the professional ranks. I went to Frank Hawley's Drag Racing School and got licensed to drive an alcohol-burning BB/Funny Car.

I developed a tremendous bond with Frank "Ace" Manzo. I raced Top Alcohol funny cars for 2½ years, went to 14 final rounds, had two national championship wins and a number of NHRA Division One wins, and was fourth on the 2007 TA/FC national points standings. That ultimately is what gave me the confidence that catapulted me into the fuel funny car ranks. However, in spite of having driven a number of different-class race cars, there's nothing quite like driving a nitro funny car. Hands down, it's truly the most amazing machine that you could ever drive!

Author: Given the odds of winning, racing the top echelon of fuel funny cars certainly is an ambitious and expensive undertaking.

Bob III: Going Top Alcohol funny car racing certainly wasn't cheap. At the time the only sponsors I could find were my family, and they were wonderful sponsors to have. However, my grandfather told me I was on my own once I went fuel racing.

That's when Ford racing came into the picture. People like Bob Glidden, John Force, and Frank Manzo. They

Renowned chassis builder Murf McKinney built the two-rail-design chassis used by all the top-name teams. The all-aluminum alloy Ford Hemi engine features a JFR block, heads with a Chuck Ford supercharger, and Todd Okuhara clutch. Crewmen on Bobby's team include Mark Denner, Chris Cunningham, and Ralph Poirier.

Chapter Seven: Bob Tasca III, Mover and Shaker   173

mean so much to me. All I want to do is make those people proud. I'm not in that race car for any reason other than to win and make the people who have supported and mentored me proud. The Ford race fans and the Ford Motor Company from Edsel II, Elaina, and Bill Ford are people who we know and love very, very much as true members of our family [to me]. That's why I'm excited about what I'm doing, and certainly with the latest move, I really believe that our success [rate] will only get better.

Trust me! By no means have I had a lousy career. I started with a ballpoint pen five years ago, been multiple times in the top 10, finished fifth in points, won four national events. I think we've been to 13 final rounds, over 30 final rounds if you figure my Top Alcohol car into the equation, so we've done an awful lot of good in a short period of time. And we're racing against dynasties like Kalitta, Force, and Schumacher.

John Force once said to me, "Kid, the first 25 years of my career, I quit 20 times! I mean I didn't even get a win. I didn't win a round for x number of years," so you've got to keep it in perspective." I'm very early in my career but my passion to win has never been stronger.

When I went Top Alcohol racing, my Mustang was obviously a very fast car [the world's quickest and fastest TA/FC in history at 5.451/263.00 at NHRA Gainesville 2007; hence re-naming his car *Mystery 5*]. It was a very intricate machine to drive, a great stepping-stone into a fuel car. I signed a deal with Ford but didn't even have a competition license, didn't even hit the throttle in a fuel funny car, but still had a contract with the Ford Motor Company.

Talk about a company who believes in you! I went to Cruz and Tony Pedregon (two of my best friends) and said, "Listen, I've got to hit the throttle on a fuel funny car at least once before the 2007 season ends (as 2008 was my first year driving an AA/FC). Do you think your brother will let me drive his car in Vegas?"

Tony said, "Yeah, I'll call him."

Cruz said, "Yeah Bobby, no problem. You can drive on Monday."

I get in the car for the first time, roll out, do a burnout, and back up. Cruz says, "Take it to 300 feet."

I take it to 300 feet. I come back and my dad asks, "How was it? What do you think of it?"

I said, "I don't know, Dad; it didn't really feel much different than the Top Alcohol car. To be honest with you, I didn't have to shift. I think it was really great."

So Cruz came over and said, "It was pretty cool, wasn't it? Now take it to half track." Whew, baby! I hit the 300-foot mark and that thing started to pull. Once the clutch, the timing, and the fuel started going into the engine, it set me back in the seat. It was scary how hard the thing accelerated. Then I made a bunch of full runs before the 2008 season. The difference between a Top Alcohol car and a fuel funny car is that a fuel car never stops pulling. It pulls right to the moment when you step off the throttle.

I feel that you don't get a true appreciation of the speed until the parachutes hit. It is unbelievable. To this day, and I've got a thousand-plus runs in a funny car, when I come up the return road at some tracks across the country (particularly on a Friday night), if you see me pull up around the starting line, I put my kickstand down, sit back, and watch a few cars come by. To this day I cannot believe that there's actually a human being in that car, and I drive one! They come by so fast that it really is one of the automotive wonders of the world that you have to see and experience in person. They are unbelievable machines that you have to give a lot of respect to.

Going back to the Top Alcohol car for a moment; that was an amazing time in my career because it gave me the belief and confidence that I could win a national event title. I am so proud to have had my grandfather see me build

Bobby III's second-oldest son, Austin, fires up Bobby IV's Junior Dragster while attending the Roy Hill Drag Racing School at Charlotte, North Carolina.

up that program. He saw me get into the fuel program and he saw me win my first race at Gainesville.

Those were special, special times for me. It was special because I got to share it with a guy who loved me as much as anyone on the planet. The greatest gift I could give to my grandfather was to have him be proud of me. I couldn't give him money. It was just to pay him back, to be proud of what I've done with my life and family; and that's what motivates me to this day.

I have a photo on the dashboard of my car, and every time I get in that car, I look him right in the eyes. Not a day goes by that I don't think about my grandfather, and how special he was!

Author: Not to mention the fact that it was your grandfather who built one of the first Ford funny cars. It's kind of like an evolution.

Bob III: That's absolutely right! It's come full circle. What is absolutely amazing are the things that Tasca and Ford have accomplished together. I remember someone saying, "What if Bob Tasca Sr. had become a Toyota dealer? What would the future have been like? It is really amazing how much of an impact he had on the sport of drag racing, and particularly the involvement of Ford Motor Company. It's a storybook scenario, and now the third generation of Tascas is carrying that legacy on at both the dealership and on the race track. All my cousins and uncles are still a part of the business, and very involved. You don't see this in life anymore, and it's special to be a part of it.

Author: Bobby, you have one of the quickest and fastest funny cars in the land and the first Ford-bodied funny car to run in the 3s, clocking a 3.988/316.97 at the O'Reilly Auto Parts Route 66 NHRA Nationals at Chicago-land International Raceway. Could this be the new *Mystery 3*?

Bob III: We had been waiting a long time to "fire a shot off," so to speak. Then at Chicago, we ran a 4.10 on Friday, and a 4.04 on Saturday, first round of qualifying. The last round of qualifying on Saturday, we're already in the show with a 4.04. I was in the trailer with the guys. To go for a national record, you've really got to go for it, and we made the decision. I knew, sitting in my car that night, thinking if I got past 300 feet [typically, that's the danger zone], it was going to haul the mail.

I remember it was unbelievably dark that night. When the tree counted down and I hit the throttle, it ran so hard that it pinned me back in the seat and I said to myself, "Whoa, I'm off on a good run." When it made it past the 300-foot mark the only thing I remember is that I couldn't see anymore. It was pitch black in front of me and I'm just punching into the darkness. The only thing I could see were the two finish-line lights on the wall. I was in the right lane and I knew I was closer to the right light versus the left light so I knew I was going straight. Unless it was on fire, I wasn't about to step off the throttle!

Author: I understand that you were involved with the Juvenile Diabetes Research Foundation, in a Ford Motorcraft/Quick Lane Tire & Auto Center–sponsored "Our Everyday Heroes Design Contest," to help raise awareness and funds.

Bob III: That's correct. Over the last five years, we have raised over $300,000 for Type 1 Diabetes research through a nationwide contest held in conjunction with the Ford Customer Service Division and the Ford Global Walk team. It is an online fundraiser and the winner participates in the unveiling of their car design at a national event. We're very grateful to the Motorcraft and Quick Lane 1 employees at Ford Motor Company for help in getting us closer to our goal to find a cure for Type 1 Diabetes.

Author: That sounds great. How can someone participate?

Bob III: Fans wishing to donate to the "Our Everyday Heroes Race Car Design Contest" can do so by texting "JDRF" once to 2022. A one-time donation of $10 will be attached to your mobile phone bill or deducted from the prepaid balance. Of course, the donor must be more than 18 years of age and all donations must be authorized by the account holder. This service is available through most carriers.

Author: Now, how about those fourth-generation Tasca racers?

Bob III: You know, I guess it was kind of an out-of-body experience to see my son Bobby IV go down the race track for the first time at eight years old driving a Junior Dragster. Over the years, I've kind of downplayed racing because I know that it will become such a force in their lives as they get older. What's important to me is that they enjoy their childhood, that they play hockey, lacrosse, basketball, and baseball so that they really experience everything before they (maybe) come into the racing side or the dealership side of things.

We'll see, but you know you can't deny the look in their eyes sitting in that car. How well he [Bobby IV] did the first time out of the gate, hitting the throttle, and driving that Junior Dragster at eight years, running over 60 mph!

I really had a lot of fun. When we first started, Bobby asked me three or four times a week, "Dad, when are we doing it again? When are we doing it again?" So I could be in trouble with my oldest son [smiling]. You see, I never had junior Dragsters when I was a kid. I had to wait until I was 16 years old to drive. To see these kids competing at such a young age with so much responsibility. It's been truly wonderful to spend the time with them.

We're going to have a big Junior Dragster Shootout this summer with my two older boys, Bob and Austin, at Piedmont Dragway, so we'll see how they do in competition. The beauty of drag racing is that it is a family sport and very, very fan friendly. It's exciting to me to have four boys, Bob IV, Austin, Cameron, and Dylan. Who knows? One of them might become a future champion.

Austin drove last year for the first time at age 8, which is the minimal age to be able to drive. Bob stepped up to a faster car, so Austin stepped into Bob's car, and really did terrific What's cool to me is that you've got 8- to 10-year-olds racing, but they're just kids. Sometimes, you want to pull your hair out. But you know something? When they get around that race car, all the games end. They become unbelievably focused on the task at hand and they can constructively channel all that energy. It's just so cool!

Author: Do the boys start talking smack with each other before a race?
Bob III: They do a little. The day before Austin first went racing, he put his fire suit on and his first question to me was, "Hey, Dad, when do I get to drive your car?" I said, "Why don't you start with the Junior Dragsters, Austin, and check back with me in about 13 years?"

Anyway, they love it. As a drag racer I have to sacrifice a huge quantity of time with the family. I mean, I'm on the road 200 days a year. However, you try and make it up with the quality of time and this is a great way to do that. During the summer I drive my grandfather's motorhome around the country, particularly on the western swing, and my kids are with me for three weeks straight. They come to Indy with me and I really get to spend a lot of time with them. In giving up the amount of time that I normally see them, those are the moments that I cherish.

Author: Do your sons want to work on the funny car?
Bob III: Absolutely! Bob takes the headers off the car. Austin works the T-shirt trailer. Cameron helps clean the car. They are greatly involved. By the time Bob becomes a teenager he'll probably be able to build and rebuild one of those race cars!

Author: Let's talk about you as an automotive businessperson and the future head of the Tasca Automotive Group.
Bob III: I'm blessed because we have a team effort here at Tasca. Of course, my grandfather was the czar back in the day. You might say he's left behind an "automotive army." There's my brother, Michael, my sister, Jaime, my two cousins Carl Jr. and David Jr., who I don't even think of as cousins. They're really more like brothers.

What makes all of us great is that we're working together as a team. This company could not have grown in the way that it has if it weren't for them. In fact, I could have never been able to go racing had it not been for them. Granted, me going racing has been healthy for the company because it's really gotten my brother and cousins much more involved with the business than when I was here each and every day. It all works together like a well-tuned race car. Some days are better than others but one thing about our family is once we make a decision and leave the room, we're all together, and we're all in on it. Nobody's pulling left and the other guy is pulling right. We're all pulling in the same direction.

That's exactly what my grandfather would want, and sometimes he didn't even agree with us. He was much more single-dealership minded. Now we're expanded into multiple dealerships and multiple brands. It's a healthy part of our growth. It's an exciting time for our family and a lot of things are going on that continue to develop and grow our family business. This is where I started, and this is where I'm going to end in the car business. Other than racing, this is my passion. I don't know anything else!

Author: You started as a lot boy, right? What was the line of progression from there?
Bob III: We all started out as lot boys! If you talk to any of the Tasca kids, it's all the same. You started out as a lot boy cleaning cars, moving cars around, changing dealer plates for the salesman. I worked as a technician. I worked as a service writer. I spent a little time in parts growing up; now I spend all my time in parts. In 2007 when Ford gave me the sponsorship for my race car, I said to them, "Not only will I win on the race

track, but I will build the largest parts operation [for a dealer] in the world. I'll do both for you."

We started doing $40,000 a month wholesale. Last month, we did a whisker shy of $2.2 million. We did that in six years. We're not number one yet, we're number five, but we're closing in on the number-one spot and we'll be there very, very soon. That's the kind of guy I am. If I get into something, I'm going all the way with it. There may be some roads I go down that don't work but trust me, I'll figure that out quick enough and we'll go down a different road.

I'm very proud of the Tasca Parts Team. My grandfather never was in the parts business on such a scale as this is. That was something that barely existed in our company but [today] we've made an enterprise out of it and the best is yet to come. That's a line that I use a lot. The sky is the limit!

Anyhow, after getting into sales, selling Ford and L-M products, and working in sales management, I ultimately started taking the reins in the dealership to promote growth. I started working on acquisitions. We bought Volvo. We bought Mazda. I was the point person on building the new dealership in Cranston, which had its ups and downs, to say the least. A new Volvo showroom expansion program was another major undertaking that hasn't really stopped.

Now that I have my brothers, sister, and cousins onboard we continue to expand our brand in the New England market. You know, it's not like we graduated to Fixed Ops. Today, there is as much focus in Fixed Operations in our family business as there is in sales. When I'm not racing, I spend 80 percent of my time in Fixed Ops because my sponsors, Ford Motorcraft, Ford.com, and Quick Lane, are all Fixed Ops–driven.

Here's my attitude: I have to be the best in that race car as a driver, I want to be the best team owner I can be, and I want to be the absolute best in front of a camera when I'm talking about Ford, when I'm talking to their dealers, when I'm talking to their distributors. In order for me to do that, I stay relevant here at the dealership; I'm not just some paid race car driver who's got a script that I'm reading from; I'm talking from the heart. This is where I live. That is our competitive advantage. There has never been a driver/sponsor/owner relationship that has more credibility with the Ford Motor Company, plus I also get to drive their car!

Roy Hill on Bob Tasca III

Bobby III came to the Roy Hill Drag Racing School 1995. I remember Richie Stevens stayed an extra day to get his Pro Stock driver's license and Bobby stayed an extra day to get his Super Comp driver's license. Bobby went on to race a Top Sportsman Capri that his daddy, Bob Jr., had. Then he came back [1998] and got his Pro Stock driver's license. He tested at Rockingham and made his licensing runs at Englishtown, New Jersey. After he got his Top Alcohol Funny Car driver's license, I would watch him run. His reaction times were tremendous and as his knowledge grew, he got better and better.

When it comes to business, Bobby has likewise impressed me tremendously. I know that, just like his grandfather and his daddy, he had to have an education to continue on in the family business. Each one of the Tasca family members has a certain part of the business they run at the dealerships. Bobby has done a tremendous job in that respect. He worked up the Tasca Parts program and put it in front of the Ford Motorcraft people. He not only became one of the top Ford Motorcraft Parts retailers in the country, he put together the Ford Motorcraft/Quick Lane Tire & Auto Center funny car sponsorship. His granddaddy was so, so proud of him.

Now, moving on into the fourth generation of Tasca kids, specifically Bobby IV, Cameron, and Austin. Bobby IV is a natural-born talent when it comes to driving a race car. His younger brother Austin has spent a couple of years acting as crew chief, and now that he's come of age, he'll be racing his own Junior Dragster as well. No doubt their two younger brothers Cameron and Dylan will also follow in their footsteps.

The Tasca family will always be a part of the Roy Hill Drag Racing School, and Roy Hill will always be a part of the Tasca family!

Carl Tasca's Storming Mustang Thoroughbreds

Carl A. Tasca Sr. has been driving fast Mustangs most of his adult life. His first car at age 16 was a Sapphire Blue 1969 Mach-1 Mustang powered by the very same 427 Ford tunnel-port engine that had formerly powered the Tasca "KR-8." Before that the engine powered Lloyd Ruby's wrecked Ford GT40, which competed in the 1967 24 Heures Du Mans in France. Running on a set of bias-ply street tires, Carl's Tunnel Port Mach-1 clocked a best of 11.88/121.00!

Carl Sr. charges hard off the Connecticut Dragway starting line in *Miss Giada*, his 2010 R-Code Mustang Cobra Jet number 027, the quickest and fastest (at this writing) manual transmission new-era Cobra Jet Mustang Super Stocker in the nation. Roy Hill, CEO of the Roy Hill Drag Racing School, holds the quickest and fastest mark for automatic transmission CJs at 7.92/172.00.

The Tasca Ford Legacy

CHAPTER Eight

Power comes from a Chris Holbrook Racing Engines 5.4L (331-ci) 12L Whipple supercharged and intercooled four-valve hemi Cammer racing engine set up according to NHRA Super Stock specifications. It produces a whopping 1,400 hp!

Carl's "office" is strictly business with its B&B Fabrications roll cage that has been updated to 2013 NHRA Super Stock specifications by Tube Chassis Design. A single fiberglass racing (bucket) seat with Simpson Safety Equipment and Auto Meter instruments is also onboard. Note the Liberty Variable-Ratio Professional Clutchless 5-speed shifter and Stroud Safety parachute release. Also along for the ride is a tunable Big Stuff Electronics engine-management system.

"I'll never forget the first day I drove that car. I stomped on the accelerator pedal and I was doing this, and doing that, and my father suddenly turned to me and said, 'This is a lethal weapon. Treat it with respect.'"

Today Carl races Ford's modern-day version of the Cobra Jet Mustang race cars that, like their namesakes, are once again terrorizing race tracks across the country. They too are "lethal weapons."

"When Ford decided to re-invent the Cobra Jet and build 50 of them, they did so to honor my father. My brother Bobby Jr. went out to the Ford River Rouge Assembly Plant with a few of the boys and they had a big ceremony."

Afterward, the Tasca Automotive Group bought two of these Gen II CJs. One they sold, one they kept. The cars arrived in February 2008. Carl's 2008 CJ featured a 331-ci 5.4L four-valve supercharged Ford Racing modular V-8 engine weighing 3,412 pounds and producing 800 hp, which was good enough to run a 9.28/147.00!

"My father walked into the shop with his coat and hat, looking at the car. I could see that his eyes were starting to tear up because it brought back such fond memories. I said, 'Dad, why don't we have some fun with this car? Let's letter it up just like our original 428 CJ Super Stock car in honor of Billy Lawton and John Healey?' He didn't say 'Yes,' and he didn't say 'No.' So I went ahead and did it, and I'm glad that I did!"

In the Tasca tradition of constant and never-ending improvement, Carl is now behind the wheel of a 2010 Mustang Cobra Jet Super Stock car, number 027 (aka, *Miss Giada*), which was named in honor of Carl's granddaughter. The following are a few fast facts.

Carl's Cobra Jet gave indications of big things to come when it became the first production-based modern-era muscle car

Chapter Eight: Carl Tasca's Storming Mustang Thoroughbreds   179

Carl Sr. (who also owned an original Gen-1 CJ Mustang back in the day) poses with his 2010 Cobra Jet Mustang Super Stock car, which has scorched the quarter-mile at 7.72/179.00.

Rear suspension on the Mustang is NHRA Super Stock specification B&B Fabrications' four-link, sporting fully adjustable electronic Penske coil-over shock absorbers and a Mark Williams Enterprises sheet-metal 9-inch rear end using DewCuDon variable-ratio gears and 40-spline Mark Williams steel billet axles. Braking is handled by a set of 11-inch-diameter Strange Engineering disc brakes.

to record a sub-8-second run (March 4, 2013) at Z-MAX Dragway, Charlotte, North Carolina, clocking a 7.738/179.23.

During mid-summer testing at New England Dragway (July 24, 2013) Carl and his Mustang reeled off a best of 7.778/175.64.00, which was particularly meaningful to Carl as the numbers "777" were the original address of the history-making Taunton Avenue dealership. They are also the racing number assigned to numerous early Tasca race cars, including the Winternationals-winning 427 SOHC 1965 Mustang driven by (the late) Billy Lawton.

Then things just got better. On August 3, 2013, Tasca's Cobra Jet clocked a career best of 7.72/177.00. Half-track numbers on that particular pass were 4.987/140.44, making it the quickest and fastest new-era Cobra Jet in the nation.

"I'm proud to say that as a testimonial to his memory, I have my father's picture on the car so he was with me in spirit when I made those historic runs. As far as the competition goes [pointing to the car], they're all chasing after this bugger!"

Twenty-month-old Giada Tasca already has her first (battery-powered) Mustang given to her by Grandpa Carl and Grandma Iuna.

Here's Carl off and running on that 7.72/177.00 pass at Connecticut Dragway. This car gets with the program, registering 4.7s at more than 140 mph in the eighth-mile.

Chapter Eight: Carl Tasca's Storming Mustang Thoroughbreds

Miss Giada at a Glance

Engine: 1,400 hp, Chris Holbrook–prepared 5.4L (331-ci) supercharged and intercooled Ford Racing mod motor
Engine Management/Tuning System: Big Stuff Electronics
Clutch: Two-disc Ram Automotive adjustable base and finger weights
Bellhousing: Browell Industries
Transmission: Liberty Variable-Ratio Professional Clutchless 5-speed, and shifter
Driveshaft: Aluminum, Mark Williams Enterprises
Rear End: Custom-made Mark Williams Enterprises sheet-metal 9-inch "DewCoDon" gears (gear ratios vary according to track) and Mark Williams Enterprises 40-spline steel-billet axles
Rear Brakes: Strange Engineering
Rear Suspension: Four-Link by B&B Fabrications
Shocks: Penske Racing coil-overs
Rear Wheels: 15x15-inch billet-aluminum Weld Racing Wheels
Rear Tires: Either 32.00 x 14.5 x 15-inch Mickey Thompson or Hoosier drag slicks, depending on track surface
Front Suspension: Santhuff Coil-Over-Strut with custom tubular front K-member
Front Brakes: Strange Engineering
Front Wheels: Weld 15x3.5-inch Cobra Jet insignia billet-aluminum front wheels
Front Tires: P8.0 x 4.5 x 15-inch Hoosier front tires
Roll Cage: B&B Fabrications with Tube Chassis Design updates
Safety Equipment: Stroud Safety parachute and Simpson Safety Equipment harnesses
Weight: 3,250 pounds
Crew Chief: Ralph Poirier
Crew: Greg Grimes, Don Belanger, "Uncle Bert" Mayer

If you take a closer look at the Hoosier-wrapped 15 x 3.5-inch Weld Racing modular front wheels, you'll notice the fancy Cobra Jet logo CNC work on the wheel centers.

Crew Chief Ralph Poirier (far left), "Uncle Bert" Mayer (middle), and Carl (right) talk performance between runs. Both longtime Tasca employees, Poirier and Mayer, collectively have about 80 years' experience with working on only the "cream" of the Ford high-performance "crop."

182   The Tasca Ford Legacy

"I have my father's picture in the car so he is always with me in spirit," says Carl Sr. "This car is a testament to his memory" and the legacy that he left behind.

Carl's Mustang may be called a Cobra Jet but its real name is *Miss Giada*, in honor of Carl and Luna's first granddaughter, whose parents are Carl Jr. and Tania.

Chapter Eight: Carl Tasca's Storming Mustang Thoroughbreds   183

In Memoriam, Robert F. Tasca Sr.

One of the saddest days in Tasca family history was saying good-bye to Robert F. Tasca Sr., who, after a lengthy illness, passed away January 8, 2010. The young man who wanted to become a Ford dealer, and did so, had accomplished so many great things in his lifetime, above and beyond his earliest expectations with his greatest accomplishment being his family.

Bob's funeral could have been likened to that of a dignitary of state as Rhode Island Interstate 95 was shut down for the funeral procession. Because he was a very religious man, there were a lot of attendees from the Roman Catholic Church. The High Mass funeral service was held at the Cathedral of Saints Peter and Paul, the mother church of the Diocese, in Providence (established 1837) with the honorable Bishop Gelleneaux coming out of retirement to preside. There was a point during the Mass when niece Jaklyne Tasca-Bulman and tenor Marc Collozzi sang David Foster's "The Prayer," which was probably the most emotional rendering of that song ever heard. It was a sad and emotional moment.

Bob was truly loved and respected by everyone locally and in the automotive realm. He dearly loved the Ford Motor Company, and the Ford Motor Company dearly loved him back. Two Ford corporate jets brought attendees from Dearborn to pay their respects. They included Bill Ford, Edsel Ford II, Elena Ford, Alan Mulally, Mark Fields, and just about every brand manager and department head from every major department within the company.

Perhaps the most inspirational moment came when young Robert F. Tasca III stepped up to the podium and eulogized his grandfather. Later, many people remarked about the admirable job he had done to get up in front of all those people and eulogize his grandfather while maintaining his composure. Bobby III did so with his son Bobby IV standing quietly by his side.

Below is "Pop's Eulogy" as delivered on January 16, 2010, by Robert F. Tasca III:

184 The Tasca Ford Legacy

CHAPTER Nine

Over the years many different articles have been written about my grandfather, Robert F. Tasca Sr. He's been called an *icon* and *innovator*, an *American* success story; I called him "Pop."

There is no question that he was one of the most intelligent, creative, charismatic individuals one could ever hope to meet. The power of his mind was eclipsed only by the warmth of his heart. Pop was the kindest, most-genuine, caring, generous person that I have ever met. And I would like to take a moment to talk about some of his key principles.

These are not business principles, like his famous commitment to customer satisfaction or his mantra of building cars for the "taker, not the maker." These are some of the principles by which Pop lived his life.

The first key principle that my grandfather lived by was loyalty. Whether it was loyalty to his wife, Josephine, of more than 60 years, the loyalty to entrust his business to his children and grandchildren, or the loyalty he showed to Ford Motor Company during his 67-year career, Pop never gave up on those whom he loved.

The second key principle in Pop's life was compassion. Whether he was speaking with an executive at Ford or an old widow at church, Pop never missed the opportunity to listen to the people around him. He never turned a person away who had a problem and looked to him for help. Pop's heart was filled with a genuine desire to help those around him, whether it was saving a school from closing or by simply listening to a friend.

The third principle upon which my grandfather built his life was an almost superhuman work ethic. Once he locked his sights on something, Pop worked longer, worked harder, and committed himself more completely than anyone I have ever come across. Unlike many men and women who achieve success in life, Pop never let today's achievements satisfy his appetite to continue to do more. Complacency was a word that was not in his vocabulary. My grandfather was born a hard worker and he remained a hard worker until his final breath. Time after time, whether in his personal or professional life, on the race track and in the showroom, Pop overcame all odds and accomplished what he set out to do.

Today is a solemn day for those who loved my grandfather. My sorrow is overshadowed only by my overwhelming feeling of pride in having had this great man as my grandfather. This feeling of pride, however, comes with a tremendous responsibility. We, who were so loved by Pop, carry the responsibility of continuing his legacy. This legacy lives on not in the bricks and mortar of the dealerships he built or in the cars he sold. Pop's true legacy, one of compassion, generosity, family, and integrity, lives on in the hearts of those who loved him.

My family and I are completely committed to upholding the morals and values that Pop instilled in us. We live our lives, raise our children, and run our business following the example he set.

Through us, Pop will live on forever!

Robert Francis Tasca Sr. was laid to rest on January 16, 2010, at Cranston, Rhode Island's St. Mary's Cemetery, just down the road from his last and greatest accomplishment, the newly opened Tasca Automotive Group super dealership located at 1300 Pontiac Avenue. At the family's request, donations were made to the Juvenile Diabetes Research Foundation in lieu of flowers.

To quote Robert F. Tasca Sr. in a 1992 interview with me, "There are a lot of things I've done in my lifetime that I'm proud of, but if anyone wanted to put something on my gravestone they could probably call me 'Mr. Quality Control at Ford Motor Company.'

"I'll tell you right now, Ford is building the greatest cars ever built by any domestic manufacturer in this country. We're going to build better cars than the Japanese. I'm an absolute fanatic about that.

"May the Lord not take me before I finish!"

Chapter Nine: In Memoriam, Robert F. Tasca Sr.

TASCA FORD TESTIMONIALS

It has been said that no man is a failure who has friends. With that being the case, Robert F. Tasca, Sr. was by far one of the richest men in the world. The following are random testimonials of just some of the people whose lives he touched!

> A lot of people are given or like to take credit for the explosive growth of drag racing in the 1960s, but very few ever had the impact of the senior Mr. Bob Tasca. "The Big Bopper," as he was known, was the man behind many of the great Ford projects of the 1960s with the 1968½ Cobra Jet being just one prime example. Tasca Ford was the classic case of "Win on Sunday, Sell on Monday!" and, ironically, they still are. I'm proud to say that through it all I have intently watched their progress and it's been a real pleasure.
>
> Bob Frey, NHRA Championship Drag Racing Announcer

Bob showed throughout his life that to serve is really to live. He was an engaged member of our One Ford team and absolutely dedicated to serving customers with the very best quality vehicles and service!

Alan Mulally
President and CEO Ford Motor Company

> Bob was a fantastic leader and partner who shared our dedication to building great vehicles. His passion and enthusiasm for racing and Ford lives on in his family today.
>
> Mark Fields, COO, Ford Motor Company

> Many years ago, I returned from a work trip in Boston and took a detour off Interstate 95 to seek out the famed Tasca Ford dealership. As it turned out, there was some kind of special event going on and the place was crowded.
>
> One of my friends in the New Jersey Region of SAAC was finishing the restoration of his 1966 Shelby GT350, which originally came from there, a car which was reportedly driven/owned/used by one of Bob Tasca Sr.'s three sons.
>
> I recounted this story to a salesman who directed me to Bob Tasca Sr. I introduced myself and explained my Shelby connection. Once again, I recounted the story of my friend Pete's car. He confirmed the connection. I noted how he did not have the dealer plate for the taillight panel. From his own desk, Bob Sr. gave me an original Tasca Ford emblem, which I was more than happy to pass along to my friend Pete.
>
> Mr. Tasca was only too happy to talk about cars, the dealership, etc.; and was a terrific host.
>
> Dan Reiter, New Jersey Region SAAC

Although we occasionally raced Tasca Ford during my "Chi Town Hustler" funny car days, I never really got to know any of those folks until I became involved with John Force Racing and Ford. Bob Tasca Sr. was a fine gentleman and had a lot of power with FoMoCo. If he said, "I will get them to do that," you could bet on it!

On a more personal note, when our female Doberman passed away Bob offered to give us one of his show-quality German Shepherd pups. My wife Lisa went to his place and visited with 100 dogs to select the one that picked *her*. Our dog Stormy is now 12 and has been a trusted and faithful member of our family. Thank you, Bob Tasca!

Austin Coil
Former John Force Racing Crew Chief
Multiple *Car Craft* magazine "All Star Drag Racing Team" Member

The Tasca Ford Legacy

> Bob [Tasca Sr.], Bill [Lawton], and John [Healey] were three drag racing pioneers who were ahead of their time, that's for damned sure. Of course, with Bob Tasca being the leader they couldn't be anything but sensational. I was very proud to have known them, and I was very proud to have been associated with them. Of course, I was probably the closest to "Mr. Bob." He and George Hurst were close friends.
>
> Tasca helped me get the Ford account. I pitched the idea of using Hurst shifters on Ford's high-performance models, which was one of the high points of my career. I really loved the entire Tasca family; all those kids and grandkids.
>
> It was real special what he did for Ford and with Ford. I was present at his induction into the 2009 Super Stock Magazine Drag Racing Hall of Fame ceremony at York [Ms. Vaughn was a 2008 inductee], and I was so proud to be sitting next to him. We reminisced a lot, talked about our old Ford days, and he asked if I'm "still with that Italian [meaning Linda's longtime boyfriend]." And I said, "Yeah, I'm still with that Italian, Bob," and we had ourselves a good laugh.
>
> I was so saddened by his passing.
>
> *Linda Vaughn, "Miss Hurst Golden Shifter" Retired*

The Tascas are one heck of a family. They are about some of the nicest people you'll ever want to meet. I've known them all, Bob Sr., Bob Jr., and also Bobby Tasca III and all his kids. Of course, we raced each other quite often back in the old days. We both had 1963½ Galaxie lightweights and we had 1964 Ford Thunderbolts. Later that year, I built my 1965 Ford Falcon and Tasca got their 427 SOHC Mustang. Then we both had the long-wheelbase 1966 Mustang match racers. The late Billy Lawton was a hell of a racer and a super-nice guy.

John Healey was one of the hardest-working mechanics in the business. And Bob Tasca Sr. was there throughout Ford's Total Performance Era when all this exciting stuff was going on. Of course, one of his greatest accomplishments was the 1968½ Cobra Jet Mustang, which I drove for them at the 1968 AHRA and NHRA Winternationals.

The Tasca family is going to be around racing for a long, long time. Bobby III's knocking on the door of his first championship and those kids of his are something else. Back in November we were at Charlotte and they were running Junior Dragsters. They're going to be the next generation of Tasca racers.

Hubert "Hube Baby" Platt
Former Eastern Region Ford Drag Team Captain
Drag Racing Hall of Fame Member

When I was younger, I looked at the Tasca family and said to myself, "Gee, there are so many sons that are interested in the car business. How is this going to work out?" But somehow over the years there's always been a place for everyone within the Tasca Automotive Group. I think that's remarkable. It's a credit to Bob Tasca Sr. and the entire Tasca family, which does a wonderful job representing Ford Motor Company and selling its products.

Edsel Ford II, Member
Board of Directors
Ford Motor Company

> Bob Tasca spent his last few months on earth coming into the dealership every day, even though his doctors were against it. As you might imagine, nobody could keep a man like Bob Tasca from doing what he really wanted to do. I had an office off the Lincoln showroom then and he made my office his headquarters during those final months.
>
> In 2007 and 2008, during the economic downturn, Ford, like just about everyone else, went through some very uncertain times. Fortunately, with the guidance of Alan Mulally, they not only got through that tough period but also came out stronger than ever.
>
> Although Bob was pretty sick I'll never forget how proud he was that Ford was doing so well, and from a product standpoint, the future looked bright. Bob had so much to do with Ford quality it was only fitting that he could see that turnaround before he passed.
>
> *Mike Perlini, Tasca University*

Chapter Nine: In Memoriam, Robert F. Tasca Sr.

TASCA FORD TESTIMONIALS

I'm a car nut, and have been building hot rods as far back as the late 1950s. I have always been a massive drag racing fan and actually in one of the NHRA's original charter clubs. I knew who the Tascas were. I knew that Bob Tasca Sr. built some of the fastest Fords in the world, Thunderbolts, Mustangs, and set many records.

When I became the Regional Manager of the Ford Pacific Region, I developed an incentive program for the metropolitan Ford dealers in Vancouver [1987], which consisted of a salmon fishing trip called the President's Reel Challenge.

Of course, we would set aside one day for business. The idea was to have a Ford dealer of some repute come in and share their thoughts about the business, then hold a Q&A and talk about how they did things and so forth. The first speaker out of the chute was Bob Tasca Sr., who also brought son Bob Jr. and grandson Bobby III along with him. The interesting thing is that Bob was a very transparent dealer. For lack of a better way to describe it, I think that he had a "customer-driven gene" in his genetic makeup. Bob spoke about his "Half a Car" program, and in his classic Rhode Island accent, said to the group, "When your neighbor is buying tires, you're changing cars."

I believe he said that at the time his company had 12,000 leases out. That was a phenomenal number. Bob went on to talk about his Team Philosophy and how it was used in customer service: Do everything in the world that you can for the customer. He spoke of his greeting program [Welcome to Tasca Lincoln-Mercury. How can we help you?] and the effect it had in "humanizing" the overall sales/leasing processes.

The other side of Bob was that he understood what he sold. He came from a technical background and he knew his customers; he knew his product. What should you stock and what kind of cars does the customer want to buy? He also discussed product repackaging, or his "TSEs" as he called them, cars that were uniquely Tasca.

Throughout it all, Bob was very transparent and very generous. He had no hesitation about sharing his knowledge with other dealers. In his opinion, he wouldn't be there if it wasn't for the customer. Based on what traditional Ford and Lincoln-Mercury dealers were doing, Bob Tasca Sr. was a definite exception.

Jim King, Retired National Director of Dealer Affairs, Former Member of the Management Policy Committee of Canada

---

I first met Bob Tasca Sr. at the Dearborn Proving Grounds in 1964 when Mickey Thompson and I were racing together. In 2004, while at the NHRA US Nationals in Indianapolis, I renewed my friendship with Mr. Tasca all over again. We had a real long talk. I asked him how things were going with grandson Bobby III's Top Alcohol funny car program. His answer typically was, "Never enough horsepower!"

Butch "The California Flash" Leal
Former Ford Thunderbolt Racer
Back-To-Back US Nationals Super Stock Champion

Bob always operated with an incredible sense of family, a spirit that continues today as new generations are brought into the Tasca family business. I think it was Bob's sense of family that made the Tasca Automotive Group so successful and what continues to drive their success today. While Bob is missed by so many people who knew him, his legacy certainly continues on.

Bill Ford, Executive Chairman
Ford Motor Company

When *Drag Times* first started up, Todd Mack asked me if I would be interested in becoming a writer for the paper. Shortly thereafter, Mike Maiatico bought *Eastern Drag News*, the parent company of *Super Stock & Drag Illustrated* magazine, and the two weekly papers were merged into one. Tasca Ford was "Jack Approved," from the start, and was a very tough and a competitive team against whomever they raced. Although I cannot remember what particular issues, Tasca frequently graced the covers of both weekly drag racing newspapers.

T. P. "Jack" Redd, Former Editor, Drag Times

The Tasca Ford Legacy

> In the 1960s through 1970s, the National Hot Rod Association's Northeast Division was a hotbed of activity in the Stock-bodied categories. The team of Bill Lawton and John Healey out of the Tasca Ford stables from New England were a pair to draw to anytime you ran a round in Super Stock eliminator (and later A/FX) and they were constantly *the* car to beat. In all the years of competition, which included stints in the altered-wheelbase and early funny cars, the team was always in the heat of the battle. Tasca ran a professional operation and they were always a most-respected representative of "The Land of NED." In fact, the Tasca name is still synonymous with championship-winning performance.
>
> *Darwin Doll, Director, Retired, NHRA North East Division One*

When it came to the 1968½ Cobra Jet Mustangs, Bob Tasca Sr. really did his homework. Those cars were magnificent. Everything about those cars was right on the money!

"Beaver Bob" McCardle, CEO
Beaver Springs Raceway,
Beaver Springs, Pennsylvania
Former Cobra Jet Mustang Owner

> I first started to take my 1965 Shelby GT350 [5S357] to Tasca Ford for servicing around 1966 or 1967. At the time, Tasca was located at 777 Taunton Avenue, East Providence, Rhode Island. When you crossed the bridge from downtown Providence to East Providence, I remember there was a huge billboard proclaiming that Tasca was the second-largest Ford dealer in the world. Tasca's dealership was huge for the day and they had acres of cars parked behind the shop. I would say that the lot was about a quarter-mile deep.
>
> The entrance to the showroom and service area was on the west side. And since the dealership was on a hill, the entire east-side entrance was below the service area and mainly used for new-car prep. The showroom always has several high-performance Fords on display and every once in a while, one of the Tasca race cars would be on display as well.
>
> After Tasca Ford closed, and the "new" had simultaneously worn off my Shelby, I started taking it to a mechanic at the local Sunoco station for service. It would be 27 years before I would find myself back at Tasca again. In 2007, I bought a Shelby GT500 and I've had it serviced at the new Cranston, Rhode Island, facility.
>
> It surprised me that Bob, "The Big Bopper" Tasca was still active in the dealership and I saw him a number of times strolling through, checking out the various departments.
>
> *Howard Pardee, Shelby American Automobile Club Board of Directors*

When I first started with Ford Motor Company, one of the first dealers that I met was Bob Tasca Sr. and the entire Tasca family. Whenever there was a management revue regarding what vehicles we were going to build for Ford or Lincoln-Mercury we would always consult with the Tascas. Now, it wasn't just a meeting with Mr. Tasca and his three sons, it was a meeting with the entire Tasca family. We would sit at a table in the conference room and Mr. Tasca would "hold court" with the Ford Motor Company executives. We would talk about what vehicles Ford would want to bring to market.

Bob Sr. spent I don't know how many days a year traveling on his bus visiting all of our assembly plants, attending the product launches. Then he would give us a performance revue on the vehicle quality that he saw during his visits, the good and the bad. He was very powerful, very forceful. This was not like a one-hour meeting. This would take two, three, and four hours that we would be in there. We would go through plant by plant, product by product on the Ford Lincoln-Mercury agenda. No one from the family spoke except for Mr. Tasca. Then when asked, sons Bob Jr., Carl, and David shared their thoughts and opinions. That's the way Mr. Tasca set it up; a family-owned, family-run business.

Generationally, the Tascas work together for the common good. It didn't matter whether you were a Ford executive or part of the Ford family, it was one family talking to another. We were all in this together. That's one of the things I miss now that "Pop" is no longer with us. Mr. Tasca loved the Ford Motor Company. His sons and grandsons love the Ford Motor Company. They truly bleed "Ford Blue" as much as we do!

Elena Ford, Director, Global Marketing
Ford Motor Company

Chapter Nine: In Memoriam, Robert F. Tasca Sr.

TASCA FORD TESTIMONIALS

> Tasca was one of the few dealers I knew that could walk into the Triple E Building at Ford Motor Company, walk right by the guard, and nobody would question him. Evidentially, he had some real horsepower there. After I got out of racing, I was involved with the company "pink report." I sat in at engineering meetings (I was in resident engineering) and would see Tasca in that building maybe four or five times a year. He would be sitting in the Chief Engineer's office or whatever, and he was privy to all of those programs. If Ford wanted to know something, they went and talked to Tasca because they knew he had the public's best interests in mind.
>
> *Bill Holbrook, Retired Ford Engineer*

> I raced at Connecticut Dragway from 1964 to 1967 and got to see the Tasca operation from the pits. East Hampton, Connecticut, was not a hotbed of factory racing teams, so it was a treat to watch the very professional Tasca operation.
>
> Tasca's 427 Thunderbolt, driven by Bill Lawton, was spectacular! The entire chassis lifted straight up when it launched off the starting line due to the unique traction bar setup that extended to the rear of the car. Bill could power-shift a 4-speed with the best of them too, usually banging second gear at the tree. When Tasca went to the injected 427 'cammer altered-wheelbase Mustang it became even more interesting.
>
> Tuner John Healey always looked like he just stepped out of a men's fashion magazine working on the car in expensive pullover sweaters. In fact, those days spent at Connecticut Dragway made enough of an impression on me that I decided that I wanted to be a part of drag racing for the rest of my life. This goal finally led to editorial positions at *Popular Hot Rodding*, and *Hot Rod* where I covered hundreds of NHRA AHRA and IHRA events.
>
> I was extremely happy to see the Tasca team return to its winning form after so many years of retirement. Even better, seeing a family member [Bob Tasca III] behind the wheel.
>
> *Leonard Emanuelson, Former Editor,* Hot Rod *Magazine*

> The Tasca Ford Group was very, very tough with Bill Lawton driving and John Healey wrenching, and no one was nicer than Bob Tasca Sr. Without them, it was a big loss to the sport.
>
> *Buddy Martin*
> *Sox & Martin Racing Team*

> Bob was such a huge person in the racing game. I mean, he was responsible for so many things that we got from Ford. I first met Bob Tasca back in 1962 while Les Ritchey and I were driving lightweight Ford Galaxies. Bob also ran one of those cars and, through that program, we became friends. If Bob really wanted something done . . .
>
> I remember in late 1962, Bob knew that we needed a lighter car, like the Ford Fairlane, to race and we needed it right away. He said, "We can't be going out to the track and have the Chevys and Mopars beat the hell out of us." So he built a 1962 Fairlane of his own, which became the foundation of the Fairlane Thunderbolt. He used a regular Fairlane body, which he lightened and installed a 406 big-block in, and it went over big time with Ford Motor Company. I don't know whom he was involved with but it was one of the top guys at Ford Special Vehicles.
>
> If he [Sr.] really wanted something done that he felt was important enough, it got done. As he was one of the biggest Ford dealers around, they [Ford] paid close attention to him. They also paid close attention to him when it came to new-car sales and advertising.
>
> Bob Tasca was a damned good man. He had a tremendous mind. He always seemed to be able to work things out and make things better, and I respected him to the end. Bob Tasca Sr. was a super, super man!
>
> *Gas Ronda, Former Ford Drag Team Member*

Bob and I go all the way back to 1961 when I first started selling cars. I had heard about Tasca through their racing program and decided that I would like to go meet the man and talk to him. What Bob taught me was mainly how to refine my skills in automotive marketing and make it one of my strongest points: to be able to take and do something differently with it than just sell "regular" cars. We used to talk many a night about the present cars and the state of the automobile industry as a whole.

What [car] was coming out, what motor should go into what car, why this should go into that car, why it shouldn't be called a Cobra, or why it should be called a Cobra.

He had a keen insight into everything that was going on around him in the automobile business.

Bill Kolb Jr.
Drag Racer
Car Salesman
Owner Bill Kolb Jr. Subaru, Orangeburg, New York

As the Tasca name and reputation grew, he [Bob Tasca Sr.] became one of the strongest individuals in Ford history that didn't have the "Ford" name. I don't know if anyone can say anything negative about "Mr. Bob." Bob Tasca Jr., Carl, David: they're all fine people and have always made me feel like part of the Tasca family!

Roy Hill, CEO, Roy Hill Drag Racing School

I have personally met Bob Tasca Sr. a few times, and I really liked the way the man presented himself. Whenever his team raced at Capitol, he used to come because he particularly enjoyed our "Saturday Night Under the Lights" events. He used to tell some amazing stories. He once said that the forerunner to the Cobra Jet Mustang, his "KR-8," wasn't dreamed up in Ford's Engineering Department. It was dreamed up right there in the Tasca Ford Service Department. He was a very interesting man!

Julio Marra, Co-Owner
Capitol Raceway and Aquasco Speedway
1957–1978

I remember Bob Tasca Sr. was always polite and courteous to me, even though he was a big-time player and I was just a kid. I always thought of him as a real gentleman, but when he had to, he was a take-no-prisoners kind of guy who could get down with the troops at any level when the timing was right.

I also felt that he always treated all the Ford guys as part of the "team" and made you feel a part of it even though we were always trying to beat each other. At that time in my life, teamwork was something I just simply didn't understand, but I did learn that from him. The Tasca Ford team always unselfishly shared their knowledge and spare parts, which I appreciated as I was competing on a shoestring budget.

Bottom line, I thought of him [Tasca] as a tough but fair taskmaster who expected excellence in return for him doing his part by supporting a top team with the proper resources. I always secretly wished that I had the same opportunity.

The last time I saw Bob (at the Legion of Honor show at York, Pennsylvania, where Bob, John Healey, Phil Bonner, and Joniec were being honored) he was in a wheelchair. He stood up and we greeted each other with a hug yet one more time.

I fondly look back on it all and feel blessed and proud to have known him, as there will most likely never be another "Big Bopper."

Al "Batman" Joniec, Ford Drag Team Star

As members of the Ford Drag Team, we always liked to stick together. Of course, I knew Bob Tasca Sr. really well. I knew Billy Lawton, who was one hell of a driver, and John Healey, who was a terrific mechanic. They worked together real good.

Of course, being that Bob Tasca was the nation's second-largest Ford dealer, he was always in on the first of everything new that came around. He would try a lot of it for Ford and proved to be a [reliable] source of information when it came to new parts and that sort of thing.

I considered Bob Tasca Sr. a very good friend.

Phil "Daddy Warbucks" Bonner, Retired Ford Drag Team Member

Chapter Nine: In Memoriam, Robert F. Tasca Sr.

Additional books that may interest you...

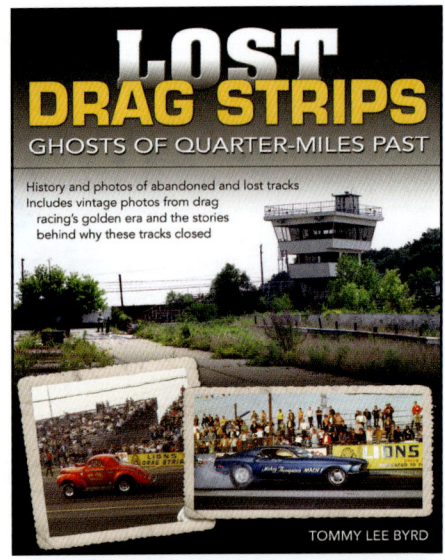

LOST DRAG STRIPS: Ghosts of Quarter-Miles Past *by Tommy Lee Byrd* This book takes a look at many of the lost quarter-mile tracks across the country. Some of them are gone completely, paved over to make room for housing developments or strip malls. Others are ghostly remnants of what once was, offering a sad and even eerie subject for the photographer. The images are teamed with vintage shots of drag racing's glory days, sharing what once was one of America's most popular pastimes with the modern reality facing these facilities today. For fans of drag racing's past, it's a sobering and interesting study. Softbound, 8.5 x 11 inches, 160 pages, 315 color and b&w photos. **Item # CT514**

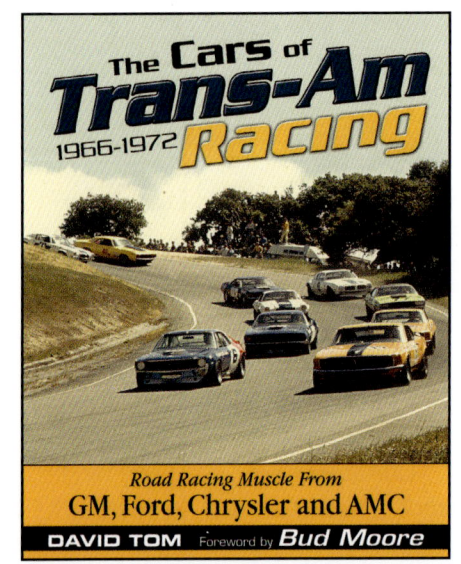

THE CARS OF TRANS-AM RACING: 1966–1972 *by David Tom* When the modified muscle cars of the Trans-Am Series were seen performing well on the country's finest tracks, fans wanted a model of their own in the driveway. These "pony cars" boasted a new look and style not seen before, and their all-around performance eclipsed anything previously accomplished by production-based American GT cars. Author David Tom covers road racing muscle from GM, Ford, Chrysler, and AMC. This book focuses on the cars used in this legendary series. Seeing them in their full competition versions when they were new brings back many fond memories. Hardbound, 8.5 x 11 inches, 192 pages, 500 color photos. **Item # CT516**

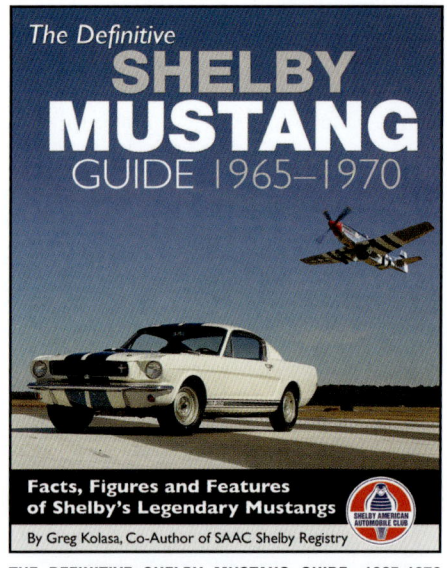

THE DEFINITIVE SHELBY MUSTANG GUIDE: 1965-1970 *by Greg Kolasa* Shelby American Auto Club (SAAC) historian and registrar Greg Kolasa details the specifics on the performance and appearance alterations. This book gives a detailed look at both the performance and styling characteristics of each year of the 1965–1970 Shelby Mustangs in text, photographs, and charts/graphs. It clears up many myths and misconceptions surrounding these legendary pony cars. In addition to his firsthand knowledge, Kolasa relies heavily on factory documentation and interviews with Shelby American designers, engineers, stylists, fabricators, and race drivers. Hardbound, 8.5 x 11 inches, 192 pages, 500 color photos. **Item # CT507**

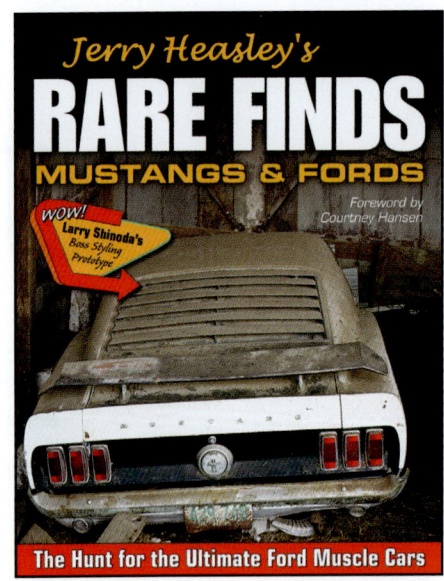

JERRY HEASLEY'S RARE FINDS: Mustangs & Fords *by Jerry Heasley* As the automotive Indiana Jones, Jerry Heasley has been tracking down and documenting the stories of the rarest and most sought-after Mustang and high-performance Ford rescue stories for years. In this follow-up to the top-selling *Jerry Heasley's Rare Finds*, Heasley has built a collection of his finest stories, including the 1969 Boss styling prototype that was owned by Ford stylist Larry Shinoda, the original 1967 Shelby Mustang prototype that became several other test cars, a rare 1965 Shelby GT350R, and a host of other rare and collectible performance Fords. Softbound, 8.5 x 11 inches, 144 pages, 225 color photos. **Item # CT509**

Check out our website:
CarTechBooks.com

✓ Find our newest books before anyone else

✓ Get weekly tech tips from our experts

✓ Get your ride or project featured on our homepage!

**Exclusive Promotions and Giveaways on Facebook
Like us to WIN! Facebook.com/CarTechBooks**

www.cartechbooks.com or 1-800-551-4754

Congratulations! ... On Your 100 Years of Successful Service to

The World's Second Largest Ford Dealer

We, Too, Have Enjoyed Success ... Because! ... At Tasca's What Was Good Today ... Will Not Be Good Enough Tomorrow!

Our Size and Leadership in the Highly Competitive Automobile Business is a Testimony of Expressed Confidence in Our Organization by the residents of Rhode Island, adjacent Massachusetts and Connecticut Communities.

In less than nine busy years, including a Hurricane disaster in 1954 that wrecked our establishment in Bristol, Rhode Island, we have grown from a two car showroom to a mammoth 12 Acre Ford Sales and Service Organization at our Present location in East Providence ... in fact the Second Largest Ford Dealer in the World.

It has been said ... "To Be the Biggest You Gotta Come Close to Being the Best," and you can be sure we are going to continue giving you the consideration, value and service that has earned for us your valued patronage and the enviable position of leadership in our business.

We really don't have a chip on our shoulder, but we are proud of our accomplishment and would like to have you visit with us and see our ...

Bigger, Most Modern Service Facility. Equipped with Every conceivable piece of equipment designed to do a complete automobile assembly if necessary and manned by the largest staff of Factory Trained Technicians in the entire area to serve you Better, Faster and Economically, Day or Night.

Our Larger Modernized Parts Department. One of the most completely stocked in the entire United States.

Our Attractively Furnished and Air Conditioned Customer Waiting Area Designed for Your Comfort and Convenience.